DATE DUE

AP 21 '99			
NO 20 '02			
DE 18 '02			

DEMCO 38-296

Friends or Rivals?

Friends or Rivals?

The Insider's Account of U.S.-Japan Relations

Michael H. Armacost

Columbia University Press

NEW YORK

Columbia University Press

New York   Chichester, West Sussex

Copyright © 1996 Columbia University Press

blication Data

count of U.S.–Japan relations

s and index.
            ISBN 0–231–10488–X
            1. United States—Relations—Japan.   2. Japan—Relations—United
        States.   I. Title.
        E183.8.J3A813   1996
        303.48'252073—dc20   95–25480

Columbia University Press thanks its friend David B. Hertz for his gift toward the costs of publishing this book.

∞

Casebound editions of Columbia University Press books are printed on permanent and durable acid-free paper.

Printed in the United States of America
c 10 9 8 7 6 5 4 3 2 1

Contents

Preface

U.S.-Japan relations are in transition. The East-West struggle supplied the motive and context for the U.S.-Japan alliance for more than forty years. The end of the cold war consequently has had a profound effect. The alliance could, of course, evolve into a more balanced and durable partnership. Alternatively, increasingly intense commercial competition could fuel renewed geopolitical rivalry. The future is not predetermined. Things could go either way.

This is a book about the efforts of the United States to adapt its relationship with Japan to the changing circumstances of the post–cold war era. It is neither a personal memoir nor an academic monograph, but an attempt to reflect analytically on the events that have been transforming that relationship. In it, I try to assess what went right, what went wrong, and how we can put this critical relationship on a sounder footing for the future.

As the U.S. ambassador to Japan from May 1989 to July 1993, I had a ringside seat from which to observe the transformation. Indeed, since I was responsible for the day-to-day management in Tokyo of our relations with Japan during this singular and fascinating period, I participated directly in implementing the key decisions. While I am not what the academics would consider a "Japan hand," neither was I without experience in dealing with the Japanese when I took up my duties in Tokyo. I taught for a year at International Christian University in Mitaka, Japan, in the 1960s. In the 1970s I served in the U.S. embassy in Tokyo as a special assistant to Ambassador Robert Ingersoll. Most of my subsequent work in Washington on the State Department's policy-planning staff, the National Security Council staff, the Pentagon's International Security Affairs Division, and the State Department's East Asia and Pacific Bureau was devoted to Asian matters. As ambassador to the Philippines from 1982 to 1984 I observed the intersection of American and Japanese interests in Southeast Asia. And as undersecretary of state for political affairs from 1984 to 1989 I exercised oversight over our policies in Asia, including, of course, Japan. Hence I had a wide range of acquaintances in Japanese policy-making circles and a substantial familiarity with the nuances of the most sensitive issues.

The late 1980s and early 1990s were a period of remarkable change in Japan. When I arrived in Tokyo, Japan was at the top of its bubble economy; by the time I left, it was experiencing one of its most prolonged and damaging recessions. Shortly after I took up my office, the Liberal Democratic Party, which had governed the country without interruption since the mid-1950s, lost its majority in the Upper House; the day before I completed my tour of duty, it lost its majority in the Lower House and was forced into the opposition. When the Kuwait crisis erupted in August 1990, the Japanese government engaged in protracted hand-wringing, unable for weeks to define a response that accommodated both the expectations of its allies and the anxieties of its own people. Three years later, a Self-Defense Force engineering battalion had completed its performance of peacekeeping duties in Cambodia as a member of the UN Transitional Authority there—the first deployment of Japanese military personnel overseas since 1945.

Some pundits claim that Japan never changes. I consider these big-time changes. They were inspired by dramatic adjustments in the underlying strategic, economic, and political realities in the world and corresponding changes in the domestic underpinnings of the governments in both countries. The end of the cold war reshuffled the cards in the great power game and raised questions about the efficacy of and necessity for the U.S.-Japan alliance. It invited officials on both sides of the Pacific to explore the wider diplomatic maneuverability that an end to East-West rivalry would afford both Japan and America. And without necessarily increasing Tokyo's readiness to reduce or eliminate the visible asymmetries that marked our bilateral economic relationship, it diminished Washington's willingness to indulge them.

The world economic system was also in the throes of a major transformation. The liberalization of financial markets accelerated international capital flows and undermined the ability of governments to control the value of their own currencies. The globalization of the production process transformed the meaning of trade. The vastly increased power and mobility of multinational firms altered the traditional links between governments and these major corporations. And if states were losing power to the private sector, they were also forced to contend with the emergence of regional trading arrangements in Europe, North America, and Asia as well. All these factors complicated the management of a complex and highly interdependent bilateral economic relationship.

Coming to grips with these changes in the strategic and economic foundations of world politics would have been challenging even in the most normal of times. The difficulty of adjusting U.S.-Japan relations to them was compounded by a basic shift in the relative strength of the two countries that then seemed under way. Nor was the precise extent and meaning of this shift self-evident. In 1989 Japan's economy was up and America's was down. By 1993 the tables appeared to be turning. The leaders and publics of both countries were uncomfortable with what they perceived to be the terms of interdependence.

The geography of international political and economic competition was also in flux. The center of gravity in the world economy was moving toward the Pacific, enhancing the political clout of Asian nations and transforming the discussion of trilateralism from U.S.-Europe-Japan to EU-NAFTA-APEC. Japan saw in this an opportunity to assert its autonomy and leadership; American leaders paid lip service to Asia's heightened importance but were heavily preoccupied elsewhere tidying up the remnants of the cold war in Europe and fighting a shooting war in the Persian Gulf.

Domestic political considerations also exerted a powerful influence on efforts to adjust U.S.-Japan relations. Americans were beginning to turn inward, yet the gridlock between the executive and legislative branches, controlled by different parties, complicated efforts to get on top of long-neglected fiscal and social problems. The Japanese, meanwhile, sought increased international recognition of their impressive economic accomplishments yet found that their political process—geared to catch-up capitalism and accustomed to leaving many security and diplomatic problems to others—stymied efforts to define clear responses to new international challenges.

The interplay between these forces of change in the international environment and within our respective societies colored all the events recounted in this volume. I make no attempt to extract novel theoretical insights from them. My objective is to reconstruct the way our attempts to adjust the U.S.-Japan relationship to these post–cold war realities looked as they were taking shape. I have added here and there suggestions as to how we might do things better.

Chapter 1 recalls the ambivalence that our growing economic interdependence seemed to evoke among Americans and Japanese at the time I was preparing to take up my duties in Tokyo. Chapters 2 through 5 describe the Bush administration's efforts to inject greater balance into the bilateral economic relationship, adjust the alliance to a less threatening security setting, elicit Japan's support for the multinational coalition that turned back Saddam Hussein's aggression in Kuwait, and devise a diplomatic partnership with Japan that had global reach.

As my tenure in Japan extended only six months into President Clinton's term of office, my analysis of his administration's approach to Japan is perforce that of a reasonably experienced spectator watching closely from the sidelines. That commentary makes up chapter 6. In chapters 7 and 8, I have tried to judge where the trajectory of change is likely to carry Japan in the coming years and the challenges this will pose for American policy makers.

I am personally convinced that close ties between Tokyo and Washington are vital to our national interests. I have made no attempt to conceal that conviction. Even so, I have tried to preserve a certain analytic detachment throughout this book; I have not exaggerated the successes or hidden the disappointments that marked these years of transition. The title I have chosen for these reflections, *Friends or Rivals?*, mirrors my hope and belief that we will remain close friends. But it is undeniable that a greater spirit of rivalry has begun to reemerge.

While I labored in the diplomatic vineyard in Tokyo, my wife, Bonny, devoted much of her time to two worthy enterprises: making music and making friends. A number of her friends were artists, and she performed ensemble and duo piano music with many of them—including Reiko Nagase, Setsuko Iwasaki, and in recent years Hiroko Nakamura, one of Japan's most renowned artists—both for personal satisfaction and in occasional public concerts for charitable causes. I often thought that Bonny and her associates provided an appropriate metaphor for the

United States' relationship with Japan: successful performances required hard work, persistent practice, and attentiveness to partners even while performing one's own role. If our countries go about their business in a similar spirit, we need not worry that friendship will turn to rivalry.

Bonny and I acquired a new stake in the U.S.-Japan relationship on August 11, 1994, when our first granddaughter—Samantha Mie Armacost—was born to our son Scott and his wife, Miho. It is to Samantha—a felicitous result of U.S.-Japanese cooperation—that this book is dedicated.

Acknowledgments

During the final months of my tenure in Tokyo, I received a phone call from Dan Okimoto, professor of political science at Stanford, inviting me to spend a year at the Asia/Pacific Research Center writing and teaching about my experiences in Japan. A/PRC offered an ideal environment for preparing this manuscript. It was sufficiently distant from Washington and Tokyo to allow some perspective, yet I was surrounded by knowledgeable colleagues whose judgment and insight proved extraordinarily valuable.

Dan Okimoto and Wally Falcon, director of Stanford's Institute of International Studies, were a constant source of encouragement and wise counsel. So was Walter Shorenstein, a good friend whose support facilitated much of A/PRC's program, including my own work. My colleagues at A/PRC—Dan Okimoto, Don Emmerson, Tom Rohlen, Larry Lau, Aki Yoshikawa, and Jim Raphael, among others—provided a stimulating intellectual environment. IIS and A/PRC—most particularly Jean Lee and Zera Murphy—relieved me of the administrative burdens associated with preparing a manuscript. Kari Hironaka, Kirsty Bez, Cindy Miller, and Sarah Holmes typed and retyped drafts swiftly and flawlessly while providing editorial and other assistance.

A number of associates both in the Foreign Service and academic life read and commented on various portions of the draft. These included George Shultz, Dan Okimoto, Harry Rowen, John Taylor, Tom Rohlen, Jim Morley, George Packard, Clyde Prestowitz, Bill

Breer, Joe Winder, Rust Deming, Jim Foster, and Mark Fitzpatrick. The usual caveat applies. I am grateful to all of them for sparing me errors of fact and judgment.

John Moore, president of Columbia University Press, prodded me to submit a manuscript and subsequently nudged me into completing the book on schedule. Anne McCoy and Sarah St. Onge provided splendid editorial assistance, and Alan Greenberg prepared the index. To all I express my gratitude.

A special thanks is due Mike Mansfield. This great American, who has made many superlative contributions to our public life, served as ambassador to Japan from 1977 to 1988. His stature and the personal qualities that so endeared him to the Japanese people enlarged the job I was privileged to perform as his successor. He and his wife, Maureen, left very large shoes to fill and extended many personal kindnesses to Bonny and me as we sought to fill them.

My wife, Bonny, helped jog my memory on many of the events recounted in this book and encouraged me to undertake it—not least because it enabled us to enjoy two very pleasant years near family members in the San Francisco area.

November 27, 1995
Potomac, Maryland

Friends or Rivals?
An Essay in Photographs

MAY 1989
En route to the Presentation of Credentials to the Emperor.

(from the author's collection)

MAY 1989
Ceremonial duties. Speaking at the Black Ship Festival in Shimoda City at ceremonies recalling Commodore Perry's "opening" of Japan in the 1850s.

(from the author's collection)

AUGUST 1989
Press conference following Prime Minister Kaifu's visit to Washington, at the diplomatic entrance to the White House. Pictured along with Kaifu and President Bush are *(from left)* Dick Solomon, Brent Scowcroft, John Sununu, Dick Cheney, Nick Brady, and Mike Armacost. *(from the author's collection)*

AUGUST 1991

With President Bush and Prime Minister Kaifu at Kennebunkport, Maine. Marlin Fitzwater and Brent Scowcroft are also pictured. This meeting brought differences over Gulf war payments to an end.

(official photograph, Office of the Prime Minister, Tokyo)

DECEMBER 1991

A golf game with Tsutomu Hata, a future prime minister, Yuzaturo Mogi, president of Kikkoman, and Toshiaki Ogasawara, publisher of the *Japan Times*.

(from the author's collection)

JANUARY 1992
With President and Mrs. Bush, wife Bonny, and former prime minister Kaifu before the opening luncheon in Kyoto during the president's visit.

(from the author's collection)

JANUARY 1992
President Bush is assisted by a security official and dinner guests after he collapses to the floor during a state dinner at the Japanese prime minister's residence in Tokyo. First Lady Barbara Bush looks on at right. Japanese prime minister Kiichi Miyazawa kneels to the right of Bush. This photo was taken from NHK television. *(AP photo)*

APRIL 1992

Prime Minister Miyazawa speaks at a dinner commemorating the seventy-fifth anniversary of the Japan-America Society that was attended by the emperor and empress. Also pictured on the dais were (*from left*) Ambassador Armacost, Mrs. Michio Watanabe, the prime minister, Mrs. Takeo Fukuda, the emperor, and the empress.   (*from the author's collection*)

MAY 1992

Presenting a letter of congratulations from President Bush to Akebono, the Hawaiian-born grand champion of sumo, after his victory in the Tokyo Tournament.   (*from the author's collection*)

MAY 1992

Performing ceremonial duties at a reception at the Okura Hotel flanked by Vice President Dan Quayle and Japanese foreign minister Muchio Watanabe (man on far right unidentified). *(official White House photograph)*

JUNE 1992

Introducing Ichiro Ozawa, the former LDP leader who in 1993 became the architect of the reform coalition that ousted the LDP from power, to President Bush at the White House. *(official White House photograph)*

NOVEMBER 1992

Checking out a mock-up of the jointly developed FSX fighter plane in Nagoya.   *(from the author's collection)*

APRIL 1993

With President Clinton, Prime Minister Miyazawa, and United States Trade Representative Mickey Kantor. The meeting was a forum for initial skirmishing over a Framework Agreement in Trade eventually concluded in July 1993 during the G-7 Summit in Tokyo.   *(official White House photograph)*

JULY 1993

President Clinton and Prime Minister Kiichi Miyazawa of Japan exchange words during a session of delegation leaders at the Akasaka Palace in Tokyo. From Clinton (*clockwise*): Belgian prime minister Jean-Luc Dehaene, EC vice president Henning Christophersen, British prime minister John Major, German chancellor Helmut Kohl, Canadian prime minister Kim Campbell, Italian prime minister Carlo Ciampi, and French president François Mitterrand.

(AP photo/Marcy Nighswander)

JULY 1993
President Clinton meets future prime minister Tsutomu Hata at a reception
at the U.S. ambassador's residence.   *(official White House photograph)*

JUNE 1995

Japan's minister for international trade and industry Ryutaro Hashimoto (*right*) and United States trade representative Mickey Kantor hold a Japanese sword that was presented to Hashimoto by Kantor when they met in Tokyo and arrived at the auto trade agreement on June 29. *(Reuters/Pascal Volery)*

I

The Promise and Perils
of Interdependence

While awaiting confirmation hearings for my assignment as ambassador to Japan in early 1989, my friend Tadashi Yamamoto—the organizer of countless U.S.-Japan exchange programs over the years—requested that I meet with a group of visitors from Japan. They asked me what I expected to be the most daunting challenges I would face in managing the day-to-day relations between our governments. I responded that months of preparation for the hearings had reinforced two central impressions about our relationship: first, the United States and Japan were dependent on one another as never before; second, people on both sides of the Pacific found this reality deeply disquieting. The trick, I suggested, was not to diminish this mutual dependence—which in any event appeared inescapable—but to make it more comfortable for both countries by assuring that its manifold benefits were equitably shared.

I traveled widely that spring to meet with leaders of U.S. constituencies with a stake in our relationship with Japan. Everywhere I went, I encountered ambivalence toward the Japanese. Almost like a mantra, Reagan administration spokespeople had reiterated the assertion of Mike Mansfield, my predecessor as ambassador to Japan, that U.S.-Japan links were our most important bilateral relationship—bar none. Yet significant elements within the Congress, the unions, the business community, the press, and academic circles believed that something in that relationship was amiss. It was reflected in a comment that circulated widely in those days: "The cold war is over, and the Japanese won!" U.S. attitudes toward Japan appeared increasingly schizophrenic. As respect for its industrial prowess had grown, so had fears of its relentless drive for market share in many economic sectors in which Americans had traditionally excelled. Lee Hamilton, longtime member of the House Foreign Affairs Committee, recalled for me an experience that typified these concerns: On a 1989 visit to Seymour, Indiana—a small town remarkable for, among other things, the fact that it still celebrated V-J (Victory over Japan) Day—the principal topic of conversation among his constituents was the recent construction of several Japanese plants in or near town. Some of the locals were enthusiastic about this development; others were agitated and distressed. The reason for the divergent reactions, it turned out, was fairly simple: those who had found employment at the plants praised the Japanese; those who had not denounced them. The impact of the growing interdependence between our countries was being felt as never before on the farms and in the factories, classrooms, and boardrooms of the United States. People held strong opinions about Japan, and they were often laced with contradictions.

The Contours of Interdependence

By the late 1980s the fates of the United States and Japan were closely intertwined. The interdependence of our economies, already vast, was growing rapidly. For each country, the other had become its largest overseas trading partner, principal source of new technology, and most valued trans-Pacific ally.

Bilateral trade approached $140 billion. Japan supplied Americans with a dazzling variety of high-quality, reasonably priced consumer products and increasingly sophisticated industrial equipment. Meanwhile U.S. farmers produced a large percentage of Japan's food; Boeing and McDonnell-Douglas furnished Japanese travelers with wide-bodied jets, and Japanese tourists were the biggest spenders at Hawaii's hotels and golf courses. U.S.-owned companies in Japan produced nearly $100 billion in goods and services. And Japanese multinationals—particularly its auto and consumer electronics companies—were swiftly building production facilities in the United States to hedge against the growing protectionist sentiment in Congress. In the process they contributed to the economic revival of the Rust Belt in the U.S. Middle West.

The rapid growth of Japanese investment in the United States provoked mixed feelings. The purchase of blue-chip properties such as Rockefeller Center and the Pebble Beach Golf Course provoked criticism and unease. Yet direct investment in production facilities offered employment to tens of thousands of U.S. workers, generated tax revenues for state and local governments, and brought technology transfers and new methods of organizing the manufacturing process. Japanese money helped to finance the U.S. fiscal deficit. And the destinies of our respective high-tech firms were becoming linked as never before through a proliferation of strategic alliances that enabled companies to pool knowledge and share the high costs and risks of developing new technology.

The growing interdependence of our countries was marked by more than increased trade and investment. Although the Soviet threat was receding, the U.S.-Japan alliance still offered both governments greater security at lower cost while providing reassurance to other Asian nations. And expanding cultural and educational exchanges enriched the lives of both peoples. By the late 1980s, Japan had become Hollywood's largest overseas market, and American popular culture was making even wider inroads in Japan. One could scarcely turn on a TV set in Tokyo without seeing Michael Jordan, Janet Jackson, or Arnold Schwarzenegger pitching one or another American product. American orchestras played Suntory Hall, Oscar Peterson and Mel Torme were headliners at Tokyo's choice clubs, and prominent country singers were featured at the annual Country Gold Festival in Kumamoto. In the USA, major sports events were regularly sponsored by Japanese companies like Toyota, Nissan, Honda, and Toshiba. Bill Blass, Donna Karan, and Oscar de la Renta were becoming household names among fashion-conscious Japanese, just as Hanae Mori's signature butterflies were recognized by stylish Americans. In San Diego you could eat sushi while watching the Padres play baseball; in Tokyo you could have Domino's pizza delivered to your home—with the price reduced if it didn't arrive within thirty minutes.

As bilateral trade and investment grew, so did travel and exchanges of all kinds. Throughout the 1980s the numbers of Japanese students and professionals temporarily residing in the United States increased dramatically. Many of these brought their families with them, with the result that many more Japanese children were educated for extended periods in this country. Relatively few Americans could be found in Japanese universities, but there was a perceptible increase in the numbers of young Americans working in Japanese banks, trading companies, security houses, and manufacturing firms.

As impressive as the extent of our mutual dependence was the complementarity of our respective national strengths. The USA extended a security guarantee to Japan; that country in turn gave the United States access to bases enabling us to project our power efficiently into the western Pacific and Indian Oceans. Japan accommodated our insatiable appetite for high-quality consumer goods; we met their needs for food, raw materials, and high-technology products. Japan's growing investments in this country helped offset our low level of national savings, while we offered Japanese investors what seemed at the time a safe haven for their assets, as well as access to financial service firms with a dazzling array of innovative products. Our oil companies supplied Japan with a substantial portion of its fossil fuel and petroleum products; Japanese firms showed ours how to utilize a variety of impressive energy-saving technologies. Japanese companies had become the principal suppliers of low-cost, high-quality semiconductor chips to the USA's computer industry; at the same time, Japanese computer firms became increasingly dependent on the microprocessors and software that only U.S. high-tech firms could provide.

The United States' excellence in basic research was matched by Japan's genius for applied engineering. Our great research universities inspired envy among Japanese educators, while specialists here examined Japan's schools for lessons on how to reform our primary and secondary educational systems. U.S. manufacturers sought to adapt Japanese lean production methods to their requirements; U.S. retail outlets—like 7-Eleven—challenged Japan's distribution system by offering lower prices and more convenient business hours. If Japanese visitors to the United States were impressed by our spontaneity, creativity, and love of freedom, Americans in Japan invariably admired the order, safety, purposefulness, civility, and decorum that were such visible features of Japanese life.

The growing interdependence of our societies was accompanied by impressive evidence that we were acquiring the habit of working effectively together. As I had learned from personal experience, this required an act of will by both sides, since the cultural and linguistic obstacles to cooperation were formidable. Government-to-government consultations were numerous, and they were elaborately choreographed. Only a true specialist could recite the plethora of channels. Discussions were often stylized and formalistic. Candor was not always at a premium; spontaneity was rare. Yet key officials on each side were regularly in touch. Each government had some access to the organs that formed public opinion in the other country. And problems tended to get managed, if not necessarily resolved.

The mutual dependence that ensnared our countries was, of course, part of a wider global process. Information-age technology—most notably telecommunications devices and computers—had shrunk distances and hastened the emergence of a global economy. Money, goods, services, and information moved around the world at breathtaking speed, with less and less reference to national borders. With multinational corporations in the lead, the production process was progressively internationalized, and the complementarity between trade and investment reinforced.

These developments brought change and competitive challenges that were unsettling to many. They also rearranged many familiar categories of thought. Even the terms *exports* and *imports* were less meaningful since many traded products incorporated parts manufactured in ten or more countries; nearly 40 percent of international trade involved intrafirm transfers by multinational companies; and statistical indices of the United States' trade performance consistently understated our exports of legal, financial, accounting, and other services since these were difficult to measure.

The growing trade deficits of the late 1980s deepened pessimism among Americans about the competitiveness of many U.S. firms, yet, ironically, information-age technologies played to American strengths in entrepreneurship and innovation. In Japan, on the other hand, although the same period brought unprecedented economic success, the forces impelling the globalization of the economy were to challenge both its society's capacity for creativity and the power of the bureaucracy that had played such a large role in designing and guiding the country's unique brand of catch-up capitalism. Moreover, as the East-West struggle faded, it was apparent that the familiar cold war rules for handling international economic and security issues were in need of revision. Since Japan and the United States together represented nearly 40 percent of the world's productive output, no two nations had a larger interest in the content of those rules or a greater capacity to redesign them. As Singapore's former prime minister Lee Kwan Yew frequently observed, when the USA and Japan collaborated effectively, the entire world shared in the benefits; when they did not, everyone experienced the baleful consequences. In short, Americans and Japanese were not the only people who had a stake in their ability to cooperate and to manage occasional differences.

The Frustrations of Interdependence

I was regularly reminded during the spring of 1989 that, despite its obvious benefits, many Americans were disquieted by the growing interdependence between their country and Japan. Increasingly familiar were complaints that the Japanese were protectionists, that they were taking a free ride on Western defenses, that they shirked their international responsibilities, and that they coveted the status of a major power without accepting the responsibilities that such a status implied. Japanese purchases of trophy properties struck a raw nerve. Congressional pique over huge and persistent bilateral U.S. trade deficits with Japan provoked the 1988 Trade Bill, designed largely to provide leverage for prying the Japanese market open wider. The terms of the FSX project involving bilateral arrangements to codevelop a new Japanese tactical fighter aircraft incensed many congressional critics, who feared it would facilitate Japan's eventual entry into the civilian aircraft market—one of the few advanced manufacturing industries the U.S. continued to dominate.

A spate of revisionist books and articles about Japan provided a more general analytic framework for specific concerns. Clyde Prestowitz, Karl van Wolferen, James Fallows, and Chalmers Johnson may not have been household names in 1989, but they had acquired a certain following in the nation's capital, changing the intellectual climate of U.S.-Japan relations at just the moment when the resolution of the cold war was altering the political atmosphere.

The revisionists differed in their analyses of the Japanese political and economic system and in their prescriptions for the USA's trade deficit, but they all maintained that Japan's brand of capitalism operated according to premises different from our own. They also regarded as hopelessly naive and unproductive the U.S. government's negotiating methods vis-à-vis Japan, alleging that U.S. economic interests were consistently sacrificed to strategic concerns. While some hoped the Japanese would become more like us and others advocated U.S. trade policies more like theirs, all believed that profound adjustments would be required to achieve a more balanced relationship. And they all disparaged many of the "Japan hands" in the government, whom they termed members of the "Cherry Blossom Protection Association" or "Chrysanthemum Club."

These revisionists changed the terms of debate on U.S.-Japan relations in Washington. Most congressional leaders I visited prior to my confirmation hearings urged a tougher stance on bilateral trade issues. Moderates like Tom Foley—a longtime supporter of cordial U.S.-Japan relations—acknowledged that leaders on the Hill were increasingly wary of defending the relationship publicly. Senator Bill Bradley, who in 1988, despite heavy opposition, had helped push through the Senate the sale of *Aegis*-class cruisers to Japan, kept a low profile throughout the FSX battle, reportedly at the behest of his domestic political advisers.

Press commentary about U.S.-Japan relations was mixed, but strident critics tended to receive the most attention. Poll results revealed, as usual, conflicting views, but an undeniable erosion of public support for the relationship appeared to be under way. In early 1989 mainstream elements of the business community—long regarded as staunch defenders of free trade—issued a report on U.S.-Japan trade issues that stopped just short of endorsing managed trade.

To some degree this mood of frustration was a natural by-product of interdependence. As transactions expanded among people as dynamic and competitive as Americans and Japanese, some friction was inevitable. We were, after all, both necessary partners and natural competitors. Competition brings change, and change breeds dislocation. The losers frequently complain. In the United States, growing numbers of them took their complaints to Washington, where they found an increasingly receptive audience.

As the cliché warns us, familiarity does not always breed greater understanding. To be sure, mutual dependence taught Americans and Japanese more about each other's systems. But as the links between our societies expanded, we became more aware of the institutional differences that separated us. Few Americans knew or cared very much about the difficulties of acquiring a Japanese bank, until Japanese interests had acquired 15 to 20 percent of the banking industry in California. Few Americans had heard of the *dango* bidding system, until U.S. construction firms managed—with help from the Reagan administration—to get themselves licensed to participate in Japanese construction projects. Few Americans knew much about Japan's industrial policy. But those who managed our major steel, machine tool, consumer electronics, and semiconductor firms had learned a lot about Japan's practice of industrial targeting, and they did not like what they had learned. The balance of our mutual dependence appeared to be shifting sharply in Japan's favor, and this was a bitter pill for many Americans to swallow.

Isolationist by tradition, America entered world politics for good only after the Second World War. At that time our preeminent power was uncontested; the other major industrial economies lay in ruins. To combat the Soviet Union we developed globe-encircling alliances and devised a liberal international economic system. To be sure, we relied on our friends and allies for military, economic, and political support, but there was always the comforting assumption that they needed us far more than we needed them. Our predominant power was generally acknowledged; our leadership evoked respect, if not always deference.

By the late 1980s, however, the efficacy of American diplomatic initiatives around the globe appeared increasingly contingent on Japan's readiness to play along and write big checks. At the same time, with the approaching end of the cold war, it seemed likely that Japan's need for our security guarantee would diminish. Our fiscal deficit made us depend increasingly on Japanese investment. Key U.S. manufacturing industries appeared to be under siege: our share of global manufacturing production had declined; our need for imported oil was growing; and we had emerged as the world's largest debtor nation. Japanese competitors seemed poised to do to our high-technology industries what they had done to automobiles, steel, and consumer electronics. Not only was there increased anxiety about our reliance on Japan for key components of even the most sensitive defense systems but a growing apprehension that the Japanese had mastered "lean production," a manufacturing methodology, regarded by many as superior, that had excited the interest of both academics and industrialists in the United States.[1]

In short, Japan's economic power was increasing relative to our own. Its banks were flush with assets; our financial system was struggling to come to terms with a profligate government and the savings and loan fiasco. Japan's manufacturers appeared increasingly formidable and were bidding for preeminence in the high–value-added sectors in which we had traditionally excelled. Despite its reputation as a nation of imitators, the Japanese were overtaking America in the development of many key technologies. As Americans awakened to the growing importance of Asia, they began to fear that Japan had positioned itself better than we to capitalize on the region's growth. This added a poignant footnote to the provocative thesis Paul Kennedy had expounded in his 1987 book *The Rise and Fall of the Great Powers* (New York: Random House): that America was in decline, a victim of imperial overstretch. Little wonder that some Americans looked on the Japanese in the late 1980s the way the British viewed the Yanks at the turn of the century—as a power to be reckoned with. To many, the challenge was profoundly unsettling. Some, to be sure, felt pride in Japan's accomplishments; after all, the United States had been Tokyo's principal postwar sponsor and ally. Some regarded Japan's growing strength merely as a reality to be accommodated. But others began looking for ways of containing Japan's surging power.[2]

The Asymmetries of Interdependence

Interdependence is rarely symmetrical. By the late 1980s the imbalances in the U.S.-Japan relationship were growing. Most appeared to favor Japan, and many seemed to reflect structural differences in our respective economies and societies. Our bilateral trade deficit, which

1. For more on Japan's production methodology, see, for example, Michael L. Dertouzas, Richard K. Lester, Robert M. Solow, and the MIT Commission on Industrial Productivity, *Made in America* (Cambridge: MIT Press, 1989); and James P. Womack, Daniel T. Jones, and Daniel Roos, *The Machine That Changed the World* (New York: Macmillan, 1990).
2. See James Fallows, "Containing Japan: Japan's One-Sided Trading Will Make the US-Japanese Trading Partnership Impossible to Sustain—Unless We Impose Limits on Its Economy," *Atlantic* 263, no. 5 (May 1989): 40–53.

exceeded $60 billion in 1988, continued to climb for two years after the Plaza Accord (1985) nearly doubled the yen's value. And Japan's resistance to manufactured imports and its low levels of intraindustry trade seemed to set it apart as an outlier among the advanced industrial economies.

The investment imbalance was even greater, and as Japanese funds poured into the United States, the obstacles confronting foreign investors in Japan were more widely publicized. Having consciously financed their postwar recovery with domestic savings rather than foreign investment, the Japanese were slow to dismantle restrictions on capital transfers. Cross-shareholding arrangements made friendly acquisitions as well as hostile takeovers of Japanese companies virtually impossible. A result was that foreign-held assets in Japan were roughly one-twentieth the level in the USA.

Trends in technology flows showed a similar pattern. As a latecomer to industrialization, Japan imported considerably more technology than it exported. By the late 1980s, the catch-up phase of Japan's industrialization was over, yet its deficit in technology trade persisted. Technology exports, to be sure, increased, but imports expanded even more. Likewise, bilateral scientific and technological exchanges appeared to be imbalanced: The United States was preeminent in basic research, which was mostly conducted at universities, with the results published openly and available to all. Japan's forte, on the other hand, was in commercializing technology, and the bulk of its R and D was performed in nongovernmental industrial laboratories. Proprietary restrictions inhibited dissemination of the results, and foreigners had limited access to the labs.

In defense technology exchanges, the imbalance was even more pronounced. During the cold war the Defense Department had transferred much technology to Japan to strengthen its defenses, promote the interoperability of allied forces, and lower the unit costs of production runs at home. Until 1983, however, Japan resisted all defense-related technology transfers to the USA—as well as to all other countries—on legal grounds. A legal basis for such transfers was established in 1983, but before the FSX project, for which a memorandum of understanding was signed in the spring of 1989, nothing of consequence flowed our way.

Educational exchanges also seemed to be largely a one-way street. By the late 1980s nearly thirty thousand Japanese young people attended university-level programs in the United States, whereas little more than a thousand Americans were taking courses in Japanese institutions of higher learning. To be sure, compared to their Japanese counterparts' interest in the USA, fewer Americans were motivated to study in Japan, let alone equipped with the linguistic skills necessary for university-level courses. But the imbalance also reflected the relatively greater access accorded foreigners in U.S. educational institutions.

Even our foreign aid programs were marked by asymmetries. Ours was driven by strategic concerns and humanitarian impulses; theirs mainly by economic and commercial considerations. Our aid went mainly to so-called frontline allies and truly destitute peoples in Africa, South Asia, and Latin America. Japan's was concentrated in Asia; it focused on countries at the threshold of industrial success, relied mainly on loans rather than grants, and was heavily oriented to infrastructure projects in which Japanese suppliers of pipe, cement, and construction services were keenly interested. In this implicit triage, we seemed to wind up supporting many of the world's poorest countries, they the emerging, middle-class, industrializing nations.

These imbalances became more consequential politically as cold war tensions subsided. Americans became more attentive to the health of their nation's industries and increasingly measured U.S. competitiveness against Japan's. A low savings rate and relatively anemic investment levels contributed to the competitiveness problems of U.S. firms at least as much as Japan's market access barriers did. But the mote in Japan's eye attracted more attention in Washington than the beam in our own. Japan's market was unquestionably tougher than ours for foreign enterprises to crack. And the American people were undeniably becoming less tolerant of this apparent lack of reciprocity. In the parlance of the day, a major objective of the Bush administration was achievement of a level playing field in Japan.

Closer analysis of the Japanese economy revealed several ways in which Tokyo used governmental power and socioeconomic arrangements to improve its international trade and investment balance:

○ The Japanese government played a more expansive role than ours in determining the conditions under which foreign goods, services, technology, and capital were allowed into the domestic market.

○ Intimate links among Japanese manufacturing companies, their suppliers, and their main banks—the so-called keiretsu system—

reinforced the government's gatekeeper role in complicating foreign access to the market.

○ The Japanese practiced industrial targeting as a means of ratchet-
  ing the economy up to progressively higher levels of technological sophistication and higher–value-added production.

Growing consciousness of these differences had inspired the 1988 trade
bill. It also redirected the attention of U.S. trade negotiators away from
the classic border controls on trade—e.g., tariffs and quotas—to structural and regulatory barriers to cross-border flows of goods, services,
and capital. Fair trade, rather than free trade, became a call to arms for
many Republicans as well as Democrats in Congress. This focus on
fairness seemed natural: equality of opportunity was a fundamental
value to most Americans.

As Americans increasingly ascribed the difficulties experienced in
trade with Tokyo to Japan's "unfair" trade policies, this label provoked
growing irritation and resentment among the Japanese. Just as we practiced different forms of capitalism, so we measured fairness by different
standards. To Americans, accustomed to winning, the very size and persistence of our trade deficit with Japan seemed sufficient evidence that
something was amiss. The recent experience of our steel, automobile,
consumer electronic, and semiconductor companies reinforced the conviction of the country's corporate leaders that the Japanese used the high
margins garnered in their protected home market to subsidize aggressive pricing practices in the United States. This precipitated more and
more charges of dumping, as well as fueling the belief that Japan routinely practiced predatory, adversarial, or strategic trade. It also prompted
growing skepticism about the possibility of obtaining genuine *national
treatment* (the principle under which a government treats firms of foreign nations the same as its own) in Japan and precipitated the search for
stronger levers with which to achieve greater reciprocity.

Finally, with the growth in Japan's industrial prowess, Americans—
particularly their representatives in Congress—expressed growing
criticism of the disparity between Japan's economic power and the
modesty of its international role. Demands for Japan to shoulder additional international responsibilities and burdens intensified. Among
other demands in the 1980s, Washington pressured Tokyo to undertake
structural reforms of its economy; to increase its conventional defense
efforts and share more of the costs of our forward military deploy-

ments; to help in convoying Kuwaiti oil tankers in the Persian Gulf; to help finance international peacekeeping, refugee resettlement, and disaster relief; to direct more of its bilateral aid to countries of strategic consequence to the West; and to share the tab for a variety of other U.S.-inspired international initiatives. Many of these requests were ultimately accommodated, but the process of achieving adjustments left raw nerves on both sides.

Bilateral negotiations over burden sharing bore a strong resemblance to the bargaining over trade. Japanese passivity invited American pressure. Pressure in turn provoked Japanese defensiveness. Frictions attracted press attention, and the issues were politicized. Negotiations were invariably protracted, and concessions came slowly and reluctantly. Exasperation mounted on both sides. The Japanese acquired a reputation in Washington for taking as long as possible to do as little as necessary. Americans in turn came to be viewed by the Japanese as likely to raise yet another demand each time they pocketed a concession. This reinforced Tokyo's disposition to take its time doling out such favors. In the end, the methods employed to cope with the accumulating problems in the relationship seemed increasingly to reinforce those same difficulties.

These then were the principal frustrations I discerned about Japan among Americans in the spring of 1989. It was a combustible mix. Yet the problems were often exaggerated. Critical attitudes toward Japan were more visible on the Hill than within the executive branch. They were more widespread in the Rust Belt than in the Sun Belt. They were more evident in U.S. firms aspiring to enter the market in Japan than among companies that already had become insiders there. They were more frequently heard in the Department of Commerce or the U.S. Trade Representative's office than in the State Department, the Pentagon, or among the National Security Council staff. Still, the criticisms affected the atmosphere; they had caught the attention of the Japanese, and they were to influence the priorities and substance of the Bush administration's approach to Japan.

Japanese Frustrations

Americans were not alone in their frustrations with the relationship. In preparing for my new duties, I had fewer opportunities to assess

Japanese views than American attitudes. But I met with Japanese business executives in New York and Chicago. I visited Mazda's new manufacturing plant in Flat Rock, Michigan. A few leading Liberal Democratic Party (LDP) politicians visited Washington and dropped by to
chat. And of course I kept abreast of embassy reporting. From these
sources I judged that, pleased with their growing power and autonomy, the Japanese were beginning to find aspects of their own residual
dependence on Washington increasingly discomforting.

No less than Americans, Japanese prize their independence and self-
reliance. Indeed the history of modern Japan features the quest to
avoid Western domination. The Tokugawa shogunate sought that
objective through stringent isolation; the Meiji reformers pursued it
through pell-mell modernization. The single-mindedness and perseverance they brought to the task was evident in the late-nineteenth-
century efforts of Japanese diplomats to terminate the unequal treaties
Western powers had forced them to sign during a period of weakness.
As Japan's power grew, so too did its ambition. In the late nineteenth
and early twentieth centuries, it staked out a sphere of influence in
Asia—in keeping with the imperialist ethic of the day. Eventually,
Japan's search for dominion in the Far East had calamitous results,
bringing the nation to defeat, occupation, and abject dependence on
American goodwill in August 1945.

Despite its more or less unconditional surrender at the end of World
War II, Japan's dependence on the United States was far from complete, even when our predominance was greatest. Since MacArthur
chose to implement the occupation through indirect rule, his reform
efforts required the collaboration of the Japanese bureaucracy, which
underwent only a brief and incomplete purge. As the cold war heated
up, moreover, Japan's strategic value to the United States provided
Prime Minister Yoshida considerable leverage in negotiations over the
restoration of sovereignty, a bilateral peace treaty, the terms of base
arrangements, and the provision of economic aid.

To be sure, Japan regained its sovereignty in 1952 at a price. It had
to accept a security relationship with the United States that circum-
scribed Japan's sovereignty and its diplomatic maneuverability. The USA
had permission to use its occupation forces to quell domestic distur-
bances, and U.S. utilization of bases in Japan was unrestricted. Domestic critics complained about a relationship of "subordinate independence" with the United States. Yet even before pressures for revision of

the terms of the agreement led to the 1960 Treaty of Mutual Cooperation and Security, the arrangement carried concrete and immediate benefits. As Prime Minister Yoshida, who regularly took the long view, observed on one occasion, "History provides examples of winning by diplomacy after losing in war."

Just as their nineteenth-century predecessors sought to eliminate unequal treaties, Yoshida and his successors worked systematically at reducing Japan's dependence on the United States. While Japanese diplomats regularly affirmed U.S.-Japanese interdependence, they devoted major efforts to altering its terms and augmenting Japan's autonomy. Seeking to limit their dependence on the United States' security umbrella, they yielded to our repeated requests for Japan's gradual rearmament, insisted on the domestic production of most weapons systems, pursued the indigenous development of technologies that could have significant military applications, and shouldered an ever more consequential share of the local costs of the U.S. military presence in Japan. Content throughout the cold war to maintain a low profile foreign policy that generally followed Washington's lead, Tokyo nonetheless skillfully utilized principles like the "separation of politics from economics" to facilitate commercial activities and quasi-official contact with nations from which it was politically estranged. The governing party even used an informal division of labor with the principal opposition party to extend its diplomatic flexibility. Former prime minister Takeshita commented on this to socialist Prime Minister Tomiichi Muriyama on July 22, 1994: "In the past," he said, "the LDP explained to the West, 'We have a clamorous group called the SDPJ.' Meanwhile, the SDPJ told the East, 'since the LDP is in power.'"[3]

Despite the impoverished conditions of their economy, the Japanese financed their postwar recovery and miraculous growth primarily out of domestic savings to avoid reliance on foreign capital. They utilized industrial policy to foster the growth of industries regarded as essential to the nation's long-term security and prosperity. Readily acknowledging the need for foreign help, particularly in furnishing advanced technology, they set the terms of foreign participation—usually through licensing arrangements—in ways that secured essential inputs without yielding significant control to non-Japanese firms. Although there were obvious limits to the degree to which the Japa-

3. Quoted in *Asahi*, July 24, 1992, p. 2.

nese could reduce their dependence on overseas sources of food, fuel, and raw materials, they went to great lengths to purchase commodities at favorable terms through long-term government contracts, reduce risks by diversifying suppliers, participate in the ownership of overseas agricultural and mining operations, extend generous foreign aid to key suppliers of raw materials, stockpile sensitive commodities, develop synthetic materials as potential substitutes, foster conservation measures for energy resources, safeguard Japan's capacity to supply its own rice, and promote the systematic development of higher–value-added industries that were less reliant on raw materials and energy.

The Japanese had traditionally ameliorated their dependence on foreign commerce by channeling the bulk of their import as well as export trade through Japanese trading companies. This facilitated their ability to buy only what they wanted while refusing to purchase goods and services that might compete with key domestic economic interests. The complexity of the domestic distribution system, meanwhile, limited direct access by foreign firms to Japan's consumers. As pressures from abroad to liberalize market access intensified, the government managed the pace and scope of liberalization in a manner that allowed its firms to adapt to increased competition without yielding much market share in key sectors. And in the face of huge and growing trade surpluses with the United States in the mid-1980s, Japan sought, inter alia, to diversify its commerce by trading more with Europe and Asia, to increase transplant factories in America, to bolster its reputation as a reliable and regular buyer of U.S. debt instruments at Treasury Department auctions, and to invest heavily in Washington lawyers and lobbyists to monitor, deter if possible, and circumvent if necessary protectionist trade bills and administrative rulings.

Undeniably, interdependence brought numerous benefits to Japan. The United States' security guarantee allowed Japan to keep its defense expenditures low. Equally significant, it enabled the Japanese to postpone or moderate an extremely divisive internal debate over rearmament and the complications it would pose for Tokyo's relations with its Asian neighbors. The United States extended Japan a continental market, and Japan was a major beneficiary of the liberal international economic system that we designed and defended. Our diplomacy was generally solicitous of Tokyo's interests.

Yet there were burdens as well. Above all, our persistent trade and current account deficits brought continuous U.S. pressure on Tokyo to adopt expansive fiscal measures, open its market, increase its aid, and share the costs of mutual defense. For Tokyo, some of these requests were easier to field than others. Increasing foreign aid was relatively simple. Current account surpluses needed to be recycled, and the Japanese were adept at using economic assistance to create new commercial opportunities for their private sector. Increased defense cost sharing was manageable, if not particularly popular. But the Japanese bureaucracy dug in its heels when the autonomy of Japan's economic policy was the issue. The key economic agencies in Tokyo viewed recurrent trade imbalances as occasions for a competitive struggle over which country had to adjust its internal policies to facilitate external balance. Throughout the postwar period, moreover, the Japanese felt that the United States had held most of the trump cards. Since unconstrained use of the dollar as a reserve currency was sanctioned, it was difficult for Japan—or anyone else—to force Washington to take the necessary fiscal and monetary steps to reduce its deficit. On the other hand, our ability to threaten to depreciate the dollar or limit Japan's access to the U.S. market gave us considerable leverage with which to press for more expansive fiscal policies or more restrictive monetary policies in Japan.

As many Japanese officials saw it, we had used those weapons in the periods from 1971 to 1973, from 1977 to 1979, and from 1985 to 1987 to force Japan to assume the major burdens of adjustment, despite their growing conviction that profligate American fiscal policies were the principal cause of our persistent trade deficits. Many influential Japanese believed that the USA periodically used raw power to force adjustments in Japanese monetary and fiscal policy because we were not prepared to pursue prudent economic policies at home. In the late 1970s, in particular, the Japanese, against their own predilections, had reflated their economy at our request. The Ministry of Finance was left struggling with the resulting run-up of government debt for more than a decade. This experience hardened Japanese resolve never again to accommodate U.S. pressures for macroeconomic adjustments that the Ministry of Finance considered imprudent.[4] American complaints about Japan's trade and investment strategies were increasingly seen as

4. See Tsuyoshi Kawasaki's analysis of these struggles in his "Structural Transformation in the US-Japanese Economic Relationship," in Henry Bienen, ed., *Power, Economics, and Security*, pp. 266–85 (Boulder: Westview, 1992).

a means of diverting attention from the U.S.'s own domestic short-comings. Clearly this bred frustration and resentment among Japanese officials as well as among politicians and businessmen.

The process that had been designed to manage these issues was also running out of steam. Macroeconomic policy coordination, under Treasury Department and Finance Ministry guidance, had achieved some notable results—particularly the Plaza and Louvre Accords. It had nurtured rapport and mutual confidence between some key play-ers—for example, Secretary of the Treasury James Baker and Minister of Finance Noboru Takeshita; Federal Reserve Bank Chairman Paul Volcker and Finance Ministry Vice Minister Toyoo Gyoten. And it probably imposed some restraint on beggar-thy-neighbor policies by both sides. Yet by the late 1980s discussions in this forum were regarded by Japanese officials as a dialogue of the deaf. We complained about their trade restrictions; they about our fiscal deficit. Neither side did much to tackle their own problems. Finance Ministry officials regarded the agenda as too heavily dominated by U.S. concerns and too driven by a desire for deals. Their confidence in our readiness to preserve a stable currency and an open market were slipping, and the suspicion that their U.S. counterparts were motivated by a quest for unilateral advantage was growing.[5]

Comparable frustrations were apparent among Japanese trade offi-cials. As Japan's persistent surplus grew, Tokyo accommodated U.S. pres-sures for restraint primarily through Voluntary Restraint Agreements (VRAs). Not that the Japanese liked VRAs; they simply preferred con-trolling Japanese exports to opening up the domestic market. Yet U.S. attention increasingly focused on market access. Beef and citrus pro-ducers had pressed hard for this, as had a host of other companies rep-resenting sectors in which the United States was highly competitive and Japanese regulatory barriers were high—for example, in industrial electronics, medical devices, telecommunications, and wood products. Growing U.S. interest in nontraditional trade barriers was scarcely wel-come to Japanese ministries, which utilized an extensive and opaque regulatory system to manage the economy. Few bureaucrats are pre-pared to cooperate in undermining their own power bases. Leaving the merits of these concerns aside, it was clear that the thinking of key ele-

5. See the recollections of Volcker and Gyoten in their jointly authored volume *Changing Fortunes* (New York: Times Books, 1992).

ments of the Japanese establishment was increasingly out of sync with Washington's views. And as Japanese power grew, its officials were less and less prepared to conceal their irritation or soften their criticism of Washington with stylized courtesy or elaborate circumlocution.

The looming end to the cold war brought other concerns to the surface. There were questions about the reliability of U.S. protection in the absence of an obvious and immediate Soviet threat. How long, many Japanese wondered, would the United States continue to extend a security guarantee to its major competitor when the Soviet threat was gone? While Japan felt domestic pressures to chart more autonomous policies abroad, it was having difficulties defining them. And it faced repeated requests from Washington for support of U.S. initiatives on regional and global problems.

As I prepared to tackle my new assignment, it seemed to me that each country reaped substantial benefits from our growing interdependence, yet both were troubled by its terms. If many Americans regarded the Japanese as predatory traders who shouldered international responsibilities only grudgingly, when pressed, many Japanese viewed the USA as a nation in decline, whining about others without being prepared to address its own problems and more solicitous of its ally's support than its ideas.

Interdependence might be inescapable. But it inspired different policy agendas in Washington and Tokyo. Americans were ready to acknowledge its virtues but were intent on ensuring a more equitable allocation of its benefits. The Japanese were more purposeful about maximizing their own autonomy, but they were also determined to achieve a wider sharing of power and to achieve the respect to which they believed their postwar accomplishments entitled them. Coming to grips with these disparate priorities and extending the considerable range of convergent interests that underpinned the U.S.-Japan relationship represented, it seemed to me, the overriding challenge of my tenure in Tokyo.

2

Reducing the Trade and Investment Imbalance

The Bush administration was dedicated to a strong political and security relationship with Japan. But it also wanted more balanced economic ties. Meetings before my departure for Tokyo with the president and his senior advisers—Jim Baker, Nick Brady, Brent Scowcroft, Bob Mosbacher, and Carla Hills—left no question in my mind about that. Consequently, I considered a sizable reduction in our bilateral trade deficit and the achievement of more equitable access to Japan's market as high-priority tasks for my mission. To be sure, the United States neither could nor should have expected to balance its current accounts on a bilateral basis. Moreover, the sources of its current global deficit were to be found in the savings/investment imbalance at home. Yet the size and persistence of the bilateral trade deficit and the perception that this reflected a lack of reciprocal access to the Japanese market undermined support for the U.S.-Japan alliance, jeopardized future bilateral political cooperation, and invited micromanagement of trade policy by Congress.

Congressional agitation over the trade issue was apparent at my confirmation hearings. Within the executive branch no clear strategy for handling trade policy had yet crystallized. Nor did I anticipate dramatic policy initiatives, although I did expect the administration to approach bilateral negotiations with a growing sense of urgency. The 1988 Trade Bill had established firm deadlines for measuring progress.

And the political climate in Washington spurred the administration to act with dispatch. The ongoing FSX negotiations, moreover, demonstrated that within the executive branch, the trade agencies had become more assertive on U.S.-Japan issues and the readiness of the White House and State Department to play down economic interests in favor of strategic concerns had diminished.

When I was pointedly asked by Senator Helms whether I intended to raise the rank of my commercial counselor to the level of minister counselor—the rank of his State Department counterpart at the embassy—in order to highlight the new priority accorded trade issues, I replied that I expected personally to serve as the embassy's "First Commercial Officer." Of course, I did not plan to supplant Keith Bovetti, a capable career commercial officer whom I subsequently promoted. But I wanted it known that I would make trade matters my personal business.

In fact, I took up my duties in Tokyo with strong convictions about several needed adjustments in the embassy's modus operandi. One priority was reestablishing the mission's reputation for credible and objective economic reporting. Preserving a balance between empathy for the host country and analytic detachment about it is one of the most demanding challenges for a professional diplomat. Among intelligence and policy agencies in Washington much of the embassy's analytic work on economic issues was widely discounted as reflecting an advanced case of "clientitis." Needless to say, there were many exceptions to this generalization: for example, the embassy conducted the analytic work that underlay the successful negotiation of a beef and citrus agreement in 1988, as well as providing input to future Bush administration proposals on distribution, land use, and tax policy in the Structural Impediments Initiative (SII) talks. Nevertheless, in the late 1980s, the Tokyo Embassy was reputed to have tilted too far in favor of its host. I was determined to effect a rapid change in this balance, for the embassy could not expect to exert influence on trade issues if Washington agencies thought it was tailoring its reports to a preconceived policy agenda.

A second requirement was a closer relationship with the U.S. business community. Many Japanese companies were beating ours badly in global competition. They could count on extensive and enthusiastic government support of their commercial activities. Given the size of the trade imbalance and the extraordinary difficulties foreign companies faced in penetrating the Japanese market, it seemed to me the least the embassy could offer was competent, energetic, proactive help to our own companies. That meant augmenting the talented group of commercial officers at our posts in Japan and displaying a receptive attitude toward any reasonable request American firms might direct our way. I wanted the U.S. business community to know that our doors were open and we were ready to lend them a hand.

A third priority was greater assertiveness in explaining U.S. market-opening requests and macroeconomic policy proposals to Japanese constituencies. The Japanese press tended to approach trade negotiations in a defensive and nationalistic spirit. I was not inclined to leave public interpretations of our proposals to them—or for that matter to Japanese authorities. So I resolved to speak straightforwardly and often to a wide variety of Japanese audiences, in hopes of broadening public understanding of the need for basic changes in the trade relationship. Blunt talk on such matters was not necessarily standard practice for ambassadors. There is an observable tendency among many diplomats speaking publicly to skate around problems and avoid controversies by relying on bland clichés. I believed, however, that if the U.S.-Japan relationship rested on the broad convergence of interests we regularly proclaimed, it could survive an acknowledgment of differences, provided they were approached in a friendly spirit. Leaving problems to fester, on the other hand, was likely to fuel resentments in United States while inviting miscalculations by Japan.

Dimensions of the Trade and Investment Problem

On substance, I had a nodding acquaintance with economics but had never borne responsibility for managing trade or investment issues. By instinct and intellectual conviction I was a free trader; more importantly, I represented an administration of that persuasion. But I also believed greater reciprocity in our economic ties with Japan would improve the competitiveness of U.S. companies, facilitate closer political relations with Tokyo, and head off additional protectionism in the United States. Ostensibly, these views had some resonance within Japan. Japanese leaders regularly affirmed their fidelity to free trade. Certainly, some barriers to Japan's market had come down. Its tariffs were relatively low, and quotas few. Steps were under way to deregulate certain corners of the market, most notably by privatizing national railway and telecommunication companies.

Yet mercantilist reflexes were alive and well in all the crucial realms of power: in the bureaucracy, which ran the government and managed the economy; in business circles, which welcomed government assistance even as it chafed under excessive regulation; among politicians, who mobilized campaign funds by guiding private interests through an extensive and impenetrable regulatory thicket; and in the press, where articles on trade were laced with military metaphors suggesting that one side's gain was another's loss. The very first question put to me by the press on my arrival at Narita Airport in early May 1989 was whether I expected a trade war. I responded that I have always regarded trade as a mutually beneficial activity, not as a zero-sum game. The remark did not seem to make much impression on my Japanese journalistic friends.

The sources of our huge and persistent global trade imbalances were complex and numerous. Both countries bore their share of responsibility. The root cause was to be found in the interaction of the fundamental economic preferences and contrasting macroeconomic policies of the United States and Japan. The difference between what Americans consumed and what they saved showed up in our external deficit, just as the discrepancy between Japan's savings and its domestic investments was reflected in its external surplus. In the 1980s, moreover, the United States attacked stagflation through an expansionary fiscal policy and tight money, while Japan stimulated growth and reduced its budget deficit with contractionary fiscal policies and cheap money. The predictable result was a growing fiscal deficit in the United States and a growing trade surplus and a foreign investment boom by Japan. Coordinated macroeconomic policies were the obvious remedy. But diagnosing the problem proved easier than treating it.

Another factor relates to both countries' trade policies. After World War II, the United States took the lead in creating a liberal international economic order based on free market precepts—most notably, transparency and nondiscrimination. We opened our market to the world and, in periodic GATT negotiations, pressed others to reduce trade barriers. Because of the many benefits flowing from widespread use of the dollar as an international currency, we accepted the constraints this imposed on our domestic economic policies. We used foreign aid, investment flows, and technology transfers to facilitate the growth of many developing countries. By shouldering the lion's share of the Western security burden, we created a stable trading and investment climate and enabled our allies—particularly Japan—to concentrate their attention and resources on economic growth. And in a host of other ways we tempered the pursuit of our own commercial interests by working to define and defend the global economic system. This was a matter of enlightened self-interest. We were the preeminent industrial power in the world, and free trade and open markets served our purposes well. We expected Japan to emulate our values and policies as their economies matured; in the meantime, we benefited from Japan's strategic dependence on us.

While U.S. companies were among the pioneers of globalization, creating many of the most impressive multinational corporations, the majority of firms were content to focus on the U.S. domestic market. Nor did Washington devote special attention to export promotion. The Japanese contention that our trade deficit was a result of the failure of U.S. companies to work hard enough at cultivating the Japanese market contained more than just a kernel of truth. By the late 1980s only about 45 percent of the United States' Fortune 500 companies had a presence in Japan, many involved in joint ventures owned only a minority share, and many local managers appeared not to have the ear of the CEO back at the home office. The Big Three auto makers had long-established relations with Japanese affiliates, for example, but none had tailored products for the local market, none controlled its own distribution system, and none appeared to accord a high priority to expanding market share in Japan or in the wider Asian market. To be sure, the Japanese had done nothing to ease their access to the market. Quite to the contrary: they had erected a complex and formidable array of barriers. But the Big Three had not undertaken credible attempts to overcome them.

Japan's approach to trade was inspired by Friedrich List rather than Adam Smith. Since Commodore Perry had forcefully opened Japan in the 1850s, its overarching national objective was to build up its economic strength in order to defend its traditional culture and national independence. The catch-up capitalism Japan practiced differed substantially from our own freewheeling, entrepreneurial style. The state played a larger role in regulating and managing markets. National power rather than individual welfare was a more central objective. Producer interests were favored over those of the consumer. The public sector was more extensive and more insulated from foreign competition than was ours. The government consistently directed capital into industries like steel, shipbuilding, autos, electronics, telecommunications, and computers, which were deemed consequential for national security. And the regulatory system kept domestic prices high and foreign competitors at bay, thus boosting profits at home and providing a protected base from which to assault foreign markets.

Bilateral and multilateral negotiations in the 1960s, 1970s, and 1980s had gradually loosened access to the Japanese market. Yet in the late 1980s it was still marked by highly internalized labor and capital markets and elaborate formal and informal barriers to market entry by newcomers—whether Japanese or foreigners. For the Japanese, the system was comfortable, egalitarian, and quite stable. For outsiders, regulatory arrangements were arbitrary and nontransparent; the costs of market entry were high; and while national treatment was affirmed, in practice insiders in Japan's clubby capitalist system were regularly accorded preferential treatment.

This is not to say that Japan's market was closed. In 1988 we exported nearly $60 billion worth of goods and services to Japan—more than we exported to the UK, France, and Italy combined. The composition of Japan's trade, moreover, was changing as more and more manufactured imports fueled the growth of its bubble economy. And it appeared that Japan had abandoned export-led growth, since from 1986 to 1990 all the nation's growth came from investment-led increases in domestic demand, as had been recommended in the widely publicized Maekawa Commission Report. Unfortunately, when the bubble subsequently burst, it was apparent that widely heralded structural changes had not taken root.

Our market was not completely open, either. In fact, we were subjecting additional sectors to protection as Japan was gradually relaxing some market access controls. While the Japanese openly practiced industrial policy, we aided sectors indirectly; for example, through government-financed R and D in such disparate sectors as energy, agriculture, aerospace, pharmaceuticals, and defense—all fields, incidentally, in which American exports were highly competitive. Nor were export subsidies entirely unknown, although ours did not begin to compare with Japan's extensive export support system.

All countries resort to protectionism to one degree or another. Some, however, are more purposeful about it than others; they protect their future rather than their past. Japan seemed determined to protect both. Its postwar industrial policy was aimed at establishing and protecting those infant industries on which Japan's future depended. Yet in pursuit of social harmony and political stability, weak and inefficient industries received plenty of government help as well: farmers got quotas and high tariffs; the owners of mom-and-pop stores successfully used the Large-Scale Retail Store Law to limit competition; the domestic financial sector remained heavily regulated by the Ministry of Finance; local construction companies divvied up contracts through the *dango* bidding system, whereby bids are rigged through collusive practices among contractors; defense suppliers were nurtured through the government's insistence on co-assembly, then co-production, and now co-development arrangements with U.S. manufacturers. In other words, both sunrise and sunset industries could count on one or another form of protection.

If the methods of protection favored by Japan were not unique to that country, neither were the rationales for it. Farmers needed protection because of their importance to the governing party; small retailers required it to preserve social stability; stringent interpretations of health and safety certification requirements were essential to protect Japanese consumers; domestic production of key defense systems was justified on national security grounds; special dispensations to high-tech industries were defended with traditional infant industry arguments.

Self-conscious awareness of Japan's protectionism seemed low among its leaders. I got a taste of this during a visit by Secretary of Commerce Bob Mosbacher in 1989. We were meeting with Michio Watanabe, an LDP faction leader and prominent member of the LDP's agricultural *zoku* ("tribe"). Mosbacher was predictably urging market openings; Watanabe responded with complaints about the failure of Americans to comprehend the demanding standards of Japanese consumers. "I visited the market over the weekend," Watanabe said, "and noticed that Bing cherries, which you prize so highly in the United States, were on the shelf alongside our Yamagata cherries. The Bings were thrown carelessly into boxes, and their quality was uneven. Though they were very cheap, there were plenty available, and sales seemed to be slow. Our Yamagata cherries, by contrast, were uniform in quality, larger in size, and packaged individually. Though they were priced four or five times higher than the

Bings, they were virtually sold out. So you see, your people just haven't paid attention to the demanding tastes of our consumers."

"I am pleased that you saw Bing cherries in the market, Mr. Watanabe," I replied, "for it took us years to wear down the Ministry of Agriculture's resistance to their entry. But if your Yamagata cherries are selling out despite this extraordinary price disparity, why was it necessary to keep ours out for so long?" I added that in fact the Bings had quickly established a significant market share, so perhaps some Japanese consumers were eating them and purchasing the Yamagatas to give away as expensive *omiyage*.

The Japanese had demonstrated the utility of invisible barriers to imports in the nineteenth century when the Western powers imposed low tariffs on them through unequal treaties. They responded with a series of import constraints including complex licensing controls, internal taxes, and subsidies to local producers. The cumulative effect of extensive market access controls, past and present, left relatively little space for newcomers, especially foreign businesses, and this became more and more galling as Japan's current account surplus mounted and its manufacturers became the benchmark firms in international competition. While some sectors were, of course, more internationalized than others, opportunities for foreigners to export and invest in Japan seemed limited mainly to those sectors in which Japanese producers were either uninterested or uncompetitive, in which foreign companies possessed technology the Japanese needed, or in which the consequences of denying foreigners access were clear and consequential.

Particularly irritating in the light of the Japanese government's free trade rhetoric, was clear-cut evidence that the public sector was especially difficult for outsiders to penetrate. U.S. construction, transportation, and telecommunications firms were among the world's most efficient. Yet in the late 1980s they won few public procurement contracts in Japan. Catch-22 situations were routine. The most bemusing, if irritating, was the arrangement until 1988 under which foreign construction firms could not operate in Japan without a license and could not obtain a license without five years' experience in the Japanese market. Little wonder that in these sectors foreign market share in Japan was trivial and Japanese price levels extremely high.

Shortly after I arrived in Tokyo, I asked the commercial section for a systematic comparison of the prices of a variety of products in Japan and the United States. Amy Anderson, a student intern from Prince-

ton, did much of the legwork, comparing prices on everything from
golf balls to theater tickets, VCRs to airline reservations, and cars to
camcorders. The results confirmed our intuitions. Many Japanese
export products could be purchased in the USA for prices 40 to 80 percent lower than in Japan. I discovered that disposable cameras with
operating instructions in Spanish and other European languages (i.e.,
exports that had been transported halfway around the world and back)
were selling as parallel imports in Tokyo at prices 25 percent lower than
those of identical products aimed at local consumers. Whether one
described this as dumping or forward pricing, the Japanese buying
public was subsidizing the welfare of foreign consumers. And from
what I could tell, they seemed neither to know nor to care very much.

Not that the trade picture was unrelievedly gloomy. Evidence of
some change in Japanese trading habits and even regulatory practices
was visible. The yen-dollar talks, initiated by the Treasury Department
and the Ministry of Finance in 1984 to foster deregulation of Tokyo's
financial markets, had brought some liberalization of access to Japan's
financial market and some decontrol of interest rates. Domestic
demand in Japan was up. Our bilateral deficit with Japan had begun to
fall. The MOSS talks (on electronics, medical devices, telecommunications, wood products, and transportation) had produced salutary
results, and exports in fields covered by those talks were growing
rapidly. Japan's investment-led boom was generating significant
demand for American capital goods. As Japanese tourism expanded,
more and more of its citizens were becoming aware of the price dis-
parities that made Tokyo the most expensive city in the world; discount stores, parallel imports, and catalog buying were among the
results. As Japanese companies globalized their operations, their business community was becoming increasingly sensitive to foreign
demands for reciprocity. The recently concluded Beef and Citrus
Agreement even suggested that further liberalization of Japan's agricultural market might be possible. And more and more Japanese were
complaining that their quality of life had not kept up with the accumulation of national wealth.

Adjusting the Balance

Our challenge was to accelerate a process of change that seemed to
be gathering some momentum. It would not be easy, for many anti-

competitive practices were deeply embedded in Japan's industrial structure and business practices. As U.S. Trade Representative Carla Hills put it, "we sometimes would need a crowbar." Given the consensual nature of Japanese society, moreover, change was destined to be slow and incremental. Our influence could be exerted only at the margins. It would only be effective if it was directed toward reforms that enjoyed significant support within Japan. I considered a GATT agreement to be especially critical, for it could provide multilateral rules for trade in areas where we encountered special problems with the Japanese—specifically, the services, agriculture, and high-technology sectors. And in multilateral negotiations we could enlist the help of other countries disadvantaged by limited access to the Japanese market.

In short, to attack a trade imbalance that exceeded $50 billion, we needed to set our own house in order, engage actively in sectoral negotiations, mount an effort to reduce structural impediments to the orderly adjustment of external accounts, and take aggressive steps to finish up the Uruguay round of the GATT. This was the agenda to which the Bush administration devoted its efforts.

"Physician, Heal Thyself"

A broad intellectual consensus among U.S. economists held that reducing the fiscal deficit and raising our savings and investment levels was central to any serious attack on our trade imbalance. The business community that submitted recommendations to Carla Hills in the spring of 1989 conceded that much. Yet support for the Gramm-Rudman-Hollings approach had flagged, President Bush had committed himself to "no new taxes," and a Democratic Congress had little interest in balancing the budget through reduced federal spending. Although the U.S. trade deficit with the world declined modestly from 1989 to 1992 as a result of a stronger yen and the U.S. recession, our fiscal deficit continued unfortunately to grow.

The Japanese, meanwhile, continued to best us on economic fundamentals. Their savings rate remained far higher than ours; from 1986 to 1992 their investment in new plants and equipment ran nearly 25 percent ahead of ours in absolute terms, though their economy was 40 percent smaller; Japan spent more than we did on civilian R and D; they were turning out larger numbers of engineers than we were; and their high school graduates consistently outperformed ours on international math and science tests.

The Bush administration acknowledged the importance of these issues. It put forward initiatives to address most of them. Few, however, emerged unscathed from Congress. In both Japan and the United States, some complained that the administration put little muscle behind its legislative efforts; others responded that a Democratic Congress was determined to block the president no matter what. The executive and legislative branches had different perceptions and priorities. It was a pity. The administration's Family Savings Plan, its proposed cut in the capital gains tax, new incentives for investment in civilian R and D, and initiatives for educational reform all had merit, though even bolder actions were warranted. The 1990 budget package was well intentioned, required political courage, and achieved some procedural results. But in the end the president paid a significant political price for abandoning his "no new taxes" pledge yet made no real dent in the savings/investment imbalance.

Improving our performance on economic fundamentals was critical not only to improving the performance of our companies but to the credibility of our efforts to alter Tokyo's economic policies. The Japanese were unlikely to accommodate our requests that they change, as long as we refused to tackle our own problems forthrightly. Our macroeconomic shortcomings provided them with ready excuses for foot dragging. Our negotiators in the SII talks were occasionally reduced to arguing that our problems would take care of themselves. I was particularly distressed by our rhetoric on the issue of savings. Washington representatives claimed that the baby boomers had come of age: they had entered the high income brackets; they had completed most needed purchases of consumer durables; their children were approaching college age; and they consequently had both the capacity and the incentives to save. It was a plausible line of argument for which, unfortunately, there was little concrete evidence. More to the point, I feared that an administration that believed the problem would resolve itself was unlikely to spend much time or political capital on fixing it. Certainly, when the Treasury Department and CEA proposed savings stimulus packages, these efforts did not appear to be central to the administration's congressional agenda. And by 1992 our savings rate remained below 5 percent, while Japan's was again climbing beyond 15 percent.

I had hopes that Secretary of State Baker might take these issues on and spoke at some length with him during one of my early trips home for consultations. He understood the problem completely and readily acknowledged its importance. Yet I sensed a certain reluctance on his part to tackle it. I subsequently recalled that in 1986, as secretary of the treasury and chairman of the Economic Policy Council, he had crafted a comprehensive package of measures to enhance America's competitiveness. Despite his devotion of much time and energy to this project, bureaucratic and political interests had altered it beyond recognition. I surmised that, as a pragmatic person with huge problems on his plate, he probably concluded that there were more promising ways of using his scarce time and political capital than hammering away at domestic issues for which other members of the administration bore principal responsibility.

The Bush administration did put together a stronger export promotion effort, and it crafted a modest, low-key technology policy to improve U.S. competitiveness. The Foreign Commercial Service was beefed up, and its director, Susan Schwab, recruited many capable officers with Japanese language credentials. Secretary of Commerce Bob Mosbacher readily supported embassy requests for additional commercial officers both in Tokyo and Osaka. The Commerce Department also initiated its promising Japan Corporate Program designed to interest middle-sized U.S. corporations in a sustained and systematic effort to crack the Japanese market. Mike Farren, Mosbacher's undersecretary of commerce, organized a binational, public-private consortium that successfully promoted design-in arrangements to increase U.S. sales of auto parts to Japanese car makers. Commerce pushed MITI to undertake complementary import promotion efforts. And Dr. Allen Bromley, the president's scientific adviser, undertook a number of steps to raise funds for technology development while easing the regulatory burdens that stifled such activity. Meanwhile, many U.S. companies, chastened by the excesses of the 1980s and alarmed by the formidable competitive challenges they confronted from the Japanese, shouldered the painful restructuring that was to revive our manufacturing industry in the 1990s.

Sectoral Negotiations

Like its predecessors, the Bush administration sought to remove barriers to market entry in Japan through sectoral negotiations. Its selection of sectors was shaped both by complaints from specific firms and industries and by a conscious effort to target industries in which Japanese barriers genuinely impeded sales by competitive U.S. firms. In every case, agreements were pursued on a most-favored-nation basis; we sought no preferential deals. Unlike its predecessors, however, the administration was armed with the Super 301 provision of the 1988 Trade Bill, many provisions of which it did not like but was required to implement. Thus in April 1989 the administration identified Japan as one of the countries that had engaged in unfair trade, specified three practices relating to trade in wood products, supercomputers, and artificial satellites that required redress, and proposed negotiations to remove them. The administration also proposed talks on structural impediments to trade but suggested that these discussions be taken up outside the framework of Super 301.

Between 1989 and 1992 thirteen bilateral sectoral agreements were negotiated. Four covered Japanese government procurement practices and procedures relating to supercomputers, satellites, construction services, and computer hardware and software; five covered Japanese government telecommunications standards, regulations, and licensing procedures; one covered technical standards for wood; and three covered market access problems involving both government policies and private practices regarding amorphous metals, semiconductors, and paper products.[1]

In some sectors, market access improvements were achieved without formal agreements. Extension of Japan's copyright laws to provide additional protection for foreign sound recordings and to curb unauthorized use of such recordings by rental stores was one example. The Commerce/MITI framework for promoting long-term relationships between Japanese auto makers and U.S. auto parts suppliers was another. The Action Plan, released at the time of President Bush's visit to Japan in January 1992, contained other informal understandings concerning glass, paper, and the treatment of foreign lawyers in Japan.

Although the administration pressed for the implementation of the 1986 Semiconductor Agreement, negotiated an action plan on automobiles in 1992 that contained specific numbers, kept very close track

1. Merrit Janow has summarized the dynamics and results of these negotiations admirably in her essay "Trading with an Ally: Progress and Discontent in U.S.-Japan Trade Relations," in Gerald Curtis, ed., *The United States, Japan, and Asia*, pp. 53–95 (New York: Norton, 1994).

of satellite and supercomputer purchases, and left a number of VRAs in place in the U.S. market, in general, it sought to improve the procedures governing market access and to avoid attempts to negotiate specific market shares for American products. This provoked scorn from some critics at home. I regarded such criticisms as misguided. No one involved was interested in negotiations for their own sake nor in achieving cosmetic agreements merely to defuse political pressures from the Congress. The negotiators—hard-nosed individuals with a detailed knowledge of the Japanese market—all realized that without concrete results, agreements were of little value. They sought in every case understandings that included elaborate provisions for monitoring results.

If the focus was on procedures, it was because that is where many of our market access problems arose. Occasionally, we had to overcome misconstructions on this score among our Japanese interlocutors. I well recall one conversation with a leading member of the LDP who had intervened effectively to break impasses on several nettlesome trade issues. The subject was construction, and our objective was to eliminate the designated bidder system in favor of open, transparent procedures for bidding on public construction projects. My interlocutor urged me to put aside the *tatemae* (formalities) in favor of the *honne* (real intentions) in our position; that is, which specific contracts, he asked, did we want for which companies? I demurred, noting that it was not possible for me to give him such an answer: I had no authorization to seek specific deals; the U.S. government could not pick and choose among competing bids from several American companies; and our request for genuine changes in the procedures reflected our real commercial interest. He remained puzzled.

Of course, his proposal would have had the merit of allowing U.S. companies to get at least a limited piece of the action while awaiting the broader systematic reforms we sought. Yet I still believe we were right to insist on transparent procedures. To obtain one or several contracts while leaving in place a dense, opaque, and, in this particular case, corrupt system for handling bids would not get at the heart of the market access problem or address the reciprocity issue that generated political resentment in the United States. This was the sort of dilemma—between standing on principle or getting a toe in the door—that we often faced.

Besides, process changes did lead to results. The results are admittedly difficult to judge, and they were surely mixed. But there was progress. Dick Nanto, who authored a study on the sectoral negotiations for the Congressional Reference Service in 1991, concluded that U.S. exports expanded dramatically faster in those sectors that had been the subject of such negotiations. By one calculation, over the thirteen sectors covered by new agreements achieved between 1988 and 1992, they increased by 57 percent. By early 1990 U.S. firms had won approximately $200 million in construction contracts. We won a significant increase in supercomputer awards from public institutions, though no U.S. bid prevailed in a head-to-head competition with Japanese suppliers. In several instances, Japanese bidders dropped out, presumably at the behest of government officials, with the result that we were not shut out of all public procurement contracts. A number of significant contracts were won by American satellite manufacturers following the June 1990 agreement. Many issues relating to standards were resolved.

Others remained, however. The supercomputer and construction agreements, for example, provoked continuing friction, mainly, in my view, because they were to be implemented by ministries in Tokyo that were either unwilling or unable to change their way of doing business. I believe Japanese officials were eager to accommodate their industry's desire to monopolize public procurement of supercomputers in order to boost their international competitiveness while preventing foreign manufacturers from gaining a strong foothold in university laboratories and corporate research centers. In the private sector, by contrast, U.S. supercomputer manufacturers earned a significant share of the market as Japanese companies sought to augment productivity by acquiring the highest-quality computing power available. Construction contracts, on the other hand, were a honey pot for the Liberal Democratic Party and *dango* bid-rigging arrangements were pervasive within the industry, so foreign pressure produced only modest results in the form of token contracts for foreign joint-venture partners of major Japanese construction firms. The administration did not respond by seeking specified market share understandings in these sectors, but it did let the Japanese know that two could play the game. Japan found itself frozen out of the U.S. public procurement market for supercomputers—mainly but not exclusively for reasons of competitiveness—and Senator Frank Murkowski (R-Alaska) regularly put legislation on the table reminding Tokyo that its entree to U.S. public construction contracts could be comparably limited.

The Semiconductor Agreement, negotiated originally by the Reagan administration in 1986, did represent a significant exception to the administration's approach. Although no explicit market share commitment was contained in that agreement, a side letter signed by the Japanese ambassador to the United States, Nobuo Matsunaga, referred to an expectation of a 20 percent share for foreign producers. In effect, this expectation was our target, and it was incorporated in a somewhat more explicit form into the revised 1991 Semiconductor Agreement.

I was not generally enthusiastic about numerical targets but came to regard this feature of the Semiconductor Agreement as not only useful but indispensable to the success our companies enjoyed in expanding their relationships with Japanese suppliers. Without the target, I do not believe the Japanese government would have pressured the major users to change their practices, nor would users have proven so amenable to design-in arrangements with U.S. suppliers. Our market share might well have languished around the 10 percent level. I believe it was not coincidental that our market share increased substantially only when the deadlines embedded in the agreement approached.

I could imagine other areas where market share targets might be salutary. But I did not regard them as generally desirable, nor was the Semiconductor Agreement a model to be widely replicated. I shared Carla Hills's contention that negotiated targets could be treated as ceilings as easily as floors. And beyond this, I had my doubts about the wisdom of leaving such determinations to bureaucrats. In any case, efforts to establish targets met with ferocious resistance from the Japanese, and even if that resistance were formally overcome, we might succeed perversely in augmenting the authority of the Japanese bureaucracy at a time when our commercial interests were best served by diminishing its power to manage markets arbitrarily.

The precedent was not repeated. To be sure, at the time of President Bush's visit to Tokyo in January 1992, Japanese auto makers did indicate their intent to more than double purchases of auto parts from $9 billion in JFY 1991 to $19 billion by JFY 1994. But that was an expression of industry intentions, not a formal government-to-government agreement. In other sectors, such as glass and paper, specific targets were forsworn in favor of generic language—for example, the promise of "substantially increased market access for foreign firms exporting paper products to Japan." The purpose was to make markets work more efficiently and competitively, not to supplant them with government-managed trade. Sadly, while the intentions of these agreements were admirable and the restraint noteworthy, the results—with respect to paper and glass, at least—were negligible. Subsequently, the Clinton administration struggled with the same problem: how to encourage efficient and competitive markets when Japan's Fair Trade Commission refuses to enforce the antimonopoly law. Expanding market access through negotiations is pick-and-shovel work, and there is no prospect that we shall be able to leave the trenches anytime soon.

The Structural Impediments Initiative

The SII talks were the Bush administration's major innovation in U.S.-Japan trade negotiations. Discussions about structural issues, to be sure, were not an entirely novel idea. Undersecretary of State Allen Wallis had chaired such discussions with Japanese counterparts during the Reagan administration. These reportedly had a rather academic character and were more useful in identifying issues than in resolving them. The Bush administration transformed the talks into a negotiating framework aimed at overcoming structural problems that impeded the orderly adjustment of external payment imbalances.

I had no hand in initiating the SII talks and first learned of the administration's decision to pursue them through a phone call from Carla Hills shortly after my arrival in Tokyo. She described the process and agenda that Washington had in mind and asked whether I thought the Japanese would play. I harbored initial misgivings about the proposal. The issues we intended to put on the table—Japan's savings/investment imbalance, its price mechanism, the distribution system, collusive business practices, land reform, and *keiretsu* arrangements—were sensitive matters that cut very close to the bone of domestic policy. They were subjects only rarely taken up in government-to-government negotiations. And clearly the Japanese had little enthusiasm for sharing decisions on these issues with foreigners.

On reflection, however, I concluded that such an effort was substantively warranted and would be politically manageable, provided we approached the talks in a collaborative spirit. The interdependence between our economies was growing; the domestic policy decisions Washington and Tokyo each made impinged directly on the other's interests; and it was only natural that some forum should exist for harmonizing our industrial structures and business practices. The EC-92 exercise under way at the time in Europe showed that sovereign governments could handle such issues successfully, and other methods of getting at the U.S.-Japan trade imbalance had fallen short. The items on Washington's agenda, moreover, had an undeniable impact on the level of Japan's domestic demand (savings/investment imbalance), the cost of market entry (land prices, collusive business practices, and *keiretsu* arrangements), and the price of imported products (distribution system).

The merits of the administration's proposal were not obvious to the Japanese. Some saw our initiative as an attempt to shift the principal burdens of trade adjustment from the deficit to the surplus country. Others saw Washington taking deliberate aim at features of Japan's economic structure and policy that were considered central to its postwar prosperity. Still others feared such negotiations would create an opening for meddlesome interference that could sour bilateral political relations without relieving the trade imbalance. The opportunity to raise complaints about U.S. policies and practices was little consolation for Japanese bureaucrats who were less interested in apportioning blame for existing trade problems than in protecting their ability to manage the Japanese economy without outside intrusion. Turning the SII talks into a cooperative venture was to prove a daunting challenge.

The formal proposal for SII talks was put on the table at bilateral talks that took place during the late May 1989 G-7 summit in Paris. The Japanese reluctantly agreed to it for several reasons: they could not deny the need to do something about the trade imbalance; the proposal was advanced by President Bush himself; it allowed talks to take place outside the Super 301 framework; and since each side would be able to present its concerns, the Japanese could construe the process as a two-way street.

An inside account of the SII talks will have to come from others. The strategy was conceived in Washington. Negotiations were carried out by subcabinet officials from the capitals. I participated in most plenary meetings and was regularly consulted by members of our team. But neither I nor other embassy representatives sat in on the restricted meetings among the principals—held outside Japan under conditions of considerable secrecy—where much of the real bargaining took place. The embassy did nonetheless exert considerable influence over the content, politics, and outcome of the talks.

For starters, we sought to counter the objections of those Washington officials who resisted the idea that the talks should be a forum in which both governments could put issues on the agenda. An effort to concentrate exclusively on Japanese structural impediments was not logically compelling and had no chance of eliciting support from the Japanese government. The Japanese were in no mood to be placed in the dock by a government they felt was guilty of fiscal profligacy and inattentive to its own competitiveness problems. Besides, I felt we would benefit from Japanese suggestions. Any pressure, I thought, that helped us step up to our own economic problems promptly and forthrightly should be welcomed. Symbolically, a two-way process could underline our resolve to achieve greater reciprocity.

In providing analytic support to the U.S. delegation, the embassy sought to discourage ideas that bore a "Made in the USA" label. Few in Washington possessed a competent grasp of the details of Japan's land-use policies, its distribution system, its price mechanism, or its *keiretsu* arrangements. In any event, proposals for reform were legion in Japan; the trick was to add our voice to thoughtful recommendations for change that already enjoyed resonance with important Japanese constituencies. Thus we compiled an exhaustive survey of suggestions that had emanated from the Maekawa Commission, the Administrative Reform Council, industrial federations like Keidanren and Keizai Doyukai, academic journals, and even the popular press.

Beyond helping to shape our side's proposals, the embassy sought, as the negotiation matured, to tease out of Washington clearer signals as to which items were critical and which were merely desirable. In any complex negotiation, many requests are put on the table. This was particularly true of SII. We had an extensive agenda; many agencies with quite different concerns were represented on our delegation, and it was easier for them to maintain internal harmony when each agency was allowed to pursue its pet projects. But the conclusion of a deal requires the assertion of priorities and tough choices among competing claims. We were interested in striking a deal, not in scoring debater's points. And we knew that getting a deal required that some of our Japanese interlocutors recognize the core elements of what we needed so that they could judge the merits of the package and figure out how to generate the necessary political support for it. So we prodded Washington to assert clearer priorities. Some in Washington were more receptive to this than others. Bob Zoellick, counselor in the State

Department and a close confidant of Secretary Baker, was particularly helpful in this regard.

The embassy also took responsibility for explaining the logic of U.S. proposals to the Japanese public and seeking support for them within the political leadership. Our best shot at mobilizing such support, I thought, lay in concentrating particularly on raising Japanese infrastructure spending to reduce the savings/investment imbalance, urging reform of the distribution system to lower prices for Japanese consumers, encouraging changes in land policy to reduce land prices—a major cost to foreigners of doing business in Japan and a major impediment to more affordable housing for the Japanese, and attacking collusive business practices that contributed to the high cost of living in Japan.

I made our case in scores of public speeches, briefings for editorial writers, lunches for businesspeople and academics, and one-on-one meetings with people influential in politics and the bureaucracy. I did not conceal the commercial motives behind our interest in structural reform but emphasized the benefits such reforms could bring to Japanese citizens, stressed the ways a successful SII negotiation could relieve pressures in the U.S.-Japan relationship, and reminded skeptical Japanese that the agenda they had set for us posed a more demanding political challenge for U.S. leaders than we were requesting of them. After all, they wanted us to consume less, save more, and work harder, while we were simply asking them to invest more of their hard-earned wealth in the welfare of Japanese citizens while making available at more reasonable prices a wider array of quality products to consumers in their own country. Not a bad trade-off—for Japan.

Pinning down the details of the deal required extensive consultations—what the Japanese termed *nemawashi*—with senior officials and politicians. It fell to me, either alone or with Washington visitors in tow, to make these rounds, outline our hopes, explain the political lay of the land at home, and urge timely decisions. My task was not to negotiate the deal but to help create a permissive political atmosphere for concluding it.

I spent considerable time with senior bureaucrats, but they were not my primary target. Senior officials from key ministries were in regular touch with our delegation, and their enthusiasm for the enterprise was distinctly limited. A few senior MITI officials proved to be unexpectedly helpful, however, and progress on loosening access to the distribution system owed much to their efforts. By contrast, some Ministry of Foreign Affairs officials were more cantankerous than I had anticipated. Generally speaking, we looked to them to represent foreign policy considerations to other agencies and to work hard to overcome obstacles to a successful negotiation. Vice Foreign Minister Takakazu Kuriyama, Deputy Foreign Minister Koji Watanabe, and Cabinet Counselor Tatsuo Arima were among those who recognized the importance of attaining an agreement and played helpful roles in reaching it. The going was frequently tough even with old friends, and some of my exchanges with them were prickly, perhaps because they bridled at some requests, considering them impertinent, resented the style of some of our delegates, and wished to preserve their well-deserved reputations for tough-mindedness with their own business and political constituencies.

I included in my rounds ministers and senior officials of particularly parochial ministries like Construction, Transportation, and Post and Telecommunications that controlled or influenced the disposition of billions of dollars worth of public contracts yet rarely took account of foreign concerns in their decisions. The involvement of these officials in the SII process served to broaden their awareness of international considerations and helped create a more efficient early warning network for identifying potential trade problems before they became politicized. It was heartening, for example, to see many of these ministries appoint for the first time vice ministers for international affairs. This institutionalized such concerns and gave us a place to register our views.

While the bulk of our political dialogue was with the LDP, I had periodic contacts with the opposition parties on SII and other trade issues. Initially I thought that the Socialists and Komeito, as parties with strong urban constituencies, might share an active interest in promoting structural reforms. The Socialists were especially disappointing in this regard. For example, I briefly nurtured the forlorn hope of enlisting the interest of Takako Doi, then the leader of the Socialist Party, in the process, but I ran into a brick wall: the Socialists appeared more preoccupied with co-opting traditional rural supporters of the LDP than in expanding their own urban and suburban political base. They exhibited virtually no interest in deregulation.

One of my early contacts with Doi, in fact, cost me a run-in with Ichiro Ozawa, secretary general of the LDP. Though my meeting with

Doi was routine, she described it to the press as a prelude to more intimate links with the embassy. Coming on the heels of dramatic Socialist gains in the 1989 Upper House elections, Ozawa presumably feared that we were giving our contacts with the opposition a higher profile in order to pressure the government in the SII negotiations. He promptly dispatched a letter admonishing me to avoid steps that might be perceived as meddling in Japanese politics during the run-up to early Lower House elections.

I had no Machiavellian purpose in mind when I met with Doi; I was simply looking, as usual, for sympathizers for market liberalization anywhere I could find them. Nor would I have been fazed by a confidential expression of Ozawa's concerns. I regarded his letter, however, as unnecessarily formal and surprisingly defensive. The Japanese embassy in Washington had maintained close contacts with leaders on both sides of our political aisle for years; we were determined to do the same in Tokyo. I told Ozawa this and also asked my deputy chief of mission to inform him quietly that I was not amused to learn that he had dispatched a letter to Secretary Baker complaining about my conduct. That missile, entrusted to an embassy acquaintance of Ozawa's (and mine), was never delivered. Overall, the episode revealed much about the LDP's nervousness over its electoral prospects, as well as Mr. Ozawa's readiness to play hardball. Happily, my subsequent contacts with him were more cordial and productive.

As the first round of SII talks reached their culmination in the spring of 1990, my contacts with senior LDP politicians became more frequent and crucial. Regular contacts included the major faction leaders and senior officials of the party. The purpose of the meetings—invariably characterized in the press as involving the unremitting application of pressure—was to be certain our proposals and priorities were understood, to encourage active political efforts on the part of those who displayed some empathy with our views, and to neutralize any misperceptions about our positions that had resulted from misleading press stories or mischievous rumors. As a result of their clout within the party or the portfolios they managed for the government, noteworthy interlocutors were LDP faction leaders Noboru Takeshita, Shin Kanemaru, Shintaro Abe, Yasuhiro Nakasone, and Michio Watanabe; Ichiro Ozawa, secretary general of the LDP; Finance Minister Ryutaro Hashimoto; and Hiroshi Mitzuzuka, minister of international trade and industry.

I did not routinely include Prime Minister Toshiki Kaifu in these consultations, and this became something of a problem for him and for me. In principle I thought it inappropriate to request appointments with the prime minister unless I had instructions. Conducting more informal *nemawashi* with political leaders was my idea; the talks were not directed by Washington. Beyond this, I assumed that my contacts with members of the cabinet were routinely reported to the prime minister. Nor did I believe I would be doing Mr. Kaifu a favor by dropping in for informal chats—even if he had had the time and inclination for them. My appearance at the prime minister's residence invariably drew extensive press attention and would have invited speculation that I was seeking to pressure him directly. Conduct that I had hoped would indicate my sensitivity to his political situation was, nonetheless, misconstrued by the media, which chose to regard the absence of meetings as reflecting a low U.S. estimate of the prime minister's power and authority. Contrary to such reports, I had a high regard for Mr. Kaifu's commitment to the bilateral relationship and his desire to attenuate trade frictions between our countries. In the end, I got Washington to send me instructions and began to make occasional well-publicized calls on the prime minister. But the rumors persisted.

Occasionally I met with larger gatherings of politicians to discuss trade matters. In the spring of 1990 Shintaro Abe invited me, along with other embassy associates, to meet over breakfast with a representative group of Diet members. Many were highly agitated about key issues. Some questions were blunt, and so were my answers. Criticism was especially intense over our insistence on changes in the Large Scale Retail Store Law, which provided extensive protection for small retailers—a significant constituency of the party. I reminded the Diet members that Isao Nakauchi, owner of Daiei Department Stores, held majority ownership of the Ala Moana Shopping Center in Honolulu, one of the biggest shopping malls in the United States. No U.S. law had impeded that acquisition; no regulation had delayed its consummation; no retailers association, to my knowledge, had attempted to forestall it; and no special public outcry had greeted its announcement. Americans would surely resent it, I observed, if Toys R Us had to wait ten to twelve years for approval of its application to set up stores in Japan—a not unlikely outcome if the Large-Scale Retail Store Law were not amended. Though this and a few other exchanges were a bit feisty, Abe later told me that the meeting had been useful in providing friendly Diet members arguments to use with constituents while allowing hard-liners to blow off steam.

A more decisive result stemmed from a private call on Shin Kane-maru during the culminating phase of the negotiations. We were seek-ing a sizable increase in Japan's infrastructure spending in order to reduce its savings/investment imbalance. Kanemaru's dialect was notoriously difficult to understand, but when I suggested a figure, he responded with a counterproposal that was crystal clear and eventually stuck.

Ultimately, the SII agreement achieved in June 1990 was hailed as a success. Certainly, I regarded it as such. Each government committed itself to a number of significant steps to ease the adjustment of exter-nal trade imbalances. The Japanese pledges were far-reaching and included

- o major increases in aggregate infrastructure spending to reduce the imbalance between domestic savings and investment;
- o potentially consequential land reform measures, including a review of the tax structure and deregulation of land-use policies;
- o steps to lower distribution costs through faster import clearance, improved import infrastructure, and a substantial liberalization of the Large-Retail Store Law;
- o more rigorous enforcement of the Anti-Monopoly Law, includ-ing criminal suits, higher penalties and the facilitation of private law suits;
- o and enhanced disclosure requirements to make *keiretsu* groups more transparent.

Needless to add, the United States made a variety of pledges as well: for example, to take concrete measures to raise the level of domestic sav-ings; to reduce the federal government's fiscal deficit; to encourage higher levels of civilian research and development; to augment export promotion efforts; and to improve the quality of job-training programs.

The Japanese press hailed the outcome. Well it should have. The Japanese people would benefit more from the concessions made by their government than we would—a point to which I referred in remarks to the Foreign Correspondents' Club of Tokyo in late April. I asked:

Is more Japanese investment on roads and airports a "concession" to outsiders? It improves the standard of living of Japanese citizens and helps Japanese businesses get products to market more quickly and cheaply.

Is the removal of restrictions on new large stores a "concession" when it permits Japanese shoppers to buy high-quality products at lower prices during more convenient hours?

Is it a concession when Japan deregulates its telecommunications sector, enabling consumers to utilize new products at reasonable prices, while stimulating technological innovation through competition?

Are changes in building codes to permit wider use of safe wood dwellings a "concession," when surveys show that 87 percent of Japanese consumers prefer to live in wooden homes?

Should one regard amendment of Japanese laws to protect U.S. sound recordings a "concession," when one of the principal beneficiaries will be CBS Records, now owned by Sony?[2]

In retrospect, the agreement contained some useful elements, but it brought no historic breakthroughs in our economic relations with Japan. Reform of the Large-Scale Retail Store Law was probably the most significant element. Substantial barriers to the distribution system remained, however, and MITI seemed to lose its enthusiasm for reform thereafter. And while the Fair Trade Commission became somewhat more active, it was positively unhelpful on key issues like paper and glass. And despite the infusion of infrastructure spending, the Japanese economy took a nosedive after the first SII report. Even so, June 1990 proved to be the high-water mark for the SII process. Successful resolution of differences over some unusually sensitive issues had been achieved without provoking a serious nationalist backlash in either country. The U.S. embassy was even hailed by some in the local press as the most effective opposition party in Japan—a tribute predictive of future difficulties. The principle that our governments should work to harmonize our industrial structures, business practices, and economic policies had acquired wider acceptance. Parochial domestic regulatory agencies had been exposed to the external consequences of their day-to-day decisions. And a follow-up mechanism was in place to monitor implementation and—at least so the U.S. delegation hoped—raise new proposals for reform.

2. "A Report on Recent Developments on Trade Issues" (Tokyo: U.S. Embassy, 1990), p. 4.

Regrettably, negotiations went downhill from there. Not that any organized effort on either side sought to roll back the commitments made. But the momentum for collaboration gradually dissipated. Both sides shared the responsibility. The Bush administration failed to deliver on many of its promises. This was a consequence of political gridlock, not bad faith, but the result was the same. To be sure, the 1990 budget package represented an effort to attack the fiscal deficit problem, but the package made scarcely a dent in the deficit, and many of the SII-related legislative proposals submitted by the administration to Congress were bottled up in committee or rejected outright.

On the Japanese side, the bureaucracy, which detested the SII process, dug in its heels about making any new commitments. More generally, the impetus for reform in Japan stalled in 1991 as the bubble economy burst. Implementing an agreement could not command the kind of press attention that negotiating it had, and the public gradually lost interest. Meanwhile, Washington moved on to other priorities, and until President Bush visited Tokyo in January 1992, the bilateral trade issues were relatively quiescent.

Personally, I felt the success of bilateral trade negotiations in the spring of 1990 was achieved at a considerable political price. Nerves were frayed on both sides; the tone of our official relationship with Japan visibly soured. I believed that we needed a breather while the dust settled and was anxious to find some framework in which we could highlight shared interests on trade matters. The Uruguay round of the GATT provided one such opportunity.

The Uruguay Round

With good reason, the Bush administration had identified a successful GATT round as its highest-priority trade objective. A more comprehensive GATT regime would serve U.S. interests well. Many of the sectors in which we were most competitive—such as trade in agricultural commodities, services, and high-technology products—were not regulated by multilateral trading rules. And few nations obtained greater benefits from a liberal global trade regime than Japan; aside from the issue of rice imports into Japan, our respective interests in the Geneva negotiations appeared substantially to converge. I hoped the political benefits of playing an active role in the GATT round would appeal to

Japanese leaders. So we sought Tokyo's help in moving the talks to an early conclusion.

On trade as well as on other matters, the Japanese government had become accustomed to pursuing its narrow commercial interests while leaving most of the responsibility for defining and defending the rules of the international system to us. In my view, the Uruguay round would test Japan's willingness to expend political capital to reshape the global trading system. It could thus serve a political purpose by reminding them of their responsibilities. The structure of the negotiations, unfortunately, limited the scope for collaboration. The centerpiece of the talks throughout the Bush years was reform of agricultural trade. This issue, regrettably, afforded the Japanese little political maneuverability. We went through the periodic ritual of enjoining Tokyo to pay its dues by taking a forthcoming position on agricultural issues, including the principle of tariffication (the process of translating all forms of agricultural protection into tariffs whose transparency made them more susceptible to multilateral adjustment through negotiations). Yet French obstructionism to major liberalization of agricultural trade rules provided Japan with a ready excuse to duck a tough issue and defer an unpalatable choice.

My predecessor had consistently urged Washington to lay off the rice issue in view of Japan's political sensitivities. I was less inclined to do so. Not that I expected we would sell much rice to the Japanese. At most, our industry analysts anticipated sales of perhaps $100 million if the market were partially opened—a figure that would make no dent in our bilateral deficit. Nor did I expect our logic to sway the politicians, bureaucrats, and farming interests that kept the import ban in place: the Ministry of Agriculture was determined to preserve its ironclad control over the market; LDP leaders were not about to jeopardize money and votes from a powerful rural constituency; and the main agricultural lobby, Zenno, had enough money and votes to intimidate any politician who even hinted at possible concessions. In practical terms, only one circumstance was likely to move Tokyo on this issue. Liberalization of the rice market would be realistically possible only when Japan had to choose between accepting a limited opening of that market or taking the blame for the failure of the Uruguay round. In the meanwhile, all we could do was explain why we wanted Japan to step up to this issue.

The argument was relatively simple. The developed countries' interests in market access, intellectual property protection, and wider opportunities to sell services in developing country markets required some accommodation of developing countries' interests in expanding their agricultural exports to developed country markets. Thus the need for reform of agricultural trade. If important countries like Japan, however, insisted on excluding commodities like rice from the negotiations, every other advanced country would demand comparable exemptions and soon there would be little scope for reform.

Japan clearly faced formidable opposition to opening this market from its rice lobby. But that did not make them unique. Farmers exerted disproportionate political clout in Europe and the United States as well. Moreover, the rice import ban had become a powerful symbol to Americans of Japan's habit, despite its enormous trade surplus, of seeking special arrangements to shield inefficient sectors from competition. Besides, contrary to warnings of the scaremongers in the Ministry of Agriculture, the market opening proposed in Geneva was limited and would be phased in over a lengthy period. The principle of tariffication foreshadowed further liberalization later, but the proposals being discussed during the Uruguay round would allow Japan to sustain formidable protective barriers around its rice farmers for years to come.

I registered these points in public speeches and private remonstrances to politicians, bureaucrats, business representatives, and journalists over many months. While individual politicians occasionally acknowledged the force of my arguments, in public I heard only excuses. The arguments found greater resonance in the business community, however, and Keidanren, Japan's most powerful industrial federation, eventually lobbied publicly for liberalization. In poll after poll, moreover, Japanese citizens appeared to recognize that liberalization of the market was both inevitable and, within limits, even desirable. Yet, as expected, the special interests exerted a controlling influence. And they left no stone unturned in their efforts to keep the market closed. The Agriculture Ministry even threatened to arrest our embassy representatives if they displayed U.S. rice at an international food fair in Tokyo in 1991.

We hoped the time for a decision on GATT might arrive in December 1990 when the GATT ministerial was scheduled to convene in Brussels. In anticipation of the meeting, I made my usual rounds. Key LDP leaders were predictably cautious and noncommittal. Some might have been prepared to accept a very limited market opening, if it were decoupled from the principle of tariffication, a step for which none appeared prepared. Former prime minister Takeshita acknowledged to me with a wry smile that when agricultural issues came up at GATT the usual modus operandi for the Japanese delegation was to look at their watches, shift uneasily in their seats, and suggest that the time had come for lunch, another meeting, or an early flight home. On this occasion, such passivity would have been welcomed. But the head of the Japanese delegation, Agriculture Minister Tomio Yamamoto, took the lead in publicly denouncing GATT Chief Arthur Dunkel's proposal that all forms of agricultural protection be converted into tariffs as a means of simplifying negotiations for the equitable removal of barriers.

The Japanese were not responsible for the impasse in Geneva. But it was disappointing to observe the leaders of the world's second-largest economy approach the negotiations so defensively. From the Geneva press reports of the negotiations, one might have wondered whether Japan was even present. Equally disappointing was the fact that when the Japanese did display modest activity, their positions rarely complemented our own. They focused the bulk of their attention on the antidumping and countervailing duties issues. On the broader questions of tariff reductions, market access, service trade, and intellectual property rights, they played their cards extremely close to the vest, shunning the lead, while seeking to withhold their offers until others had disclosed their bids. Their negotiating tactics were a logical means of defending their nation's commercial interests, but they provided dispiriting evidence that Japan's leaders were unprepared to incur significant political risks to facilitate an agreement. A GATT agreement was eventually concluded, but not on my watch. My tour in Tokyo ended, as it began, with little discernible progress on this front.

Macroeconomic Coordination

Coordination of macroeconomic policy was central to any serious effort to reduce our trade imbalance: we could not reduce our trade deficit without saving more and consuming less; Japan could not control its trade surplus without investing more of its savings at home. Regrettably, while thoughtful individuals on both sides understood this, neither side took effective action. Bilateral communications on the subject were at best sporadic, and they rarely inspired mutual confidence. Bureaucratically, the U.S. Treasury and the Japanese Ministry of Finance controlled macroeconomic discussions. While our respective officials worked very effectively on a number of international questions (e.g., Mexican debt, establishment of the European Bank for Reconstruction and Development), I saw little evidence of effective macroeconomic coordination. The bureaucratic fit was not perfect. Japan's MOF possessed authority for managing both tax policy and budget compilation; Treasury did not. In the U.S. Treasury, political appointees controlled policy decisions; in the MOF, the bureaucrats were a law unto themselves. In fact, no component of the U.S. government could begin to match the MOF's considerable power. It recruits the best and the brightest from the finest university in Japan; it dominates the budgetary process; it controls the nation's financial system; it places its retiring senior officials in charge of many of the key private banks, research institutes, insurance companies and securities firms; and it utilizes its control of the tax system to deflect private and public attempts to bring outside pressure to bear on its decision-making process.

I was never much of a player on macroeconomic policy issues, and I learned early that MOF officials did not take kindly to suggestions from me. In my first call on Finance Minister Tatsuo Murayama in May 1989, I asked what I considered an innocent question about why the ministry sought to maintain a sizable surplus in its consolidated budget despite high levels of private savings and widespread complaints about the inadequacies of Japan's public infrastructure. The minister changed the subject. I subsequently learned that his associates were offended that I had even raised it. My subsequent encounters with MOF officials, while invariably cordial, were rarely productive.

It was apparent that both MOF and Treasury preferred to keep discussion of macroeconomic issues, as well as other matters for which they bore responsibility, strictly within their own channels. MOF resented the SII framework not least because it exposed the discussion of financial issues to other Japanese agencies. MOF regularly excluded the Japanese ambassador in Washington from its discussions with Treasury, and I sensed that Treasury would have been happy to reciprocate. At the culmination of the SII discussions on savings/investment issues, the ministry sought—unsuccessfully—to exclude me from a meeting between Minister Ryutaro Hashimoto and Assistant Secretary of the

Treasury Charles Dallara. I informed Vice Minister Makoto Utsumi that how the Ministry of Finance chose to deal with the Japanese ambassador in Washington was its problem, but as long as I was ambassador to Japan, I would decide whether to accompany senior U.S. officials to meetings with ministers.

The need for a discreet channel between central bankers and financial officials is, of course, widely acknowledged. Sensitive subjects like exchange rates cannot be handled in wider fora without chaotic results in the foreign exchange market. Consequently I neither had nor sought any role in deliberations about exchange rates, and I made it a practice never to comment publicly on the subject. Nor was I consistently well informed regarding MOF-Treasury discussions on other issues. The telephone provided a direct line of communications between them, and the gist of such discussions was closely guarded.

Though mostly out of the loop, I was concerned that the discussions between MOF and Treasury did not appear to inspire mutual confidence. Momentum in the yen-dollar talks had dissipated. David Mulford, undersecretary of the Treasury and a frequent visitor to Tokyo in the past, showed up only rarely and appeared preoccupied with other issues. Personal relationships at both ministerial and working levels appeared stiff. As far as I could discern, the cooperative language contained in G-7 summit communiqués regarding macroeconomic policy was not matched by complementary work programs to assure its realization.

In truth, MOF had a decidedly different agenda from ours. Its highest priority was "fiscal reconstruction"—reducing the public indebtedness Japan had incurred from fiscal expansion measures in the late 1970s. The attitude toward deficit financing in the ministry was "Never again." Cheap money, rather than fiscal stimulus, was used to fuel growth in the late 1980s. This allowed Japanese companies to finance the adjustments required to remain competitive in the face of a stronger yen. Improving the social infrastructure of the country was accorded priority only insofar as it could be accommodated within the framework of tight budgets.

Nor did MOF appear interested in rectifying the savings/investment imbalance through more expansive use of the off-budget Fiscal Investment Loan Program, through which postal savings funds were channeled into capital investment projects. The U.S. Treasury believed that Japan possessed the fiscal flexibility to augment such spending dramatically because it was running a large surplus in its consolidated budget. That budget included social security funds, however, and the Japanese argued that prudence required them to build up their reserves to cope with the future burdens of an aging population. This struck our experts as excessively cautious since the real financial burdens of an aging population were at least a decade away. Investments in infrastructure could be amortized so that funds would be back in the treasury when most needed; besides, the elderly population would benefit to a disproportionate degree from improved public facilities such as transportation, hospitals, housing, and other social amenities. But given that Japan's public finances were in better shape than ours, our advice was, perhaps understandably, discounted.

I did consistently urge the Japanese in both public remarks and private conversations to rely more heavily on domestic demand as a means of reducing its external surplus. The Japanese government had ostensibly embraced that concept when the Maekawa Commission Report was issued in 1986. Certainly their government regularly reaffirmed this intent in G-7 communiqués. And, in fact, from 1986 to 1990 domestic demand growth, driven by robust investment levels, was very impressive: imports grew rapidly; Japan's global surplus diminished; and so did our bilateral current accounts imbalance. Yet when the bubble economy burst and the Japanese economy slipped into recession in 1991, domestic demand weakened, and the Ministry of Finance strenuously resisted fiscal stimulus measures that could not be financed within a balanced budget.

Some in Washington suggested that we address the savings/investment imbalance by encouraging the Japanese to save less. This struck me as wrongheaded, and I felt the Japanese would regard such advice as both gratuitous and perverse coming from a nation as improvident as our own. Moreover, since other industrial countries also were saving too little, the global economy depended increasingly on savings generated by Japan and other East Asian nations. Consequently, I preferred to urge Washington to save more, while prodding Japan to channel more of its savings into public investments at home.

Why, I asked, did it make sense for Japan's general government budget to generate high surpluses at a time when personal savings rates remained extremely high? Why was the proportion of GDP devoted to personal consumption declining at a time when most Japanese complained that their national wealth was not matched by the standard of living to which their hard work and prolonged effort entitled them? Wouldn't it be sensible, I asked, for the government of Japan to direct more of its savings into investments in public infrastructure and housing for the Japanese population? The suggestion found some resonance in the Japanese press, if not in the Ministry of Finance.

As Japan's recession deepened and our recovery commenced, I was asked by Washington with increasing regularity to encourage the Japanese to apply more fiscal stimulus. This pressure heightened particularly on the eve of President Bush's visit to Japan in January 1992. Treasury Secretary Nick Brady believed a strong mutual commitment to complementary macroeconomic measures would contribute to the success of the trip, could help stimulate U.S. exports in an election year, and would put pressure on the Germans for comparable steps on interest rates at the upcoming Bonn summit.

The Miyazawa government was preparing to submit its budget for fiscal 1992 to the Diet. It envisaged a 3.5 percent growth rate for the year, with all growth projected to come from domestic demand. Economists at the embassy and many of Japan's most respected private research institutes, however, dismissed the government estimates as highly implausible. I made the rounds of government officials and LDP politicians, soliciting their support for fiscal stimulus measures. It was tough going, but former prime minister Takeshita, Shin Kanemaru, and some members of the LDP Policy Research Council showed some flexibility. When Bob Zoellick, undersecretary of state for economic affairs, came to Tokyo to finalize advance preparations for the president's visit in late December, I took him to see many of the same contacts, as well as Prime Minister Miyazawa, underscoring the U.S. government's interest in this issue.

Negotiations over communiqué language were, of course, conducted by the Treasury and MOF. The latter was predictably unsympathetic. We anticipated some help from Prime Minister Miyazawa, who was widely regarded as a fiscal expansionist and had been the architect of a major public works package in 1987 during his stint as finance minister. This time, however, Miyazawa appeared reluctant. Negotiations continued up to and through the visit. A joint statement was eventually issued. The operative clause from Washington's standpoint involved a reference to the Japanese government's plans to submit to the Diet a budget designed to strengthen domestic demand by increasing public investment and to monitor the progress of those measures in order to assure that the desired effects would be realized.

It soon became evident that the Ministry of Finance did not regard the communiqué as a commitment to undertake any special measures—at least not for the moment. Having front-loaded the disbursement of planned public works expenditures during the first half of the fiscal year, MOF resisted any supplemental expenditures until the effects of the front-loading could be assessed. By the time even they acknowledged that those disbursements had had little effect on Japan's sluggish growth, months had passed. A substantial supplemental public works package was submitted to the Diet in late fall. But it was provoked more by the free fall of the Japanese stock market in August 1992 than by any commitment to coordinated macroeconomic policy.

Unfortunately, Japanese officials could judge our macroeconomic performance just as harshly. In both countries, policy coordination fell victim to gridlock: in the United States, between the executive and legislative branches; in Japan, between politicians and bureaucrats.

More Balanced Investment Flows

While the magnitude of Japan's new investments in the USA—$16 billion in 1988—attracted criticism and some legislative proposals to monitor or even restrict those flows, the Bush administration opposed limits on foreign investment for both ideological and practical reasons. With savings low, foreign funds helped finance our fiscal deficit and created new jobs. My main concern on arriving in Tokyo was to reassure the Japanese that the United States would remain receptive to foreign investment, while encouraging them to avoid actions—for example, hostile takeovers or speculative real estate deals—that could provoke negative political reactions.

A steady stream of prominent Americans visited Tokyo in those days to solicit investment funds, particularly direct investment in new plants and equipment. In my first couple of years in Tokyo, nearly a score of state governors made the trek. More than forty states maintained trade offices in Japan, and their principal aim was to attract Japanese investment funds. They openly competed with one another in putting together attractive packages of tax, zoning, and financial inducements to lure Japanese companies to their states.

The benefits of these investments were increasingly apparent. By

1990 Japanese corporate affiliates in the United States employed as many as 629,000 Americans—at high-quality, well-paying manufacturing and services jobs, to boot. The by-products of those investments—Japanese design, technological, and manufacturing expertise—helped improve the competitiveness of many U.S. industries. Japan's greenfield plants forced companies to compete or lose market share, but they also brought new technology to the United States and encouraged civilian R and D here as Japanese companies established more and more technical design centers.

Of course, these investments were not gifts to the American people. They were motivated by the prospect of high rates of return, the need to hedge against future protectionist sentiment in the Congress, the desire for a direct presence in a consequential market, the lure of lower costs, and the desire to acquire access to new technologies. The last point was especially salient: in the late 1980s Japanese venture capital investment in U.S. high-technology firms quadrupled, from $42 million to $166 million.

In view of these advantages, the Japanese were understandably nervous about the crescendo of criticism their investments were attracting. They noted that British and Dutch investments were larger yet drew scant hostility. Some attributed this to racism. I offered a different explanation: Japan's investment was more recent and was growing more rapidly. Japanese firms—perhaps because of their relative lack of familiarity with our market—tended to stand out. Their affiliates had fewer expatriate managers, procured less from local suppliers, and were less attuned to the philanthropic traditions of our business community. Equally important, Americans accepted British investment, even in sensitive sectors of our economy, without alarm, because they knew that it was just as easy for Americans to invest in comparable activities in the UK. By contrast, foreign investment in Japan at the time was only about 0.3 percent of GNP and falling. This was the lowest figure in the industrial world—low even in comparison with the less developed countries.

In the 1990s the focus of U.S. concerns shifted away from investment in the USA to promoting American investment in Japan. As Japan slipped into recession, it began to dawn on more and more Americans that they needed to worry about obtaining too little rather than receiving too much Japanese investment. At the same time, Japanese barriers to investment became a source of greater concern. Increasing numbers of U.S. companies recognized that a local presence in Japan was critical to their export prospects. Such a presence enabled a firm to tailor products to local tastes, to monitor technological developments in Japan, and to develop local marketing and distribution channels.

A study done at the embassy turned up the fact that only 45 percent of our Fortune 500 companies had such a presence in Japan and frequently they had only a minority stake in a joint venture. Of Japan's top five hundred companies, more than 65 percent were present in our market, invariably in majority-owned ventures. In 1990 the Japanese invested $57 billion overseas, and 48 percent of this investment was in the United States. The same year, U.S. firms invested $32 billion overseas, of which only $1 billion went to Japan—a disparity that can hardly have reflected market considerations alone.

Not that the legal barriers to investment in Japan were particularly formidable; they corresponded roughly to those of other OECD nations. But a host of informal barriers existed, and in conjunction with high land prices and the difficulties of recruiting local staff, these discouraged many investors. Few ventures undertaking their first investment in Japan could expect to turn a profit swiftly. The time horizons of U.S. shareholders permitted all too few companies the luxury of taking a longer strategic view.

The embassy sought to focus more attention on this problem. We worked with the American Chamber of Commerce to identify the practical obstacles to investment in Japan. We sought to get Washington interested in the issue. During trips home, in public speeches, briefings for business groups, and consultations with executive branch officials, I emphasized the need for more investment. I even pressed the AFL-CIO's Tom Donohue on the matter, though to little avail: the unions were persuaded that foreign investment would lead to the migration of U.S. jobs overseas rather than to the creation of new export-related jobs in the United States.

The administration also sought to persuade the Japanese to take initiatives to facilitate inward investment flows. Displaying some interest, MITI cobbled together a package of tax and credit incentives, together with a scheme for bonded warehouses that foreign companies could use to reduce investments in land. Ministry of Finance opposition, however, vitiated these initiatives, and they never got far off the ground. Nor was there much steam behind them in the U.S. business community. Thus I began my tenure worrying about the high levels of

Japanese investment in the United States and finished it anxious about the paltry levels of American investment in Japan.

Gaiatsu (or "Foreign Pressure")

The visible application of U.S. pressure was a common thread in all these trade negotiations. It attracted much press attention and earned me the sobriquet "*Gaiatsu-san*," or "Mr. Foreign Pressure." In the end, its seeming necessity reinforced the frustration of Americans, even as its frequent use provoked nationalist reactions from many Japanese.

Pressure—broadly defined—is present in most negotiations among nations as they seek to remind one another of the incentives for agreement and the consequences of failure to achieve it. In this respect, our trade negotiations were quite typical. What was unique was the degree to which the pressure was palpable, overt, and apparently one-sided. To an unusual degree, we used pressure tactics to precipitate negotiations, move them forward, and bring them to a conclusion.

Of course, Japan directed pressure our way too—mainly toward U.S. competitors in the marketplace, where it belonged. But because Americans accurately perceived that Japan's market was less open than ours, the inclination was greater to respond politically. I used to explain this to Japanese friends by noting the differences in our auto trade with Japan and Germany. Both were formidable manufacturers of cars and major factors in the global market. Yet while we had experienced constant strife with Japan over autos, rarely had we encountered such difficulties with Germany. The main reason was that the Germans were both a major importer and exporter; Japan essentially exported, confining foreigners to a trivial share of the local market. Since our producers knew that they could sell in Germany, when sales there went down they examined their product, its price, and their marketing efforts. Slow sales in Japan, where they had not been able to establish even a toehold, they tended to attribute to Japanese barriers, which prompted them to turn to Washington for help.

And Washington was increasingly inclined to provide it. In some respects it had no choice. The 1988 Trade Bill, which was mainly targeted at Japan, required the administration to remove unfair trading practices through negotiations and invited retaliatory measures when bargaining failed. This congressional search for leverage was scarcely disguised, and the pressure was brandished openly.

The Japanese capacity to resist pressure or to absorb it without yielding much of substance was about as skillful as I have ever seen. The special interests that benefited from protectionist arrangements demanded their retention; the bureaucracy energetically defended them; and the politicians readily acquiesced. As usual, the consumer paid the bill but either did not notice, did not bother to complain, or could not figure out how to translate indignation into effective action. Yet Japanese supporters of market liberalization—both in the private and public sectors—often solicited our pressure to help break bureaucratic and political logjams and to galvanize support for change—although, of course, they did so in confidence and would have been embarrassed to have their fingerprints on such requests exposed. Local agents of change naturally had their own objectives, and once we put pressure on the system, they could utilize it to promote their own agenda. At times our interests converged. For example, at a crucial juncture in the SII talks, I went to LDP faction bosses Takeshita and Kanemaru in search of help in getting the Japanese government to increase its public infrastructure budget dramatically. Both were receptive. I had no doubt that more influential than the persuasiveness of my arguments was the interest of the construction *zoku*—with which both had tight connections—in expanding public works expenditures.

Japan's negotiating style also prompted us to rely on pressure tactics. Ministry officials were staunch defenders of constituency interests. Their defensive skill in deferring or avoiding concessions was widely and justly renowned. Indeed, the personal reputations of their negotiators with their peers and the press seemed to depend on their exhausting every defensive tactic before yielding even the most modest concession. Consequently, all negotiations seemed to end only at the last hour of the last day of talks—if then. These difficulties were compounded in the SII talks, because there were many issues, which touched on the jurisdiction of many ministries. Each official sought to shift the burden of adjustment onto other agencies, and since political leaders were generally weak, impasses were not easily broken.

When agreement was achieved, Japanese politicians often explained the outcome publicly as a compromise necessitated by their interest in getting the Americans off their backs or, more diplomatically, in preserving the U.S. connection. Usually the only concrete benefit highlighted was the negotiators' success in holding concessions to a minimum. While Japanese government spokespeople embraced the rhetoric of free trade, the negotiations increasingly resembled a zero-sum game, and that is how the press portrayed them.

The Japanese press targeted me as the principal practitioner of pressure tactics, but others were equally or more deserving of the compliment. President Bush was among the most skillful. Shortly after the February 1990 Lower House elections, he invited Prime Minister Kaifu to Palm Springs, California, for a working summit. The talks were wide-ranging, but the principal focus was trade. The key discussions were conducted tête-à-tête. The president appealed to Kaifu as a friend and leader who shared responsibility for protecting the bilateral relationship. Politician to politician, he explained the political forces in the United States that could imperil the future of the relationship if trade frictions were allowed to accumulate and current negotiations failed. The president issued no threats. He avoided any attempt to address the details of the negotiation and did not suggest that Japan alone was responsible for the trade imbalance, readily acknowledging the United States' need to bolster its competitiveness and attack the fiscal deficit. And he posed no deadlines (he did not need to: the administration was required to report the results of negotiations with Japan to the Hill by April 30). Instead, the president explained, he sought the prime minister's help in arresting drift toward trade conflict that could poison our political relationship and play into the hands of trade hawks in Congress. And he found a receptive audience in Mr. Kaifu who, with the help of associates at home, produced impressive results in the ensuing negotiations.

In the weeks just before President Bush's visit to Tokyo in January 1992, the pressure was more pointed and less subtle. For domestic political reasons, the president and his entourage were themselves under the gun to produce results. The proximate aims—pledged increases in U.S. auto parts sales, resolution of a host of safety and certification issues, achievement of an agreement on government procurement of computers, and some movement on market access issues in the glass and paper industries—were identified only days before the trip. The inclusion on the trip of U.S. business leaders, including major figures in the auto industry, suggested that the results would be appraised by knowledgeable skeptics. And the unstated message to Japan was clear: throw the incumbent president a lifeline through some tangible concessions on these issues, or risk the prospect of a Democratic president more inclined to economic nationalism and more susceptible to pressure from protectionist legislators on the Hill. Given the brief time available to put together a package, what President Bush got was not insubstantial. But the public paid little heed, since the media focus was on the inclusion of business leaders in his entourage and his unfortunate illness at the prime minister's banquet.

Reliance on *gaiatsu* posed dilemmas for Japanese politicians. It facilitated their efforts to build a consensus for change, but it also exposed them to domestic criticism. During the later years of my tenure in Tokyo, I observed that thoughtful Japanese acknowledged with growing candor the need to take the steps necessary to truly open Japan's market and hasten its deregulation. Akio Morita was perhaps the most visible spokesman for this view. It was evident as well in the Okawara Report, commissioned by the Foreign Ministry and published in late 1992. Japanese calls for reform were generally accompanied by the proviso that Japan should undertake such steps of its own volition. Unfortunately, during my tenure there, resentment of and resistance to our pressure grew more rapidly than Japan's capacity or willingness to undertake needed reforms without it.

Given the size of our bilateral trade and the degree of our economic interdependence, each government's interest in the other's laws and administrative rulings that could affect its economic fortunes was perfectly natural. So were both governments' active efforts to influence these matters. Yet here, as in so many other areas, our relationship with Japan seemed to be structurally out of balance. In undertaking lobbying—that is, in applying pressure—the Japanese enjoyed a distinct advantage: Given the disparity in market access, they were normally seeking to prevent new trade restrictions in the United States, while we were seeking to remove old ones in their country. In the U.S. political system, veto points are legion, hence Japanese representatives could quietly shop around for an amendment here, a procedural delay there, a veto elsewhere, in order to block new trade restrictions. And they encountered little difficulty in recruiting capable help, since many former U.S. trade officials were readily available for an appropriate retainer.

We, on the other hand, were nearly always seeking to get the Japanese government to take positive action to reduce or eliminate formal or informal trade barriers. Such actions usually required an energetic local sponsor and broad support within the bureaucracy, business community, and LDP. Even when we could find allies within the Japanese government, they invariably encountered difficulties in securing the cooperation of problem agencies such as Construction, Transportation, Post and Telecommunications, Health and Welfare, Justice, MITI, and MOF. And whereas in the USA delays left the market open, in Japan they left trade barriers intact. Beyond this, I had no money to utilize for lobbying and would have found it exceedingly difficult to recruit knowledgeable Japanese for this purpose had I tried. Since the contest was so unbalanced, I was bemused to find that most of the accusations of using pressure tactics were directed at me.

A Balance Sheet

I left Japan in mid-1993 somewhat dispirited about our economic relationship. The bilateral trade imbalance was climbing back toward the 1989 levels, despite a substantial appreciation of the yen. Our business cycles were again out of sync. Support in Japan for major adjustments in the saving/investment imbalance was only lukewarm in political circles and virtually nonexistent in the Ministry of Finance. Even though the Japanese had slipped into recession in 1991, in 1993 it surpassed the United States to become the world's largest manufacturing economy. Its savings continued to outpace our own, and the USA had solidified its position as the world's largest debtor nation. And whereas in 1989, when the Tokyo Stock Market was at its peak, Japan's economy was roughly 55 percent of America's economic size, by 1993 that figure exceeded 65 percent. The Clinton administration had taken its time to formulate a trade policy toward Japan, and clumsy talk about numerical targets allowed the Japanese trade bureaucracy—in a monumental act of chutzpah—to seize the high political ground by posing as a world champion of free trade. A framework agreement signed during the president's visit to Tokyo in July 1993 merely papered over decidedly different and conflicting agendas. And the prospects for Japanese market-opening initiatives were scarcely promising in the midst of a recession. Another collision between an irresistible force and an immovable object appeared imminent.

In other respects, however, the situation had improved. Undeniably, the Japanese market had become more porous. Sectoral and structural agreements had broken down many obstacles to market entry. More and more American firms acknowledged the need to be in Japan. The success of U.S. companies in virtually every segment of the market—

producers of consumer products such as Procter and Gamble or Kodak; industrial giants such as Motorola, GE, Monsanto, or Merck; high-tech firms such as Intel, Applied Materials, Apple, Compaq, and DEC; service companies such as McCann Erickson, McDonald's, AFLAC, Peat Marwick, and Kentucky Fried Chicken; financial firms such as Salomon Bros., Morgan Stanley, and Goldman Sachs; even auto parts producers such as TRW—provided evidence that highly profitable operations could be undertaken in Japan in virtually all sectors. And U.S. companies, spurred in many cases by Japan's ferocious competition, had undergone restructuring that had resulted in leaner staffs, lower costs, greater attentiveness to quality, renewed interest in the manufacturing process, and growing skill in capturing the rents from innovative technology.

Even in politically sensitive sectors such as cars and consumer electronics, we were slowly reclaiming market share. By 1993, if one included Japanese transplants, the United States was the low cost auto producer in the world; the Big Three were increasing their market share at home against both German and Japanese competitors; through design-in arrangements with Japanese makers, our auto parts manufacturers were beginning to make some headway into Japanese supply networks; and exports from Japan's U.S. production sites were gaining momentum. Between 1989 and 1993 our share in Japan's semiconductor market increased from less than 9 percent to more than 20 percent. The USA had also reasserted its technological leadership in many fields, including a number on which Japan had set its sights—for example, HDTV, the high–value-added sectors of the computer industry, telecommunications, and multimedia products. While a strong yen cut the profit margins of Japan's flagship exporting firms to the bone, the Clinton administration made it a priority to reduce the fiscal deficit and promised a new partnership with the United States' exporters.

Meanwhile, Japan was forced to pay for the excesses of the 1980s. A Bank of Japan–triggered recession continued much longer than anticipated. By mid-1993 the Japanese stock market stood at roughly half its 1989 value. Property values continued to depreciate. The banking sector struggled under a mountain of nonperforming loans. Business community confidence was at its lowest point in decades. And these developments—with the help of a series of scandals—pushed the LDP out of office for the first time in decades. Its successor—a fragile, somewhat conservative, yet reformist coalition—proclaimed its interest in political reform, deregulating the economy, promoting fiscal stimulus through tax cuts, and readjusting the balance between producer and consumer interests—all in all, an agenda Americans could applaud.

Strategic alliances between U.S. and Japanese firms continued to proliferate, and more and more frequently the Japanese took the initiative for them. More broadly, some convergence was evident in our decidedly different forms of capitalism. In the United States, Japan was no longer perceived as invincible, and successful restructuring was reviving the productivity of our manufacturing sector. As we regained our self-confidence, we were likely to be easier for others to live with; in Japan, sobering reminders of their own vulnerability had pushed into retreat the hubris and arrogance that had accompanied the bubble economy. Thus, though trade rivalry remained inevitable, some of the objective conditions that threatened to transform commercial competition into a broader political conflict appeared by 1993 to be in retreat.

Only some, however. Because the U.S. and Japanese business cycles were again out of sync—ours in a strong recovery phase, theirs mired in recession—the trade imbalance was destined to grow. More importantly, the Clinton administration seemed inclined to adopt a more confrontational stance on trade issues, and 1993 proved to be a year that did in fact bring more intense political conflict.

3

Redistributing the Burdens
of Mutual Security

As the Bush administration sought more balanced
economic relations with Japan, it began to adapt
the U.S.-Japan alliance to the exigencies of the
post–cold war world. The potential effects of declining East-West tension on the alliance were profound; however, in practice, they provoked only modest adjustments of long-standing patterns of defense cooperation. The subsequent collapse of the Soviet Union had potentially farther-reaching effects, yet those, too, were, at a minimum, delayed.

Arguably, the reduced Soviet (later Russian) military threat diminished Japan's need for our nuclear deterrent and allowed Japan greater diplomatic maneuverability without fear of U.S. reactions. It also permitted Japan to move forward its relations with other communist countries, without necessarily coordinating very closely with Washington. And to some degree it extended the range of Japanese diplomatic options in the Middle East—a region in which U.S. and Japanese interests did not inevitably coincide—partly because they were less likely to run afoul of American sensitivities about Moscow's role in the area, partly because Russian influence there declined, and partly because that influence was no longer reflexively deployed to block U.S. initiatives.

By the same token, a reduced Soviet threat potentially relieved Washington's need for access to Japanese bases, and to this extent it diminished the USA's need to tailor its commercial diplomacy to strategic concerns. It freed Washington's as well as Tokyo's hands to explore new approaches to erstwhile adversaries. And it shifted attention away from grand strategic issues to economic matters where the United States and Japan were competitors. In all these respects, the alliance was subject to new pressures and strains.

The Legacy of the Cold War on the U.S.-Japan Alliance

Yet the legacy of the cold war was not easily set aside; after all, the U.S.-Japan alliance was a by-product of that struggle. Soviet provocations in Central Europe, Mao's victory in the Chinese Revolution, and the outbreak of war on the Korean Peninsula shifted the focus of the United States' Pacific strategy in the late 1950s from demilitarizing and democratizing Japan to creating a globe-encircling system of alliances. Washington regarded Japan as a major strategic asset in the East-West competition; for Japan, defense cooperation with the United States was the price it paid to regain its sovereignty.

In the 1950s the alliance offered something to both sides. For the USA, it added Japan's weight to the Western camp in the cold war, enabled Washington to recruit a major Asian ally for the global political-ideological contest, allowed the United States to project its power efficiently into the western Pacific through bases in Japan's main islands and Okinawa, and thereby facilitated support for defense commitments Washington had undertaken to Korea and other Asian countries. Washington also pursued a variety of derivative aims through the alliance: It sought to limit Tokyo's diplomatic maneuverability in dealing with communist adversaries. It encouraged Japan to assume wider responsibilities for its own conventional self-defense. It urged the Japanese to adopt policies on regional and global issues in harmony with its own. Most particularly, it sought progressively larger contributions from Japan to support the United States' forward military presence and at the same time resisted limitations on its flexible use of bases in Japan. Recognizing that only an economically strong and politically stable Japan could play an effective supporting role in its grand strategy, Washington readily contributed to Japan's economic recovery and encouraged and assisted its reentry into regional and global politics.

At the outset many Japanese vigorously opposed the alliance with the United States. The conservatives, however, led by Prime Minister Yoshida, considered the alliance at worst a necessary evil and at best a heaven-sent opportunity to regain Japan's sovereignty, reclaim its lost territories, recover its economic strength, increase its diplomatic autonomy, and restore its international status. Despite critics' claims that the Japanese government had accepted a form of subordinate independence, the alliance afforded Japan huge benefits: access to the U.S. nuclear umbrella, American help in providing for its conventional defense; protection of its supply lines for imported raw materials, food, and energy; access to the U.S. market on an unreciprocated basis; and an abundance of diplomatic, political, and technological assistance.

In recurrent negotiations with the USA to define the contours and conditions of defense cooperation, the Japanese concentrated principally on avoiding foreign policy distractions and defense obligations that could delay their economic recovery, while limiting the United States' use of bases in Japan to purposes related directly to their own defense. Above all, Prime Minister Yoshida—and those who subsequently practiced the so-called Yoshida doctrine—attempted to use the time afforded by the U.S. security guarantee to rebuild Japan's economic base and catch up with the West.

The alliance therefore rested on a solid foundation of converging interests. Yet there was plenty of room for tough bargaining over the details of defense cooperation. The dynamics of U.S.-Japanese negotiations on security issues reflected to some degree the pattern of our bargaining with other allies; that is, Washington sought to minimize Japanese intrusions into its management of grand strategy while maximizing their support of its implementation. Tokyo in turn attempted to maximize the protection the U.S. guarantee afforded, while minimizing the costs and risks Japan shouldered in order to sustain it.

Nevertheless, while the U.S.-Japan alliance resembled in some respects other American alliances, it was marked by a number of special features. First, it was fundamentally asymmetrical. The United States was obliged to come to Japan's defense; Japan assumed no comparable commitment to help defend the USA. Nor could it, since the constitution MacArthur helped draft proscribed Japan from assuming overseas military obligations. Since the Japanese had forsworn offensive capabilities and developed a doctrine of exclusive defense, they relied on U.S. forces both to deter and to repel even conventional attacks. This asymmetry was balanced by another, which occasioned concern among Japanese: the United States' freedom to use bases on Japan's territory to pursue policies vis-à-vis other parts of Asia with which the Japanese government might not fully concur.

Second, there was ambivalence on both sides about the purposes the alliance was to serve beyond the general objective of containment. Some Americans saw the security treaty as a means of nestling Japan comfortably under its wing, thereby reinforcing the pacifist instincts that many Japanese embraced following the war. Others, however, were eager to use Japan's industrial power and military potential to limit our own cold war burdens. This produced repeated disagreements in Washington about how actively to press for Japan's rearmament. Some Americans seemed to want Japan to be strong enough to deter the Soviets without becoming so powerful as to frighten the Koreans—a neat trick. For their part, some Japanese considered the alliance as a necessary precursor to the recovery of Japan's major power status; others regarded it as a welcome brake on the buildup of its defense forces. When Major General Hank Stackpole, the U.S. Marine Corps commander in Okinawa in the early 1990s, inadvertently described some Americans as regarding the U.S. military presence in Japan as a "cork in the bottle"—i.e., a check on Japan's rearmament—some Japanese took umbrage; others regarded it as an accurate description of the situation.

Third, perhaps because of the ambivalence of both parties, the U.S.-Japan alliance enjoyed relatively soft support on both sides of the Pacific. Until the 1980s, in fact, few prominent Japanese politicians risked more than a halfhearted public defense of the alliance. A by-product of the occupation, it had not been a matter of free choice. Conservative politicians recalling the turmoil surrounding the revision of the treaty in 1960 preferred an arm's-length relationship to the alliance. Senior bureaucrats, eager to restrain U.S. requests for burden sharing, highlighted the residual opposition that the treaty inspired among domestic constituencies. And the major parliamentary opposition—the Socialist Party—continued to oppose the treaty and its associated arrangements as a matter of principle well into the 1990s. In this light, it is not so surprising that as recently as 1981, the characterization of the U.S.-Japan relationship as an "alliance" in a joint communiqué issued during Prime Minister Zeuko Suzuki's visit to Washington almost brought down his government. And while U.S.

administrations consistently affirmed support for the alliance, it evoked neither the widespread public enthusiasm nor the wide-ranging institutional infrastructure that surrounded the USA's involvement in NATO.

Fourth, Washington and Tokyo approached defense cooperation with quite different agendas. Washington was largely preoccupied with the East-West balance and was willing to pay a commercial price for Tokyo's strategic cooperation. The Japanese, on the other hand, valued the alliance precisely because it gave them access to a host of economic benefits while allowing them to remain aloof from international security issues and avoid a contentious domestic debate over rearmament. Two consequences followed from this. First, on security matters, the Japanese concentrated more on what they could not do than on what they could do. Thus the most familiar hallmarks of Japan's security policy became a series of self-abnegating guidelines: e.g., no overseas deployment of troops; no more than 1 percent of GNP on defense; no arms exports; no manufacture, possession, or introduction of nuclear weapons; no acquisition of offensive weaponry; no military use of outer space. These guidelines, whether matters of law or policy, placated left-wing domestic opponents of the government while reassuring Asian neighbors that Japan had renounced militarism for good. They also provided a serviceable means of limiting U.S. requests for defense cooperation. Second, when international conflicts surfaced, the question of Japan's direct involvement was moot. Its security concerns were limited to defense of its own territory; the United States would take care of everything over the horizon. For a generation, Japan's contribution to international security focused essentially on how the Japanese might help indirectly by augmenting support for U.S. forces in Japan.

Fifth, the corollary of Japan's passivity on defense matters was an assertive and impressive effort to rebuild the economic sinews of its national strength. The proximate goal was to augment the competitiveness of those industries that were considered crucial to Japan's security. Reducing its vulnerability to disruptions in the importation of food, energy, and raw materials was another aim. The alliance was helpful in this regard, since the United States was a prime exporter of food and raw materials, and its oil companies dominated the petroleum market. Key industries were encouraged through industrial policies emphasizing structured competition among domestic firms, the systematic promotion of exports, incentives to secure the most advanced technology available on favorable terms, and heavy protection of the home market. Thus another asymmetry appeared.

Sixth, nowhere was the economic/security imbalance greater than in the flow of defense technology. The United States consistently and liberally transferred high-quality defense technology to Japan throughout the postwar period. Washington, of course, preferred to export end items, but it regularly yielded to Tokyo's insistence on co-assembly, then on co-production, and more recently on co-development arrangements. This was consistent with Japan's approach to technological development. Bolstering its indigenous technological strength was a critical component of Japan's economic security strategy. The resulting flow of defense technology moved essentially in one direction. The Pentagon generally assumed that Japan had little defense technology to offer; in any case, well into the 1990s it advanced remarkably few specific requests for Japanese defense-related technology—vivid evidence that the "not invented here" syndrome was alive and well in Washington. Besides, the Japanese were more inclined to receive than to give, and Tokyo used legal arguments to bar—until 1983—all exports of defense technology, even to Japan's strategic guarantor.

Seventh, because of Japan's strong aversion to military matters and the intense controversy surrounding the treaty within Japan, the alliance was not fortified by strong supporting arrangements between U.S. and Japanese military establishments. No attempt was made to integrate allied forces. No joint command was contemplated. Indeed, the Japanese military does not even have its own integrated command. Until the late 1970s talk of joint planning was taboo, joint exercises were out of the question, and intelligence exchanges were thin. Naval cooperation was the furthest advanced, but this was carefully shielded from the public. And though the Japanese relied on our nuclear umbrella, they preferred to keep it at arm's length. Elaborate circumlocutions evolved to handle the issue of transit and port calls by U.S. naval vessels that might carry nuclear weapons.

Eighth, consultative arrangements between our governments on security issues occasioned special problems. The principal mechanism for such consultations—the so-called Security Consultative Committee (SCC)—was elaborately structured, dealt mainly with base-related problems, and had unequal representation. It matched Japan's foreign minister and Defense Agency director general with the U.S. ambassador and commander-in-chief of U.S. forces in the Pacific. Exchanges in the SCC were highly formalistic. It last met in the 1970s. The Security Subcommittee (SSC), created to allow a more informal venue, brought senior civilian and military officials together to deal with broad security issues. A more lively and useful body, it continues to provide a forum for thoughtful exchanges.

The nub of the consultation issue was substantive. The Treaty of Mutual Cooperation and Security was designed to contribute to both the defense of Japan and the stability of the Far East. The Far East clause prompted concern among Japanese officials who feared our use of their bases could draw them into quarrels they preferred to avoid. Provisions were thus incorporated into the 1960 treaty revision that required us to consult with Japan in cases in which we planned the "use of bases . . . for military combat operations" other than those conducted in response to an armed attack on Japan. The Japanese government also formally defined the Far East as a limited geographic area north of the Philippines and south of the Kurile Islands.

The consultation provision was a mixed blessing for both parties. The Japanese did not want to be uninformed about actions undertaken by U.S. forces deployed in Japan, but neither did they wish to shoulder responsibility for U.S. actions outside Japan—as an acknowledgment of prior consultation might imply. Formal consultations posed a corresponding dilemma for the United States. Our commanders wanted maximum operational flexibility, yet they recognized that publicized failures to consult on consequential matters could undermine Japanese support for our continued presence. The upshot was that we never asked for consultations and tended to interpret the provision narrowly—an interpretation the Japanese government did not contest. Instead, informal arrangements tended to fill in much of the gap. The substance and timeliness of such exchanges depended heavily on the personal skill and inclinations of our commanders. In Lieutenant General J. B. Davis, I was blessed with one of the best.

This then was the legacy of our cold war security ties. The Japanese were dependent on the United States for their defense yet remained curiously disengaged from regional and global security issues. Regional security problems provoked negotiations over the level of Japanese assistance for U.S. forces in Japan rather than over joint efforts to deal directly with the external sources of instability. This pattern of defense cooperation left its imprint on U.S. conduct as well. Since we maintained larger forces, sustained bigger budgets, and assumed greater risks, U.S. officials got into the habit of calling the tune on security issues of possible interest to Japan, expecting the Japanese to follow Washington's lead while paying a growing share of the financial costs of mutual security. Our burden-sharing requests took many forms, among them larger financial subventions for our presence, growing Japanese responsibility for their own defense, greater equity in defense technology transfers, and closer coordination of economic aid to countries of strategic consequence.

To be sure, with the adoption of Japan's comprehensive security policy in the late 1970s, opportunities expanded for enlisting Tokyo's diplomatic and economic support. Although Tetsuya Kataoka characterized even this innovation as largely cosmetic, "embellishing the status quo with slightly increased foreign aid and a little more active diplomacy such as an Olympic boycott,"[1] the anomalies of U.S.-Japan defense cooperation were gradually attenuated, and a more normal alliance began to take shape. This evolution was spurred by the United States' defeat in Vietnam, the Russian military buildup in the Far East, security challenges that prompted the diversion of U.S. attention and defense capabilities to the Middle East and Persian Gulf, and the congenial partnership between Prime Minister Yasuhiro Nakasone and President Ronald Reagan. For the first time, joint planning was undertaken, intelligence sharing expanded, and joint exercises authorized. Japan increased its defense budget in a more robust and consistent fashion. One effect of a new division of roles and missions was the extension of the perimeters of Japan's maritime defense one thousand miles to the south of Tokyo. Host nation support increased dramatically. And Japanese law was amended to permit an exception for the United States to its strict ban on the export of military technology. Operationally, Japan's ability to supply Air and Maritime Self-Defense Forces to contribute air defense and antisubmarine warfare capabilities in areas adjacent to Japan's territory assisted the United States in complicating Moscow's access to and from its ballistic missile submarine bastion in the Sea of Okhotsk.

These changes notwithstanding, continuities of the old policy were evident when I arrived in Tokyo in 1989. While Japan's defense

---

1. Quoted in Chalmers Johnson, *Japan: Who Governs? The Rise of the Developmental State* (New York: Norton, 1995), p. 269.

budget had grown dramatically in absolute terms, it still claimed only 1 percent of GNP. Host nation support had expanded, but the Japanese continued to resist picking up many of the yen-based costs of our forward presence. Japanese air and naval capabilities had improved, but restrictions on acquiring offensive or power projection capabilities remained firmly in place. While legal obstacles to two-way defense technology exchanges had been removed, little Japanese technology had been passed to the United States, and the FSX dispute, described later in this chapter, highlighted Japan's continuing drive for technological autonomy. Although the Japanese government contemplated the dispatch of minesweepers to help protect the safety of maritime shipping in the Persian Gulf in 1987 (when the United States and several European allies were providing protection to Kuwaiti tankers), domestic considerations ultimately blocked the initiative. In short, although the alliance was functioning better than at any time in its history, fundamental asymmetries persisted. And impatience with them was growing in the United States—particularly on Capitol Hill.

Adjusting the U.S.-Japan Alliance to the Post–Cold War World

At the highest levels of the Bush administration, the alliance with Japan was considered a cornerstone of U.S. foreign policy. The president underlined this by personally attending the funeral of Emperor Hirohito, within weeks of his inauguration. The strength and cohesion of U.S. alliances with Western Europe and Japan were regarded as essential to the further easing of East-West tensions and the gradual integration of former communist adversaries into the international, economic, and political system. At the same time, pressures on the U.S. budget and the evident strength of Japan's economy made a more equitable sharing of the burdens of security a high priority.

Managing these adjustments was a delicate task. As East-West tensions subsided, many Americans and Japanese would begin to question the further necessity of defense cooperation. As security concerns diminished, moreover, a huge and persistent trade imbalance guaranteed that the competitive aspects of U.S.-Japanese relations would come more and more sharply into focus. And without the sense of shared danger which the Soviet threat had provided, the Japanese were less comfortable with American tutelage, while Americans were less tolerant of what they perceived as Japanese free riding. Congress had taken up this last refrain with growing vehemence. Why, more and more senators and representatives asked, should we continue bearing a disproportionate share of the burden of defending Asians who were edging us out of key world markets?

The Treaty of Mutual Cooperation and Security

Although officials in both capitals recognized the opportunity and the need to adjust the U.S.-Japan alliance to new realities, few felt that radical adjustments were appropriate. No significant pressure emerged in either country to amend, let alone terminate, the Treaty of Mutual Cooperation and Security. This treaty, after all, was more than a defense alliance; it provided the political framework for the entire relationship. The language of the treaty was framed broadly enough to transcend the conditions of the cold war. And its defense provisions retained their relevance in a post–cold war setting. The treaty allowed the United States to project its power into the western Pacific and contribute a stabilizing presence to the East Asian balance of forces. It permitted Japan to assume larger international responsibilities without stimulating anxieties among its friends or reawakening fears among its neighbors. And it provided reassurance to all Asian nations that the United States and Japan were partners rather than rivals.

In any case, although the Soviet threat was receding, the Asian security environment was by no means free of danger. Soviet military strength in the Far East remained formidable, and the durability of glasnost and perestroika in the Soviet Union were scarcely assured. Tensions persisted between North and South Korea, and there were disturbing hints of North Korean nuclear ambitions. No one could know whether China's growing economic prowess would reawaken its ambitions for Asian hegemony. Internecine fighting continued in Cambodia. And the U.S. base presence was under attack in the Philippine senate.

Political leaders in Japan and the United States thought it imprudent to compound these uncertainties by raising doubts about the future of the security treaty. It was, however, essential to explain to the people of both countries how the alliance continued to facilitate the protection of durable American and Japanese interests in the Pacific—

for example, commercial access, freedom of navigation, regional stability—in a post–cold war environment. Both the U.S. and Japanese governments consequently began to shift the public rationale for the alliance, emphasizing its importance as a prudent, low-cost insurance policy in a highly uncertain and unpredictable world. Secretary of Defense Richard Cheney outlined the revised U.S. rationale in remarks to the National Press Club in Tokyo during his visit in February 1990. His speech was noteworthy in another respect. Instead of soft-pedaling trade problems in the interest of alliance solidarity, as many of his predecessors had done, he reminded the Japanese that unless the trade imbalance were reduced, public support in the United States for defense cooperation could atrophy. While this facet of his speech was not heavily reported in the Japanese press, it was not lost on Japanese officials. It was a dose of Tokyo's own medicine. The Japanese had frequently argued that Washington's pressure for economic concessions might undermine Japanese public support for the alliance. They were now being told the reverse: failure to provide a greater measure of reciprocity could diminish support for the alliance in the United States.

U.S. Force Levels

Secretary Cheney also heralded adjustments in U.S. force levels in Japan. Maintaining the security treaty did not mean that U.S. force levels were sacrosanct. On the contrary, a receding Soviet threat and growing U.S. fiscal deficit made some reductions inevitable. Mindful of the unhappy consequences of the precipitous dismantling of U.S. military strength after World War II, the Bush administration was eager to control the pace of force adjustments in Asia as well as in Europe. Yet the liberation of Eastern Europe and the demise of the Warsaw Pact altered the strategic situation more dramatically on the Continent. It seemed therefore appropriate to focus the largest initial reductions there. To assure a disciplined pace of adjustment in the Pacific, the Pentagon formulated the East Asia Strategy Initiative as a means of preempting haphazard congressional cuts through a process of controlled reductions. In Asia this initiative—which laid out a plan for consolidating U.S. military strength through the 1990s—provided a timely means of combating fears of American retreat from its security responsibilities in the region.

Thus, while Cheney confirmed in early 1990 that U.S. force levels in Japan, Korea, and the Philippines would be reduced, the cuts that he announced were modest (roughly 10 to 12 percent over a three-year period); they were to be implemented gradually; initial cuts were to concentrate primarily on personnel at headquarters rather than in combat units; and force reductions were to be carried out only after thorough discussions with local authorities. Cheney foreshadowed the likelihood of additional adjustments between 1992 and 1995 but noted that a further review of the regional security environment and the impact of initial cuts would be completed before determining further steps.

Nearly six thousand U.S. military personnel in Japan were affected by the initial cuts. Most were withdrawn from Okinawa. The cuts occasioned little adverse Japanese reaction, either officially or through the press. All in all, the Japanese appeared reassured that the initial adjustments would be modest, that their views would be taken into account, and that the pace and scope of future reductions would be based on the regional security situation rather than on U.S. budgetary politics.

Such fears as may have existed then and later about deeper U.S. troop reductions from Japan were attenuated by three developments. First, growing concerns in the early 1990s about North Korean nuclear ambitions prompted Washington to place projected reductions from Korea in abeyance (projected cuts anticipated for U.S. forces in Japan during that time frame were in any event inconsequential). Second, following the Philippine senate's decision in 1991 to terminate its base agreement with the United States, some functions and some personnel were redeployed from the Subic naval base and the Clark air base to other bases in the Pacific. Finally, operational and budgetary reasons prompted the navy to homeport additional ships at Sasebo naval base in Kyushu in 1992.

Cost Sharing

Even without congressional prodding, the prospect of more stringent defense budgets put cost sharing near the top of the administration's agenda. Congressional pressures were intense, prompting the administration to appoint Alan Holmes as an ambassador-at-large, charged with tackling the question of burden sharing with the Germans, Japanese, Koreans, and other allies. I had become quite familiar with this issue during my service at the Pentagon in the late 1970s. At that time, our status of forces agreement (SOFA) required Japan to furnish "facilities and areas" without cost to the United States while leaving us to bear all other expenditures associated with the maintenance of U.S. forces in Japan. Agreements struck in 1977 and 1978 prescribed that the Japanese assume some of the costs of locally hired labor at the bases. In addition, the Japanese offered financial support for upgrading our facilities. This improved the morale of U.S. military personnel, relieved pressures on the Pentagon's military construction budget, and deflected congressional criticism from Japan. Yet the United States continued to shoulder many of the yen-based costs of our military presence, including those associated with labor, utilities, transportation, and communications.

On my arrival in Tokyo, I encouraged the embassy's political section, headed by Rust Deming, to collaborate closely with its U.S. military counterparts in exploring the possibilities for a new cost-sharing agreement. The section found the Japanese surprisingly receptive. Both sides recognized the advantage of a bold move that would put cost-sharing arrangements on a more durable footing, offer clearer guidelines for allocating the burden, and result in an equitable formula that could elicit public support in both countries.

The concept they promoted was simple and straightforward: Japan should finance all the yen-based costs of our forward military presence. Nearly two years were required to define with precision what all those costs were. In the end, the Japanese agreed to assume responsibility for all the labor and utilities expenses at our bases. Over the five-year life of the agreement that was signed in January 1991, we estimated that these arrangements would cost Japan about $1.7 billion; total host nation support for the period—including indirect support and construction projects—would approach $17 billion (calculated at an exchange rate of 126 yen to the dollar). Excluding the salaries of U.S. personnel, and depending on the exchange rate, Japan assumed, as a result of this agreement, 50 percent or more of the total costs of our presence. This understanding brought no new limitations on our flexibility in operating the bases and appeared equitable. It was roundly applauded in the Congress.

It deserved such applause. It was by far the most generous offset agreement the United States had ever concluded with any ally. While it fell short of the goal of 100 percent of the cost of U.S. forces set forth in a congressional resolution passed in the fall of 1990, it was a reasonable understanding. Indeed, were Japan to pay the salaries of U.S.

troops, we would become mercenaries. The 1991 agreement resolved the cost-sharing issue well into the mid-1990s. But the Gulf war, which provided a catalyst to bring these negotiations to a conclusion in early 1991, broadened the scope of our burden-sharing discussions well beyond Japanese support of U.S. troops in Japan.

Japan's Defense Budget and Its Roles and Missions

In the late 1970s the United States began diverting resources devoted to security in the western Pacific in order to build a stronger position in the Persian Gulf. It consequently sought stronger Japanese efforts to relieve the USA of security responsibilities associated with Japan's conventional defense. This prompted Jimmy Carter's secretary of defense, Harold Brown, to press the Japanese publicly for substantially greater real increases in its defense spending. The Reagan administration downplayed such public pressures on Japan's defense budget but sought Tokyo's agreement to more ambitious defense roles and missions that by inference would necessitate higher levels of defense spending. Specifically, Japan agreed to assume responsibility for surveillance and defense of two sea lanes within one thousand nautical miles south of Tokyo. In addition, it accommodated U.S. requests that it take on added responsibilities for monitoring movements of the Soviet submarine fleet and be prepared to block Russian access to and egress from the Sea of Okhotsk. This expansion of defense missions underlay Japan's procurement of a substantial fleet of P3C and F-15 aircraft, along with other advanced equipment.

These equipment acquisitions were included in the 1986–1991 Mid-Term Defense Plan. When the SSC met in Tokyo in the summer of 1989, the U.S. participants (myself included) were astonished to learn that, two-thirds of the way through Japan's five-year defense program, all acquisitions had been accomplished or were projected to be completed on schedule with the minor exception that a slightly smaller number of F-15s than planned had been procured because the attrition rate had been lower than anticipated. The Pentagon's surprise at this accomplishment was readily comprehensible: given the vicissitudes of our budgetary process, we were rarely able to stick to a midrange plan for more than a year or two.

With East-West tensions fading, the Bush administration had little reason either to prod the Japanese to increase their defense spending or to redefine the division of labor between us on roles and missions. On no occasion was I instructed to make such requests, and I certainly felt no urge to seek Washington's authorization to reopen these issues.

There were, however, sporadic—occasionally intense—pressures on Japan to procure specific items of equipment—most notably the AWACS aircraft. Some Pentagon officials regarded such off-the-shelf purchases of U.S. equipment as an important offset from Japan. This was a perennial topic in exchanges between Department of Defense and Japanese Defense Agency officials. Pressures to buy the AWACS also reflected the desire of the Boeing Corporation to keep their AWACS production line open as demand for this aircraft from the U.S. Air Force and overseas customers waned. Such commercial concerns played well on the Hill. A variety of considerations—principally related to the very high price of the aircraft—repeatedly delayed Japanese decisions. Vice President Quayle spearheaded the last major effort to sell the AWACS during the 1992 election campaign. In the end, the Japanese government agreed to purchase four AWACS aircraft, but the decision came too late to be of any help in getting President Bush reelected.

With respect to certain kinds of defense capabilities, the Defense Department did draw a line in the sand, provoking at the time considerable uneasiness among Japanese military leaders. For several years, elements within the Japanese Maritime Self-Defense Forces, perhaps encouraged by their counterparts in the U.S. navy and air force, had conducted a quiet campaign to procure a helicopter carrier, along with tankers to give them an aerial refueling capability. This capability was obviously relevant to its sea lane surveillance and defense mission but signaled possibly larger ambitions as well. Since the United States possessed ample carrier strength and had traditionally provided long-range sea lane protection, these extensions of Japan's capabilities appeared redundant to U.S. officials. In the Pentagon's 1991 Defense Posture Statement, Washington openly expressed reservations about the acquisition of power projection capabilities by Japan. Subsequently, Japanese pressure to acquire such systems temporarily abated, though I suspect this was attributable more to budgetary pressures in Japan than to any special deference to U.S. views.

In 1992 it became evident that Washington was reconsidering the fundamentals of U.S.-Japan defense cooperation in the wake of the

Gulf war. A Department of Defense press guidance leaked to the *New York Times* in the spring of 1992 hinted that in the future the United States would devote itself to discouraging regional powers like Japan and Germany from acquiring the attributes of major military powers (in particular, nuclear weapons and power projection capabilities). In the furor provoked by the leak, this policy guideline was modified, but the episode was instructive: with the end of the cold war, United States incentives to press Japan to increase its defense power diminished.

The Nuclear Issue

I received a pleasant surprise in September 1991: an instruction to brief the prime minister on a major decision to reconfigure U.S. nuclear deployments. In a nutshell, the United States planned to transfer tactical nuclear weapons currently deployed abroad to storage sites back home; concurrently, it intended to remove such weapons from naval ships and aircraft. The prime minister welcomed the decision and promised public support. He expressed no misgivings. Nor did I encounter subsequent expressions of second thoughts.

Politically, the decision removed the vulnerability of the Japanese government to speculation about whether U.S. ships homeported at the Yokosuka naval base were equipped with nuclear weapons. Diplomatically, the Japanese hoped the removal of tactical nuclear weapons from South Korea might open the door to progress in containing North Korea's nuclear ambitions and stimulating a more substantive dialogue between Pyongyang and Seoul. And as further evidence of adjustment in major power nuclear policies, it signaled another lessening of the dangers associated with the East-West struggle. As long as the Japanese were assured that they were still protected by our nuclear umbrella, the announcement was an unmitigated blessing.

The decision was to be implemented gradually, and the administration did not foreclose the possibility of a reversal should international circumstances warrant. In any event, the Pentagon would sustain indefinitely its standard procedure of refusing to confirm or deny reports about the weaponry aboard specific ships (the Japanese had their own standard formula for handling this delicate issue: namely, prior consultations were required regarding matters bearing on Japan's nuclear principles, and when no consultations had been requested, it was presumed that no nuclear weapons were aboard U.S. vessels transiting Japanese ports). Press reactions in Japan to the president's announcement were extremely favorable. Even the socialists applauded, though they had lost one of the issues on which they had enjoyed harassing the Japanese government for years.

More Balanced Exchanges of Defense Technology

Assuring greater balance in defense technology exchanges had been a long-standing U.S. objective. An agreement signed in 1983 provided a legal basis for Japanese exports of defense technologies to the United States, but few such transfers had actually taken place. The FSX dispute—which flared prior to my confirmation hearings—provided the first genuine test of Japan's readiness to establish practical arrangements to facilitate a more balanced two-way flow of defense technology.

The Japanese Air Self-Defense Force and aerospace and industrial circles had long urged the development of a new tactical fighter plane for both military and industrial reasons. U.S. defense officials had consistently opposed Japan's autonomous development of such an aircraft on grounds that it was an inefficient use of the country's limited defense funds, would diminish the interoperability of our respective air forces, and was unnecessary since the United States could supply a superior aircraft. More broadly, an independently developed aircraft was widely regarded—particularly on the Hill—as signaling Japan's determination to challenge U.S. dominance in the aeronautics industry.

There was also a growing concern, rarely articulated but lurking just beneath the surface, that a failure to redress the asymmetries in our bilateral technology trade with Japan could have lasting consequences for our future security. Japan had developed a highly efficient lean production system with an architecture of supply that strongly favored its own firms. The Japanese understood that what some economists called "the law of increasing returns" made high-technology markets unpredictable, extremely lucrative, frequently volatile, yet possible to corner—at least for a while. And the Japanese were very good at cornering such markets, utilizing their capacity for high-volume exports and aggressive pricing policies—aided by a protected home market—to lock in an early advantage. Japan's concentration, moreover, on low-cost, simple technologies for general-purpose commercial applications had growing military relevance. High-volume commercial electronics, for example, began to drive the development, costs, quality, and manufacture of technology crucial to many military systems. Thus the Japanese had quietly developed a "spin-on" system for moving from civilian to military technology that rivaled our own "spin-off" method for exploiting defense technology in the civilian market.

During the cold war, Washington typically sought to transfer defense technology to Japan to deepen its dependence on us while expanding our own exports. By the late 1980s, however, some began to worry that Japan's technology development trajectory offered it growing independence from the United States, even as we were becoming more dependent on Japanese defense technology. Clearly, the technology exchanges in the defense sphere were becoming too one-sided.

By the end of the Reagan administration, the Japanese had given up on an independent FSX project and agreed on a memorandum of understanding (MOU) with the Defense Department that established the work shares and general contours of a joint development project. Key members of the Bush administration—most notably Secretary of Commerce Robert Mosbacher—were, however, disposed to reopen the terms of that agreement in the early months of 1989. The battle to revise the terms, which unfolded as I awaited confirmation, reproduced in microcosm the tensions that had crept into our bilateral relationship.

Japanese Defense Agency officials considered the project a crucial means of achieving greater technological independence. MITI saw in it possibilities for cracking the global commercial aircraft market. The Ministry of Foreign Affairs presumably sympathized with these aims but was charged with preserving the alliance with the United States. All shared a desire to maximize the indigenous development of technology, to domesticate the production of key defense capabilities, and to avoid an open break with the United States.

Washington, meanwhile, was eager to keep Japanese defense capabilities lashed closely to the United States, to avoid inadvertently propelling the Japanese into competition with our commercial aviation industry, to prevent U.S. aircraft manufacturers from giving away critical technology that had been developed with taxpayers' money, and to maximize the USA's share in the development and production of a next-generation fighter aircraft in Japan. The modified MOU negotiated by the Bush administration was superior in all these respects to the deal the Reagan officials had struck. But, as always in negotiations with the Japanese, the signing of a document did not terminate the bargaining.

The deal provided that General Dynamics would supply Japan with highly sophisticated F-16 technology and help it with systems integration, in return for free access to any improvements the Japanese made in that technology plus access on request and with remuneration to so-called nonderived technology utilized in the project. As Richard Samuels later wrote, "In effect, the United States was betting that Japanese firms could improve U.S. military aerospace technology by spinning on commercial expertise, that U.S. firms would learn and exploit these improvements, and that the interests of both countries would be served by such an arrangement."[2] The Japanese made a comparable bet: namely, that the joint project would address virtually all their technological gaps (except propulsion), would allow them to lead a major project, would give them hands-on experience with a company possessing superior system integration capabilities, and would still largely retain for them control over the procedures governing the flow of Japanese technology to the United States.

The new deal, struck in the spring of 1989, increased the U.S. work share (to 40 percent), and confirmed that it would apply to the production as well as to the developmental phase. It denied Japan access to flight control source codes with commercial applications. It gave the U.S. Air Force the right to post officers at Mitsubishi Heavy Industry Nagoya Works to participate in design efforts. And it sought to differentiate between derived and nonderived technologies in order to facilitate the expeditious flow of technology to the United States— not so successfully, as things turned out.

Defining the procedures for technology exchange under this project was time-consuming and frustrating. Delays were frequent and seemed interminable. Japan's reluctance to facilitate prompt transfers of technology was confirmed repeatedly. Hard bargaining was required—including on one occasion the suspension of all defense technology transfers from the United States—in order to overcome obstacles. Cost overruns plagued the project, and the schedule repeatedly slipped. How many FSX aircraft will ultimately be produced

2. Richard Samuels, *Rich Nation, Strong Army* (Ithaca: Cornell University Press, 1994), p. 241.

remains to be seen, but a model of the plane has now been flight-tested. And notwithstanding the difficulties, the FSX deal was gradually transformed from a huge political controversy to a collaborative project from which both countries appeared to derive benefit.

Two other episodes cast light on the balance of interdependence in the defense field. During the Gulf war rumors circulated that Japanese manufacturers withheld supplies of key components to U.S. air defense systems in order to meet the priority needs of Japanese civilian industries. Such claims seemed implausible to me. It made little sense for Japanese companies to risk their reputation for reliability at a moment when U.S. defense production was being ramped up. Nor would the Japanese government countenance decisions that could place its security relationship with the United States in jeopardy. The embassy staff never found evidence that lent credibility to the rumors.

Another incident revealed how dependent Japanese forces remained on U.S. support. In 1993 JAE, a Japanese defense electronics firm, was caught violating agreed-on export controls, and its contracts with U.S. suppliers were consequently put on hold for months while the allegations were investigated. Before the issues were resolved, officials throughout the Japanese Self-Defense Forces became increasingly frantic as airplanes, missile guidance systems, and other key defense systems came close to being grounded as parts supplies dried up. It provided a timely reminder to Americans who worried about excessive dependence on Japanese suppliers that this dependence was mutual—and indeed substantially greater for the Japanese.

Adjustments Promoted by the Japanese

Naturally the Japanese had their own ideas about adapting their alliance with us to new circumstances. Their agenda was familiar. For one thing, they wanted the consolidation and return of bases and facilities no longer needed by the United States—a natural and understandable desire of long standing. Yet demands on this front were never particularly acute during my tenure. Since many Japanese worried about a precipitate U.S. withdrawal from Asia, they had no desire to accelerate our retreat. Understandably, the pressures were greatest in Okinawa, where our presence was ubiquitous and the inhabitants have historically expressed antimilitary sentiments. Governor Ota, a socialist elected in 1990, became a pen pal of mine, peppering me with letters requesting the reversion of key facilities, particularly those located at the port of Naha. The U.S. military command undertook an extensive review of the possibilities but volunteered few facilities for early transfer. Some of the most intensive bureaucratic infighting focused on golf courses and recreation centers. The Japanese wanted their return for commercial development purposes; the U.S. military argued that their retention—or replacement—was essential for morale. The proposed trade-off was the construction of alternative facilities, but with the bursting of the economic bubble, funds for such trade-offs dried up. Thus, with a few minor exceptions, our base presence in Okinawa was only slightly smaller in 1993 than it was in 1989.

A second Japanese government concern involved night landing practice at several of our air bases located in urban communities that were sensitive to noise and safety problems. This problem most acutely affected the Atsugi Naval Air Station in Kanagawa Prefecture. Training requirements for U.S. fighter pilots onboard carriers homeported at Yokosuka were extremely rigorous. Hence our military commanders were wary of adjustments that limited training opportunities. But they reached an agreement with the Japanese Defense Agency that a new training facility would be created in Iwo Jima, a remote island with no civilian inhabitants. The Japanese built an appropriate airstrip and agreed to offset some of the costs we incurred by having to fly to a more remote location. This did not eliminate all night landing practice at Atsugi or other bases on the main islands. But it did permit its substantial reduction.

A third concern related to unequal representation in the SCC, the highest-level body for consulting on security issues. In a nutshell, Japan was represented at a ministerial level and the United States was not. The Japanese felt this disparity was anachronistic and proposed the creation of what came to be termed the "two plus two committee"— a ministerial-level forum composed of the U.S. secretaries of state and defense, the Japanese foreign minister, and the director of the Japan Defense Agency. Washington readily agreed that such a forum was symbolically appropriate and could have genuine utility in reshaping the alliance to the needs of a post–cold war era. Coordinating the schedules of four busy cabinet officials proved to be challenging, however. Despite good faith efforts on both sides and a government-to-government agreement to create the new forum, the first meeting did not take place until the spring of 1994 and then at what might be called the two plus one-and-a-half level, with our Defense Department represented by Under Secretary Frank Wisner.

A final concern involved Japan's desire to extend the range of its security consultative links as it groped for a post–cold war role. One expression of this was Tokyo's interest in closer ties with NATO and CSCE in Europe—an interest we heartily endorsed. Will Taft, the U.S. ambassador to NATO, encouraged more frequent high-level Japanese visits to that body's headquarters and invited Deputy Foreign Minister Hisashi Owada to participate in a NATO-sponsored conference. We also sponsored Japan for observer status in CSCE, and Ambassador Nobuo Matsunaga attended the meeting in Helsinki in 1993.

In Asia, Foreign Minister Taro Nakayama was an early enthusiast of an Asian forum to discuss regional security issues, and as early as the spring of 1991, he proposed a ministerial-level dialogue. Washington was less keen about this idea, preferring to rely on bilateral arrangements for managing Asian security issues. But sentiment in Asia in favor of a regional security dialogue grew. There were a variety of motivations. Some Asians saw a regional dialogue as a way of hedging against a U.S. retreat from overseas security responsibilities. Others perceived it as a means of bringing greater influence to bear on Washington's security policies. It seemed a timely moment to consider post–cold war security challenges confronting a region in which economic cooperation was accelerating. And it promised to draw former adversaries into more constructive ties with their neighbors.

These advantages appeared less compelling to Washington. But it was increasingly apparent that some forum of this kind was likely to emerge with or without U.S. participation. When Larry Eagleburger visited Tokyo in October 1992 to attend a ministerial-level pledging session for aid to Russia, I made the case for acquiescing to such a meeting. It was like leaning on an open door: I met no resistance, perhaps because the secretary had already decided to go along with the emerging Asian consensus. He announced that the United States would no longer oppose a regional security dialogue, and it was launched early in the summer of 1993.

All these adjustments served to keep defense cooperation on track while beginning the task of adapting the practical arrangements for cooperation to a new international security environment and changing political realities in both capitals. If the adjustments themselves were rather modest, that simply reflected the persistence of unresolved security problems, most notably in Korea, which emphasized the continuing need for defense cooperation. This perhaps explains why the security side of our relationship with Japan by and large worked smoothly, and the links between our respective armed forces grew closer. But the most demanding test of these ties came in response to the Gulf crisis, which raised some new issues and gave some old ones a new spin.

4

The Gulf War

The war in the Persian Gulf in 1990–91 was a defining moment in the evolution of U.S.-Japan relations. For the United States, the challenge was to organize a broad international coalition under UN auspices in order to reverse Iraq's brazen aggression against Kuwait; for Japan, it was whether the nation could transcend the policy reflexes of the Yoshida doctrine and participate in defining new rules for handling international security issues in the post–cold war world.

For the Bush administration, victory in the Gulf war was a triumph of crisis management and coalition diplomacy. The president's popularity surged, and the United States emerged with its reputation as the world's only remaining military superpower enhanced. By contrast, the Gulf war experience left most Japanese distressed, some embittered. Despite Japan's economic power, its political role in the anti-Iraqi coalition was marginal; its reluctance to dispatch noncombat support personnel to the Gulf exposed it to sharp criticism from Western and Arab countries alike, and even its financial contributions—which ultimately exceeded those of any country outside the Gulf region—earned Japan faint praise and little gratitude.

The conflict surfaced latent tensions in the relationship between Washington and Tokyo. It prompted some Americans to question Japan's reliability as an ally and reinforced doubts about Japan's willingness to play a global political role commensurate with its economic power. In Japan, it heightened suspicions that the global partnership Washington urged would allow the United States to call the tune while leaving Japan to pay the bill and aroused in many Japanese a desire for a foreign policy less dependent on the United States and more focused on Asian regional concerns.

This outcome scarcely seemed foreordained. In many respects, the Gulf crisis appeared ideally suited for close U.S.-Japanese collaboration and a redefinition of Japan's international security role. Iraq's attack on Kuwait was an act of blatant aggression; Saddam Hussein, a reckless egomaniac who had devoted a decade and incalculable resources to military adventures against his neighbors, squandered billions to develop weapons of mass destruction and displayed open contempt for the international community by providing a haven for terrorists. By occupying Kuwait and threatening Saudi Arabia, Saddam appeared determined to acquire a hammerlock on the Middle East's oil—a matter of considerable consequence to Japan, 70 percent of whose petroleum was imported from the Gulf area. The multilateral effort to respond to Iraqi aggression was centered in the United Nations, an institution to which Japanese leaders had for decades expressed a special devotion. And the Gulf conflict erupted at a moment when Japan was groping for a larger and more ambitious international role in concert with the United States and Western Europe.

Tokyo's first reactions to Kuwait's invasion were encouraging. Prompted perhaps by a telephone call from President Bush on August 2, Prime Minister Kaifu immediately condemned Iraq's blatant aggression. The following day Tokyo froze Iraqi and Kuwaiti assets, and Prime Minister Kaifu expressed Japan's readiness to comply with sanctions imposed by the Security Council. Tokyo subsequently supported UN resolutions calling for the withdrawal of Iraqi troops from Kuwait, the restoration of Kuwait's legitimate government, the safe release of all hostages, and the maintenance of security and stability in the Gulf.

After these initial steps, however, the going got considerably tougher. While this occasioned frustration, it came as no particular surprise to me. Japan's postwar history had left its government ill equipped to respond decisively to international security crises. Japan's involvement in UN peacekeeping was confined to the provision of financial support, and it had no tradition of expending political capital or assuming major political risks on behalf of general principles. Confronted by external difficulties, Japanese leaders had become accustomed to react by keeping their heads down, minimizing risks, and leaving security responsibilities to others—mainly to the United States.

The Bush administration, outraged by Iraq's disregard for the UN charter, moved by the fate of a small nation whose territorial integrity was violated, alarmed by the strategic consequences of Saddam Hussein's increased influence over the international oil trade, and braced by the steely resolve of UK Prime Minister Margaret Thatcher, was determined to respond. It consequently mounted a multilateral effort to protect Saudi Arabia and drive Iraq out of Kuwait. By contrast, the Japanese business community was not nearly as alarmed about Iraq's growing power. As they saw it, those who controlled oil could not eat the commodity; they had to sell it to realize any benefit from it. And as a huge customer with reasonably diversified sources, Japan, its leaders confidently assumed, could obtain the energy supplies it needed, even if it had to pay a higher price.

More fundamentally, Americans and Japanese tend to draw diverging lessons from twentieth-century history. For U.S. leaders, Munich provided the enduring lesson of history and a source of policy guidance: aggression must be promptly stopped; appeasement merely breeds greater dangers. For most Japanese, Hiroshima is a reminder that resorting to arms—at least by Japan—leads to disaster and defeat.

A reflection of these fundamental differences in our historic memories and policy reflexes was the absence in Japan of much public debate about the justice of the allied coalition's cause or, for that matter, about the policy choices facing Japan. Another was a lack of public clamor for action by the government—except to secure the release of Japanese hostages. For most Japanese, the conflict between Iraq and Kuwait was a "fire on the other side of the river": let those closer to the blaze risk getting burned trying to put it out. Naohiro Amaya, former vice minister of MITI, likened Japan's performance to that of an ostrich confronting a lion: despite its agility, the bird will panic and seek to avert danger by burying its head in the sand. In this context, it was not surprising that Tokyo's actions, when they came, appeared to be prompted more by the sting of external criticism or the fear of diplomatic isolation than by the pursuit of a clear-cut foreign policy design.

Sharing the Costs and Risks

I first learned of Iraq's invasion on CNN while vacationing with my wife, Bonny, in Sun Valley, Idaho. I returned to Tokyo promptly and immediately initiated informal soundings of senior government and party officials. I had no instructions, but experience prompted me to forewarn Vice Foreign Minister Takakazu Kuriyama, Deputy Foreign Minister Hisashi Owada, and LDP Secretary General Ichiro Ozawa about the likelihood of early U.S. burden-sharing requests. An administration that was preparing to deploy troops halfway around the world to defend oil regarded as more critical to European and Japanese prosperity than to its own would surely expect its allies to help with the costs and risks of that effort.

I believed that the U.S.-Japan alliance reflected a wealth of converging national interests. But in a democratic era, a durable alliance required strong emotional and psychological underpinnings as well. The crisis in the Gulf would have a powerful effect on these underpinnings, I felt, for when a nation risks its sons and daughters in combat, it discovers anew who its real friends are. The future of the alliance would depend importantly on whether Americans saw Japan standing shoulder to shoulder with them in this test of wills. I recognized, of course, that Japan had a unique history and constitution with respect to military engagement abroad, and I had no desire to see Japan dispatch combat troops overseas. But I urged Japanese leaders to think of ways in which Japan could perform noncombat duties in the Gulf region so that it would be seen as an active participant in the broad multilateral effort that was taking shape.

Kuriyama, Owada, and Ozawa all appeared to recognize the dangers this looming crisis posed for Japan. Regrettably, the press and general public continued to view the crisis as someone else's problem, and most key members of the political establishment did little to counter that complacent view.

The first hint of future difficulties came on August 12, when I accompanied Secretary of Agriculture Clayton Yuetter to a Sunday morning call on Prime Minister Kaifu. The prime minister had been scheduled to embark on a previously planned visit to the Gulf region on August 14. Clayton and I urged him to go through with the trip, which now offered a timely opportunity to extend forthright political support to Egypt, Turkey, Jordan, Oman, and Saudi Arabia—nations facing severe internal and external pressures. Kaifu was noncommittal. Senior Foreign Ministry officials were reluctant to see the prime minister travel into an area of tension. And they did not wish to expose him to Arab requests for help since he would be in no position to respond. Presuming that swift decisions regarding Japanese assistance were impossible, they opposed the trip, which hours later was abruptly postponed.

My first instruction to seek specific Japanese help arrived that week, and I discussed its contents with Vice Minister Kuriyama on August 15. The general outline of our desires were known, for the president had talked to the prime minister by phone two days before. Washington requested financial support for the coalition; economic assistance for Turkey, Egypt, and Jordan; additional host nation support; and Japanese personnel contributions to back up the coalition. I mentioned a variety of possible responses to this last request: medical volunteers, logistic support in transporting personnel and equipment to Saudi Arabia, Japanese help in managing the anticipated exodus of large numbers of refugees from Kuwait, and participation in the multinational naval force through the dispatch of minesweepers to help clear the Gulf and transport vessels to carry equipment from Egypt to Saudi Arabia. What Washington initially seemed to want most was the deployment of a Japanese ship manned by Japanese personnel and bearing a Japanese flag as a symbol of Tokyo's involvement in a common effort.

I had known "Kiki" Kuriyama for nearly twenty years and had the highest respect for his intellectual acuity and commitment to the U.S.-Japan alliance. Personal friends, we had consulted on many occasions during my tenure as under secretary and had always leveled with one another. His response to our request was mixed. He readily acknowledged the importance of a substantial Japanese contribution; while consultations within the government were clearly required before decisions could be announced, he hinted at Japan's readiness to offer support that went beyond financial subventions. But he emphatically noted the political and constitutional difficulties that would attend any involvement of Japanese Self-Defense Forces in an area of strife and clearly signaled that there was no likelihood that Japan would dispatch minesweepers.

His reaction came as no surprise to me; I had thought it extremely improbable that Japan would provide even nonlethal military support to the coalition. True, the Japanese had quietly performed minesweeping tasks during the Korean War, but at the time, Japan was still under occupation, so that did not constitute a precedent for the voluntary contribution of such support. Beyond this, Tokyo had contemplated dispatching vessels to the Gulf in 1987 in support of U.S. and European efforts to provide protection for Kuwaiti-flagged tankers. Then–prime minister Nakasone was among those favoring the deployment, and, though the Japanese government eventually demurred, some of the arguments raised against the deployment of minesweepers in 1987 were now moot; for example, by contrast with the war between Iran and Iraq, Japan could not be neutral in this conflict since it supported the UN resolutions and Iraq did not, and this time the multilateral force in the Gulf would operate under explicit UN Security Council sanction.

Still, aside from the fact that I was instructed to do so, I felt no qualms in proposing the dispatch of minesweepers or transport vessels. Japan possessed these capabilities; the purpose was clearly defensive and related to Western commercial as well as security interests; there was an obvious need; and the vessels would be involved in a multilateral venture under UN auspices. If the Japanese were willing to provide such nonlethal support, all the better; if not, they might compensate by further sweetening their financial contribution or providing other forms of nonmilitary backup support.

I had numerous opportunities during the following weeks to echo the points I registered with Kuriyama in encounters with other Japanese leaders. In public remarks I concentrated on a few broad themes: the threat Saddam Hussein's aggression posed for the future viability of the United Nations; the danger to the world economy and Japan's prosperity of Iraq's controlling such a large share of the world's oil resources; the determination of the United States and its friends to mobilize a broad coalition to resist Iraq and to shoulder whatever costs and risks this entailed; and the importance of quick, substantial, and visible Japanese contributions if our bilateral relationship was to be maintained in good health.

Detailed conversations about what the coalition required and what other allies were planning to supply were held in Washington as well as in Tokyo. Bob Kimmitt, my successor as under secretary of state, was the point man in that effort. He spoke authoritatively, enjoyed full access to Secretary Baker, had a good feel for Japanese sensitivities, and kept the embassy fully informed. Subsequently he dispatched an inter-agency team of State, Defense, and NSC professionals to Tokyo to encourage, influence, and accelerate Japanese decisions. This team—lead by Desaix Anderson, Karl Jackson, and Carl Ford, supplemented by uniformed officers from our armed forces—provided timely liaison with key Japanese officials who were pressing their government for more decisive action. But decisions did not come easily or quickly.

Throughout August, Japanese authorities struggled inconclusively to determine the appropriate forms and levels of their support. My advice—and that of my fellow ambassadors from the United King-dom, Kuwait, Saudi Arabia, Egypt, and Turkey, with whom I consulted regularly—was simple: aim high! The biblical injunction "From those to whom much has been given, much will be asked" seemed pertinent. That notwithstanding, the request to send minesweepers was quietly dropped. Keeping the request alive would have invited journalists to criticize U.S. judgment rather than urge a prompt Japanese response.

The Japanese government seemed unable to approach decisions regarding its role in the Gulf crisis boldly or with a sense of urgency. All the usual constraints were evident: the Finance Ministry's reluc-tance to release funds, the political establishment's reticence to con-sider novel security measures, the "business as usual" inclination of industrial circles, the vulnerability of labor unions to leftist pressures for political correctness, and the sectionalism and parochialism of the bureaucracy. This is not to say that stronger political will could have overcome resistance. Even those eager to help were in a quandary as to what to do. No emergency legislation existed that could have been used to compel civilians to staff commercial vessels to carry out sea lifts. Such legislation could have been proposed; however, its passage would have been time consuming, and its fate uncertain. Such con-cerns reinforced the disposition of a weak leadership to delay hard choices. Delay, moreover, allowed various Japanese officials and special envoys—some self-appointed—to shop around in Washington in order better to judge U.S. officials' expectations of Japan.

I could not keep track of all these contacts, but I did worry about them. I knew that a number of midlevel Washington officials tended to express personal views to Japanese friends with a ring of authority greater than they deserved. I was aware that special Japanese representa-tives often heard only what they wanted to hear. The inevitable result was confusion. One senior Ministry of Foreign Affairs official later told me that a well-placed Japanese visitor to Washington had been told in late August by a senior official—whom he would not identify—that the U.S. government would be satisfied, though scarcely thrilled, with a Japanese contribution of $1 billion by the end of the year, with increased monthly payments in 1991. This fictitious figure proved to be a substantial misjudgment, not least because by this time the Pentagon was projecting its own incremental spending at about $1 billion per month.

Japan announced its first official support package on August 29. It included unspecified loans and grants to Egypt, Turkey, and Jordan; one hundred medical specialists; a pledge to supply refrigeration equipment, water, and other goods to help coalition forces cope with the desert heat; and a commitment to transport various nonlethal items on civilian aircraft and ships, as well as to pay for military equipment to be flown to Saudi Arabia on planes chartered from other nations. The issue of additional Japanese host nation support was not addressed in the package because contingency funds were limited and some bureaucratic resistance had yet to be overcome. But we were assured by the Ministry of Foreign Affairs that the subject would be handled before the next fiscal year's budget came into effect.

Unfortunately, the announcement raised as many questions as it answered. It was difficult to judge the overall value of Japan's support, since many details were to be filled in later. The projected economic aid to the frontline states was to be released only after the conclusion of painstaking negotiations over specific projects. The Ministry of Finance insisted on channeling aid through a consortium that included the IMF, and since the IMF was already pressing Egypt for extremely tough austerity measures, Japan's pledge of assistance would scarcely serve the immediate political goal of bolstering the solidarity of Muslim countries confronting Iraq. The offer of medical support personnel was welcome, but press reports and other sources indicated that only a handful of individuals were likely to volunteer. In any event, Arab governments appeared interested in receiving medical personnel only if hostilities broke out.

Washington wanted logistic assistance, but many of our specific requests were parried or refused. We asked Japan to provide transport aircraft to carry military supplies. The request was denied on legal grounds. Requests for supply ships and military tankers evoked a similar response. When friends in the Foreign Ministry came up with their own offer to charter nonmilitary ships for supply runs, delays prevented the finalization of arrangements until late September, when the heaviest demand for such logistic assistance had passed. In response to our request for the airlifting of troops and supplies to Saudi Arabia, prolonged consultations among the Ministry of Foreign Affairs, the Ministry of Transportation, and Japan Airlines yielded a cumbersome and ultimately unworkable plan that would have required several transfers of equipment to different planes at stops en route. Only non-military supplies were to be transported, and JAL insisted on reserving the right to inspect cargo. Ultimately the plan was dropped in favor of chartering U.S. planes.

Hopes that Japanese auto companies might fund or lease vehicle transporters came to naught. A proposal that Self-Defense Force aircraft might be used to transport refugees out of danger zones was dropped, after brief consideration, for fear of domestic criticism. And transportation services for which Japan paid the bill were limited to carrying food, medicines, and noncombat gear—a condition that seemed extremely fastidious to Americans, who would bear the burdens of combat if conflict erupted.

One of the episodes I found most irritating received little public notice back home. Japanese ship repair facilities at the Yokosuka naval base were among the most impressive in the world. During normal times, the efficient management of Seventh Fleet repairs was aided by dispatching key workers to Bahrain to assess the condition of ships returning to their home port in Japan, so that work schedules could be formulated in advance and implemented with greater efficiency. During Desert Shield, however, leftist unions resisted the dispatch of Japanese workers to the Gulf area on grounds that it would engage them too deeply in support of our operational requirements. The implication was perverse: Japanese unions would support the U.S.-Japanese alliance only when their help was not urgently needed.

I complained about this incident during an office call on Shin Kanemaru, whom I had first met when he was serving as director of Japan's Self-Defense Agency in the 1970s. He asked whether I had discussed the matter with Makoto Tanabe, a senior member of the Socialist Party who was reportedly close to the seamen's union. I said no. He immediately picked up the phone, called Tanabe, and requested that he make himself available to discuss the matter with me. I met Tanabe at my residence later that day. He offered to be helpful, but the problem remained unresolved.

During those weeks of August and early September 1990, Japan's conduct distressed its friends and angered its critics. While Washington's official response to Japan's August 29 package was politely affirmative, unofficial reactions were more telling. One unidentified U.S. official commented sarcastically to the press that we faced a demanding military challenge in the Middle East, and "there's a limited number of Girl Scout cookies that can be used there." Nor was the disappointment confined to Americans. Motoo Shiina, a respected defense expert in the Japanese Diet observed, "This was a time when Japan was really tested to see if it could bear its international responsibility. I am disappointed that Japan could not show the will and the courage to do something more."[1]

I became increasingly blunt about expressing to Japanese editorial writers and others my exasperation with the delays in Japan's announced plans, the uncertainties surrounding its promised assistance, and the detailed conditions that restricted the operational and political value of its support. I had numerous chances to discuss Japan's principled refusal to involve itself in military activities and to draw parallels with our own concept of conscientious objection to military service. I regularly noted that in our culture the concept of conscientious objection did not exempt its practitioners from sacrifice and risk; for example, those who opted for service in the Medical Corps often operated under conditions of maximum danger. COs merely shouldered such risks on terms compatible with their religious or moral principles. This pitch generally elicited pained or puzzled silence.

Washington's muted reaction to the announcement of the August 29 package prompted the Japanese to assess its value at $1 billion. That helped some, but with the costs of the coalition effort mounting, President Bush decided to send cabinet-level envoys around the world to dun key allies for augmented support. Secretary of the Treasury Nick Brady and Deputy Secretary of State Larry Eagleburger were designated to visit Japan. They arrived on September 7 with little advance notice. Though they were on the ground only a few hours, they managed to outline their requirements and hopes—$2 billion in aid for the frontline states, with $600 million of this available for quick disbursement, and an additional $1 billion to support the multilateral force—

1. Both quotations from the *New York Times*, August 30, 1990, p. A14.

in separate meetings with Prime Minister Kaifu, Foreign Minister Nakayama, and Finance Minister Ryutaro Hashimoto.

Many Japanese evinced surprise, even consternation, at the inflation in our requests. But, as I subsequently reminded key officials and politicians, we were not asking Tokyo for more help in order to shave our own contributions. Far from it. Aside from putting our military forces at risk, we were already contributing more than $2 billion annually in aid to Egypt, most of it in the form of grants, and we were now offering to write off $7 billion in FMS (Foreign Military Sales) debts. If we had not acted with dispatch in sending troops to Saudi Arabia, Japan would probably have seen a swift and dramatic increase in its oil bill.

Having just come from stops in London and Paris where Mrs. Thatcher and President Mitterand had enthusiastically volunteered increased support for the coalition, Brady and Eagleburger found the meetings in Tokyo—particularly the detailed and extended dinner discussion with Mr. Hashimoto—disappointing. Hashimoto possessed no authority to commit to a specific level of support; he represented a ministry whose traditional role in budgetary matters was to hold the line, and he conducted the meeting as if its principal purpose was to determine the strength of U.S. pressure. I guessed that Hashimoto was on the spot. He had pressed MOF bureaucrats to support the recently announced $1 billion package and wasn't pleased to be asked to go to the well again so soon. At the dinner with us, in the presence of his MOF associates, he chose to assert the tough line that no further contributions would be possible during the current fiscal year—a position that Brady and Eagleburger characterized firmly as a huge mistake. Overall, the discussion lacked a spirit of cooperation and impressed my Washington visitors as more akin to negotiating with a competitor than consulting with an ally. Brady and Eagleburger departed without making much visible effort to conceal their irritation. I shared their frustration but urged patience and reminded them that haste was not a noteworthy attribute of Japanese decision making. I could only hope that the strength of their representation would produce a worthy result. As it happened, they got some unsolicited help.

If the administration was irritable, the Congress was angry. My visitors had scarcely departed Tokyo when the House of Representatives voted 370 to 53 for an anti-Japanese amendment attached to a military spending bill sponsored by Congressman David Bonior. This bill provided that Japan pay all the expenses associated with our military presence in that country, including the salaries of U.S. personnel. If Japan refused to pay, our forces were to be withdrawn at a rate of five thousand a year. The amendment was silly; its logic contradictory. If implemented, its consequences would have been counterproductive for both countries. Still, it provided a fair barometer of sentiment on the Hill. For its part, the Senate unanimously passed a resolution warning of a serious downgrading of relations with allies that were deemed not to have made appropriate contributions to the Gulf coalition effort. Its ostensible targets were Bonn and Tokyo.

Within a week, Prime Minister Kaifu called President Bush to inform him that Japan would provide an additional $3 billion in support—$1 billion for the multilateral alliance and $2 billion for the frontline states with $600 million of the latter funds earmarked for rapid disbursement. The decision was announced formally on September 14. A marked improvement also appeared in other cooperative activities. Thanks to imaginative and energetic efforts by younger Foreign Ministry officials, led by Minoru Tamba and Yukio Okamoto, the Japanese shared with the Pentagon lists of equipment they could supply. This enabled Defense Department officials to check them against the coalition's requirements, thereby expediting deliveries. Eight hundred Toyota Landrovers were included in one major shipment to Saudi Arabia. The legal entity Japan needed to channel financial contributions to the Gulf coalition was formally established. And on September 14 Prime Minister Kaifu publicly announced plans to seek legislation to create the United Nations Cooperation Corps, a civilian agency that would enable Japan to perform support functions for UN peacekeeping forces

Just as the Japanese began to get their act together, I was reminded that Tokyo had no monopoly on nit-picking. Officials in Washington, noting that the Japanese government had pledged another billion dollars in support of the multilateral alliance, instructed me to seek confirmation that the full amount would be supplied exclusively to the United States.

Japan's first billion contribution had been committed to the coalition, although the lion's share was provided to Washington. This arrangement had been devised to allow Tokyo to demonstrate that it was participating in a multilateral undertaking. The Japanese were extremely unlikely to deviate from that precedent. Moreover, Sir John Whitehead, the UK's able ambassador, told me the British were already anticipating a modest contribution to their forces from this second tranche, and I knew that the Japanese wished to extend at least some modest support to certain troop-contributing Arab governments in order to cover their flanks politically in the Middle East. These seemed reasonable concerns, and I expressed my misgivings to Bob Kimmitt and others about carrying out the requested demarche. Over my objections, the instructions were confirmed, and I took up the matter with Vice Minister Kuriyama. As expected, he reiterated that the bulk of Japan's support would go to Washington but maintained firmly that since Japan was contributing to a multilateral coalition, it could not ignore all claims except our own.

Personal Concerns

The quest for financial and other forms of support did not exhaust my concerns during the fall of 1990. One was a purely personal matter. *Bungei Shunju*, one of Japan's most prominent intellectual magazines, ran a major article on me in its October 1990 issue. Dubbing me "*Gaiatsu-san*"—"Mr. Foreign Pressure"—the article was laced with criticism of my allegedly blunt methods. In some respects the central theme of the article—that I had figured out the Japanese political system and knew where to apply pressure in order to achieve results—was a backhanded compliment. But I was uncomfortable with the direct criticisms it contained from senior LDP politicians like former chief cabinet secretary Masaharu Gotoda, for whom I had great respect.

Similar criticisms had been conveyed privately some months earlier. Bill Franklin, a good friend and former president of the American Chamber of Commerce in Tokyo, had come to me in the spring of 1990 to report complaints from two "very prominent members of the Japanese business establishment" to the effect that I was insufficiently solicitous of the interests of "my hosts," i.e., the Japanese government. I asked Bill who had passed on this observation, but he had promised them he would not disclose their identities. I told him I would be happy to discuss the situation with them but couldn't very well do that without knowing who they were. I suggested he go back and inform them that while I attempted to assure that Washington had a decent appreciation of the situation in Japan, the Japanese government had a very able ambassador in Washington whose job it was to safeguard

Tokyo's equities in the relationship. My legal obligation was to look after our interests. Fortunately, on many issues U.S. and Japanese interests converged. I heard nothing further about this from Bill.

Some of the commentary in the *Bungei Shunju* article—for example, that I had breached protocol by making my case outside usual bureaucratic channels—was galling. The Japanese ambassador in Washington routinely met with politicians on both sides of the aisle in Congress, and its embassy lobbied energetically on behalf of Japanese interests both directly and through a stable of lawyers and public relations specialists. I figured that what was sauce for the goose was sauce for the gander. Still, my concern about the article grew when other journals picked up the story and embroidered the critical commentary. Whether this was the herd instinct of Japanese journalism in action or a more calculated and orchestrated official effort to diminish my standing, I never knew.

I was especially apprehensive about rumors suggesting that former prime minister Takeshita, perhaps the single most powerful member of the LDP, had voiced some of these same criticisms and expressed questions as to whether I retained the confidence of the White House. A related but separate concern involved suggestions that my frequent calls on Secretary General Ozawa and various LDP faction leaders, juxtaposed against infrequent calls at the *kantei* (the prime minister's official residence), implied a lack of respect for Mr. Kaifu. I reported the rumors concerning Takeshita to Washington and later learned that Secretary Baker had sent him a private note not only affirming that I enjoyed his full confidence but urging Takeshita to use me as a channel for passing sensitive messages to the secretary. Evidently this had some effect, for all my subsequent meetings with Mr. Takeshita were thoroughly cordial.

The Japanese press displayed an unusual interest in my relationship with Ichiro Ozawa. The contents of confidential meetings that I had with him at my residence seemed to circulate informally among Japanese correspondents, and occasional references to them showed up in the papers. According to the conventional wisdom I exerted exorbitant influence over the Japanese government through Ozawa. In truth, my relationship with him was less intimate than the press often suggested. But I liked and respected him. I enjoyed our conversations, which were straightforward and direct. He had an interest in the big issues, and his focus was on fixing problems, not merely analyzing them. He wanted to make things happen, and he knew that politics was the art of the possible. He was self-assured without being cocky. He understood the value of the U.S.-Japan relationship, and he was willing to utilize his considerable political skills to solve problems when they emerged.

Hostage Diplomacy

A more significant concern to Washington was the danger of diplomatic freelancing on the hostage issue. One hundred thirty-nine Japanese hostages were being held in Baghdad, and another one hundred sixty-six Japanese nationals, while not formally detained, were unable to secure exit visas from Iraq. It was clear that Saddam Hussein intended to use hostages as a lever not only to deter attacks but to divide his opponents. He was eager to lure countries into deals for the release of their nationals, and Japan may have appeared susceptible to blackmail or blandishment. The U.S. Government, on the basis of extensive and occasionally bitter experience, was convinced that the chances of securing hostage releases on terms compatible with other objectives would be increased if all countries stood united in their resistance to Saddam Hussein's ploys, forswearing any attempt to negotiate special deals.

In previous episodes, the Japanese government had displayed a readiness to negotiate for the release of hostages. Financial inducements were not excluded as a matter of principle. The Kaifu government was under intense domestic political pressure to demonstrate that it would leave no stone unturned in seeking the release of Japanese hostages. And certain LDP and opposition politicians were eager to get into the act.

One of these, former prime minister Yasuhiro Nakasone, utilizing contacts he had established with senior Iraqi leaders during his tenure as MITI minister in the 1970s, announced that he would visit Baghdad in early November to explore possibilities for accelerating the release of the hostages. Washington reacted nervously to this report. It came at a time when the efficacy of our sanctions policy was subject to growing doubts. Difficult decisions consequently loomed, and sensitivities to alliance solidarity were heightened. Washington's doubts about Japan's fortitude were rekindled at this time by reports that its consul general in New York, Ambassador Masamichi Hanabusa, was publicly expressing doubts about the wisdom of U.S. policy in the Gulf. And the Japanese press and media were, as usual, full of commentary questioning Washington's inclination to confront Saddam Hussein.

Fortunately, Mr. Nakasone forewarned me about his plans before his trip was publicly announced, and he promised to brief me prior to his departure. In this meeting, which took place on October 29, Nakasone emphasized that he was going as a former prime minister invited by an Iraqi-Japanese friendship group, not as a representative of the LDP or the government. The meeting allowed me in turn to convey to the former prime minister the decided lack of enthusiasm his proposed trip had evoked in Washington and to emphasize the devastating effects a separate deal for the release of Japanese hostages would have on the alliance. I expressed concern about the procession of Western leaders beating a path to Baghdad. Such visits relieved Saddam's isolation, provoked speculation about cracks in alliance solidarity, and gave the Iraqi leader potential diplomatic leverage. I also expressed uneasiness about hints in an article Nakasone had recently published suggesting the possibility of a mediating role for Japan rather than highlighting Japan's firm adherence to all UN resolutions.

Whether Nakasone needed any reminders on this issue was an open question. He was an experienced politician who had cultivated close relations with the United States throughout his tenure as prime minister. Nonetheless, since his involvement in the scandal that resulted after the Recruit Corporation made improper political contributions to the LDP in return for help in working around government regulations, his influence had diminished, and there was the possibility that he might attempt some high-visibility diplomatic maneuvering to enhance his standing at home. Another source of inspiration may have come from former president Jimmy Carter, with whom Nakasone had met during Carter's visit to Tokyo a few weeks earlier. During our conversation, I noted that Carter's publicly expressed views were sharply at variance with the administration's and urged Nakasone to remind Saddam forcefully that settlement of the Persian Gulf crisis required his compliance with *all* UN resolutions. In any event, his trip did result in the release of seventy-four Japanese hostages but, as far as I could judge, he had done no major harm to allied solidarity nor gained much political mileage in Japan. His jaunt to the Middle East drew criticism, however, from the Bush administration's spokesperson,

Marlin Fitzwater, and from Vice President Quayle, who was visiting Tokyo for the enthronement of the emperor.

Nakasone made one further attempt in early January 1991 to mediate a compromise in the Persian Gulf. He sent a personal emissary, Bunsei Sato, to Baghdad to test reactions to a compromise proposal involving concessions—including a guarantee of access to international waterways for Iraq—that were opposed publicly by both the American and the Japanese governments. Nakasone defended his effort, saying that a solution required mediation and compromise. The initiative died of its own weight, however. Events had acquired a momentum of their own, and Nakasone's views were neither backed by his own government nor taken seriously by the parties concerned.

Peacekeeping Operations Bill

Pressure on Japan to contribute personnel as well as financial support to the coalition effort in the Gulf, as noted, prompted Tokyo to seek a new legal basis for supporting UN-sponsored peacekeeping activities. Theoretically, the government might have attempted to undertake such activities on the basis of a reinterpretation of what the constitution and Self-Defense Force Law permitted. But the prevailing consensus was that new legislation was required, and Prime Minister Kaifu announced in early September 1990 that a new law would be drafted and introduced within weeks.

The drama that unfolded over the next two months—and was to be replayed periodically for nearly two more years—involved the interplay of two considerations: international concerns encouraged the LDP to seek the swift passage of a peacekeeping operations bill, while domestic realities required it to secure the acquiescence of some opposition votes to put together the necessary majority in the Upper House. The desire for a quick result enhanced the leverage of opposition parties, thereby enabling them to impose a host of detailed conditions on Japan's participation in peacekeeping activities—not that the governing party sought a legislative carte blanche. But divisions within the LDP left it unable or unwilling to focus the public debate on broad foreign policy and constitutional guidelines and principles. The result was confusion and a series of compromises that managed, in Professor Takashi Inoguchi's subsequent comment, "to combine absurdly detailed and limiting provisions with an astonishing overall vagueness."[2]

Prime Minister Kaifu initially proposed the creation of an unarmed, civilian, volunteer "UN Cooperation Corps." The idea was for this force to provide communications, surveillance, and medical support for UN peacekeepers while staying well away from the front lines. The proposal drew attacks from virtually all ends of the political spectrum. Socialists as well as moderate opposition groups saw it as a dangerous step down a slippery slope. The military establishment was offended by its exclusion from participation in peacekeeping activities. Within the LDP, members of the defense caucus contended that without the discipline of military training, such a force would be ineffective and potentially vulnerable. Poll results suggested that the public was skeptical.

Former prime minister Takeshita and Secretary General Ozawa proposed that instead of submitting brand-new legislation, the government seek a revision of the Self-Defense Force Law to permit military units to take part in peacekeeping activities in the Gulf. This was reportedly opposed by Prime Minister Kaifu and Foreign Minister Nakayama, among others, reportedly out of concern that such a move would trigger adverse reactions in neighboring Asian countries while providing new and unwelcome authority and prestige to the Defense Agency and Self-Defense Forces.

After several false starts, the cabinet finally approved a plan on October 14 that would allow soldiers to go to the Gulf area to perform tasks behind the lines but bar them from the threat or use of force. Specifically, the bill limited Japanese units to the surveillance of cease-fires and elections and the performance of telecommunications, maintenance, medical care, transportation, and disaster relief activities. Despite its modest scope, few political analysts thought much of the plan's prospects.

I was determined to keep the United States out of this political maelstrom. The Japanese would have to sort out for themselves the precise nature of their future security role in the world. We would only compound the confusion in Tokyo and complicate our relations with Japan if we intruded in this highly charged debate. I addressed the issue

2. Quoted in Kiyofuku Chuma, "The Debate over Japan's Participation in Peacekeeping Operations," *Japan Review of International Affairs* 6, no. 3 (fall 1992): 248.

in a speech to a large gathering of young LDP political leaders in Ito on September 9, 1990. As delicately as I could, I urged the audience to extend Japan's contribution to the multilateral alliance beyond mere financial support. As for its direct involvement, I said:

> I do not wish to take a position on the legal or constitutional issues the crisis in the Gulf poses for Japan. They are important issues. We know their sensitivity. They are properly yours to define and to resolve. Your friends abroad have a stake in the outcome, however, because your answers will indicate to others what role you are ready to play in future UN peacekeeping ventures and what share of the costs and risks you are prepared to shoulder. Naturally we would expect your response to reflect what your national interests and your stature in the international community require. Predictably, your American friends hope you will be generous and far-sighted.

On the golf course that afternoon, Tsutomu Hata, one of the hosts of the meeting, expressed some misgivings about my remarks. He suggested that if I wanted a better understanding of Japanese sensitivities on this issue, I should talk to Masaharu Gotoda. Gotoda, who had served as chief cabinet secretary to former prime minister Nakasone, was widely known as a man of probity, independence, and political courage. I had met him only at large functions and asked my political section to arrange a meeting. A lunch was set up in mid-October, and on the appointed day Gotoda arrived at my residence with two other LDP Diet members—Koji Kakizawa and Kazuo Aichi—at hand. Both were younger; both, it turned out, disagreed with Gotoda on the issue of Japan's participation in UN peacekeeping.

Gotoda expressed strong reservations about any Japanese involvement in peacekeeping because of his evident doubts about Japan's ability to sustain effective civilian control over a military force whose capabilities and responsibilities had grown substantially over the years. He recalled a Chinese proverb—"The dike crumbles from a single ant hole"—to emphasize the need for vigilance to prevent even a modest initiative from escalating into a decisive shift in the nation's direction. He implied that if Japan were to take one step toward deploying its military forces abroad—even for benign and internationally sanctioned purposes—other unanticipated steps might follow. Both Aichi and Kakizawa demurred, avowing that Japan's democratic institutions were secure, its military forces professional, and its mechanisms for civilian control firmly in place.

The conversation reinforced my own disposition to keep the United States out of the debate. I thought Aichi and Kakizawa made an impressive case, but if an experienced and seasoned politician like Gotoda harbored such doubts, it was no wonder that other Asian countries remained apprehensive. Resistance to Japan's involvement in peacekeeping activities was most visible in China and Korea. Australia openly welcomed a Japanese role in the Gulf. The views within the Association of Southeast Asian Nations (ASEAN) appeared mixed. The Thai seemed relaxed; the Singaporians nervous. Japanese authorities, of course, monitored their neighbors' reactions to the proposed legislation carefully.

Since the 1990 peacekeeping operations (PKO) legislation inspired divisions at home and ambivalence abroad, it is scarcely surprising that many observers regarded the LDP's effort to pass the UN Cooperation Bill as somewhat perfunctory—an effort destined to fail, designed more to deflect foreign criticism than to accomplish a legislative result. My own discussions of this issue with key LDP leaders such as Secretary General Ozawa and Executive Secretary Takeo Nishioka persuaded me that at least they gave the effort a good college try.

For example, when I called on Nishioka on October 22, he requested my help in dispelling an impression he said was circulating among LDP members; namely, that the United States was not genuinely supportive of the UN Cooperation Bill. He claimed that many Diet members were reluctant to work hard to pass a bill that was controversial at home and unappreciated in Washington. I emphasized that Washington eagerly sought allied support for the multinational coalition, but in the end each country had to determine for itself what kind of contribution was appropriate. I was reluctant, I said, to offer detailed advice on a sensitive national issue like this, and I noted that comments by U.S. officials on the pending legislation were likely to complicate the political debate further.

Nishioka characterized my position as "very prudent," adding with a smile, "perhaps too prudent." I was subsequently surprised to read in the afternoon newspapers that I had expressed "high expectations about passage of the UN Cooperation Bill" to senior LDP executives. Since the prime minister and other LDP leaders had been laboring to refute inaccurate but persistent opposition charges that the bill was drafted under U.S. pressure, this rather imaginative characterization of my remarks appeared to reflect the growing apprehensions in LDP leadership circles about the bill's prospects in the Diet.

Those prospects did not improve, and Mr. Ozawa looked genuinely pained when he informed me in mid-November that the votes were not there to pass the bill and LDP leaders were consequently inclined to withdraw it from the Diet without submitting it for a vote. I expressed disappointment at this news. It came at a time when the release of French hostages, some increased resistance in the Security Council to the use of force against Iraq, and recent visits to Baghdad by Willy Brandt and Yasuhiro Nakasone suggested cracks were appearing in alliance solidarity. Yet I had to acknowledge that little purpose would be served by revealing the lack of support for the measure by pressing it to a vote. I added my hope that the party would persevere in its quest for legislation of this kind during the next session of the Diet.

The party leadership was somewhat noncommittal about its future plans for peacekeeping legislation. But I suspected that the effort would gather strength. Progress was being achieved in negotiating a peace agreement for Cambodia. While there was little enthusiasm in Japan about participating in peacekeeping ventures in remote regions such as the Middle East, such activities in Asia entailed a different foreign policy calculus. It seemed to me unlikely that the Japanese would allow legal impediments to bar them from a consequential role in resolving a major regional issue at just the moment when support for the so-called Asianization of Japanese foreign policy was gathering momentum.

Desert Storm

While Japan was prepared to support sanctions against Iraq, some feared it would lose its nerve in the event sanctions failed and force proved necessary. Henry Kissinger, who visited Tokyo in mid-October, questioned me closely on this point. My own soundings with senior officials and political leaders convinced me that the Japanese would support Desert Storm provided the policy of sanctions was given an honest try, the coalition exhausted all reasonable possibilities for resolving the conflict, and Saddam Hussein continued to respond with defiance. In this connection, the late November announcement that Iraq faced a deadline of January 15 to withdraw from Kuwait and

Secretary Baker's expressed readiness to go to Baghdad and meet Vice Premier Tariq Aziz in Washington helped prepare the political ground in Japan for governmental and public support of Desert Storm. The secretary's readiness to have face-to-face talks with the Iraqis was welcomed as a last-ditch effort to avoid war, though it heralded no substantive change of position: he offered no concessions, no political solutions, and no deviation from his past insistence that Iraq honor all UN resolutions.

As the January 15 deadline for Iraq's withdrawal from Kuwait approached without any signs of conciliatory gestures from Saddam Hussein, I urged the Japanese government to prepare for new and substantial requests for additional financial support. Deploying troops for deterrent purposes was not cheap; employing them in combat would be truly expensive, for when many lives are at stake, money is no object. Though I had as yet no precise idea what Washington's expectations of Japan might be, I wanted to be sure that Tokyo did not shoot too low again. I consequently made my rounds to key government and party leaders, emphasizing to each the importance of being prepared to respond quickly to new and ambitious requests.

During meetings in January, while renewing my request for political and financial support for Desert Storm, I also urged prompt and forthcoming Japanese initiatives in tackling the refugee problems we all anticipated. I recommended that those who dwelt on the political problems Japan would face in coping with these issues should view their situation with some sense of proportion. The Bush administration was staring war in the face with Congress in the hands of the opposition. Authorization to use force had been supported by a thin majority on the Hill, and if casualties were high, criticism would be fierce. I observed that crises have a way of rearranging relationships. With war imminent, our people would be taking careful note of who our friends were. And I suggested that the Japanese offer whatever practical help they could, manage their politics with resolution, and announce their decisions expeditiously without awaiting pressure.

A particularly key figure was Finance Minister Hashimoto, for he would have to manage any specific requests for funding through the Ministry of Finance, whose bureaucracy was notoriously unreceptive to political direction. Nor was my relationship with Hashimoto an easy one. I had found him a somewhat prickly individual with whom I felt little personal rapport. I initially had expected to develop a comfortable relationship with him. We were virtually the same age, and he had a reputation as a strong and highly capable "take charge" guy. Yet in our first meeting—a courtesy call in the spring of 1989—he seemed to have a chip on his shoulder. I particularly recall his assertion, "The trouble with you Americans, Ambassador Armacost, is that you cannot forget that you won the war." (The evidence Hashimoto offered to support his proposition—e.g., our bilateral civil air agreement, one of the few that seemed to work to the United States' economic advantage, and U.S. pressure to open the Japanese cigarette market despite our domestic regulation requiring notices on each package that smoking was injurious to health—struck me as, at best, strained.) I assured Hashimoto that since I was only eight years old and lived on the East Coast in 1945, the war with Japan had exerted little influence on my outlook. I expressed the hope that, as members of a younger generation, we could overcome the unfortunate legacies of the past. But I left the meeting doubting we would become close. Subsequent events confirmed that intuition.

But Hashimoto was a key player. And I did not have the luxury of approaching him through his associates in the Ministry of Finance, for I did not enjoy the easy entree to senior officials there that I had developed in most other ministries. In general, MOF bureaucrats appeared ill-disposed toward taking up much substantive business with ambassadors, preferring to tackle macroeconomic and foreign exchange issues directly with their Treasury counterparts in Washington either by phone or by fax. Given the sensitivity of such issues on markets, this was neither surprising nor inappropriate.

Beyond these natural inclinations, I had perhaps burned some bridges with MOF officials during the SII talks. Though I had not set the agenda for those negotiations, I energetically pursued U.S. objectives, including the effort to alter the savings/investment imbalance in Japan by encouraging increases in its infrastructure spending. MOF professionals regarded almost any advice from foreigners on such issues as gratuitous and unwelcome. They undoubtedly found U.S. suggestions particularly offensive since they had little respect for Washington's management of public finances. Whatever their concerns, when I sought to arrange a meeting with the finance minister through the usual channels, unexplained difficulties frequently appeared.

Impatient with such delays, I asked my deputy, Bill Breer, to use his personal contacts with political associates of Hashimoto to arrange a private meeting at my residence. In this fashion I met several times with Hashimoto in December 1990 and early January 1991 to review the landscape in Washington and obtain a better understanding of the political and budgetary realities Hashimoto would have to accommodate in formulating Japan's response to new aid requests. I cannot judge the value of these sessions to Minister Hashimoto or their effect on his thinking. But he headed for New York in mid-January briefed by more than just his own colleagues and subordinates and in a mood I judged to be constructive and helpful. On the margins of the G-7 ministerial meetings, he met privately on January 21 with Secretary Brady to discuss the multilateral coalition's financial requirements now that hostilities had commenced. The meeting was one-on-one, with only a Japanese interpreter present. Secretary Brady appealed for $9 billion in additional support—a figure I suspect was considerably higher than the Japanese anticipated and greater than Secretary Brady realistically expected Tokyo to provide. To Hashimoto's credit, he secured his government's official response in little more than forty-eight hours—an extremely rapid turnaround when so much money was involved. More astonishing yet was the fact that the answer was thoroughly positive. Indeed, the Japanese coupled their announcement with a pledge of an additional $38 million in refugee assistance and an offer to supply military aircraft for evacuating refugees from the war zone.

As usual, the devil was in the details. Compared to the generosity of the offer, the problems that subsequently surfaced were small potatoes. But they were sufficient to take some of the gloss off a notable display of alliance solidarity. Washington wanted Japan to eliminate its strings on aid during Desert Storm. Japan's contribution was to be financed through new taxes on cigarettes, gasoline, and corporations; treasury bonds were to be issued to supply funds until the government was reimbursed out of these new tax revenues. To secure passage of a supplemental budget to provide new funds, however, Tokyo needed the concurrence of the opposition-controlled Upper House. This gave the swing votes to the Komeito Party and the Democratic Socialists, who used them to force Prime Minister Kaifu to agree that Japan's financial contribution, which was provided for logistical purposes, would not be spent on arms, ammunition, or other lethal purposes. In the bargaining with the opposition, moreover, the proposal to utilize military aircraft to transport refugees was ultimately abandoned; it was also agreed that some of the funds would be obtained through expenditure reductions rather than tax increases, and the Komeito Party exacted a pound of flesh politically by securing Ozawa's promise that the LDP would support a mutually acceptable candidate for the Tokyo gubernatorial election later that spring. Despite these conditions, Tokyo's generosity, the timeliness of its decision on aid, and its steadfast political support helped dissipate criticism of Japan within the administration, the press, and Congress. Indeed, in late February 1991, before the ground war in Kuwait commenced, Moscow solicited Japan's support for a conditional Iraqi withdrawal from Kuwait—a measure designed to help Saddam Hussein off the hook without requiring his full compliance with all UN resolutions—but found no daylight between Tokyo and Washington.

Unfortunately, the Brady-Hashimoto meeting left several loose ends that occasioned some trench warfare between our respective bureaucracies. Two unresolved issues in particular provoked friction. One was the old question of whether Japan's support would be allocated exclusively to the United States or shared with other members of the coalition. The other involved the exchange rate used to calculate the dollar value of Japan's contribution. The first issue surfaced immediately; the latter when the dollar appreciated rapidly in the wake of the coalition's decisive military victory.

In truth, these issues were discussed at least briefly by Assistant Secretary Dallara and Vice Minister Utsumi, following the Brady-Hashimoto meeting. No agreement was reached, however. Washington was obdurate on the first question, but it overreached. The Japanese, as noted above, had allocated their earlier contribution to the coalition. This served their political needs, and we, however reluctantly, had accommodated their wishes. There was no chance the Japanese would deviate from this precedent, and I saw no reason why we should challenge their judgment. Tokyo had been generous, and our demarche struck me as nit-picking. Nevertheless, I dutifully raised the matter, but with little conviction and no effect.

The exchange rate issue turned out to be more consequential financially, for the appreciation of the dollar against the yen diminished the value of Japan's contribution to us by roughly $500 million. A strapped Treasury Department was perhaps destined to raise the issue, but our position suffered from two defects: first, we had reached no clear-cut understanding on the exchange rate matter back in January; second, previous precedents worked against us.

The Ministry of Finance routinely calculated the dollar value of its assistance to foreign countries by averaging the dollar-yen exchange rate over the fifteen-day period prior to its submission of a supplemental budget bill to the Diet. Based on this procedure, the government calculated its contribution at 115 yen to the dollar. The Diet naturally appropriated the money in yen, and dollar payouts were subject to future currency fluctuations. The Japanese had followed precisely this procedure in the fall of 1990. At that time, the yen was appreciating against the dollar, and the United States earned a $40 million windfall on the exchange rate fluctuation. Treasury had expressed no complaint and offered no rebate. This time, however, with the dollar appreciating rapidly, Treasury cried foul. Predictably, the Finance Ministry reminded Washington of its normal procedures and rested its case. But the issue would not go away.

Congressional pressure for additional money was not particularly subtle. Pending supplemental amendments to the Gulf war provided that the United States would neither sell nor deliver weapons to any country that did not promptly pay its pledged assistance, and the Treasury had publicly expressed the view that as far as it was concerned, Japan's pledge was for $9 billion. Administration officials told the Japanese that they did not support this legislation but thought it would become law. Sure enough, the so-called Byrd Amendment was passed, but in signing the bill the president emphasized it was up to him to determine the timeliness of contributions.

Washington's pursuit of the matter led to some delicate public diplomacy challenges for the embassy by midspring 1991, since recurrent newspaper reports hinted that financial contributions from allied nations by then exceeded the Pentagon's total outlays during the surprisingly swift military campaign. Prime Minister Kaifu's scheduled meeting with President Bush at Kennebunkport in midsummer 1991 provided a convenient deadline for putting the issue behind us.

To the end the Japanese refused to recalculate their exchange rate. But before Kaifu's visit to Kennebunkport, which eventually took place in early August 1991, they did offer to provide $500 million—an amount roughly equivalent to the shortfall—to tackle postwar problems in the Gulf area, such as environmental issues, humanitarian assistance, maintenance of the UN embargo, destruction of mines, and the phasedown and redeployment of U.S. forces. The president highlighted the positive contributions Japan had made to the multilateral effort in the Gulf and agreed to schedule a visit to Japan later in the year. An official visit would provide possibilities for accentuating the positive features of U.S.-Japan collaboration. And in fact these had multiplied in the wake of the Gulf war.

The Japanese took one unexpected step in tackling postwar problems when they dispatched four minesweepers to the Gulf in April 1991 to help clear that international waterway for commercial traffic. They took this initiative without prompting from us, although they did wait until after the April 1991 local elections, ostensibly to avoid putting the Komeito Party on the spot. Admiral Makoto Sakuma, chairman of the joint staff, had long urged the deployment of Japanese minesweepers to the Gulf; stung by international criticism, key Foreign Ministry officials were now more receptive to the request. In any case, the military risks had declined with the end of the war, and Japanese oil companies in Saudi Arabia, not to mention merchant shipping interests, had an obvious stake in clearing mines from the Gulf. And since Japanese crews on vessels transiting the Gulf were among those exposed to danger, the maritime unions no longer resisted. The government, moreover, could point to the precedent of a recent German decision to send minesweepers to the Gulf. Not the least of the ironies in this affair was the fact that Japan's deployments were undertaken without benefit either of PKO legislation—the UN Cooperation Bill having failed in the Diet—or a revision of the Self-Defense Force Law. As usual, the Japanese government demonstrated flexibility when it perceived compelling reasons to do so.

Tokyo was eager to assert a more active diplomacy in the Middle East and Gulf region in the postwar period. Promising opportunities included closer ties with Israel, political initiatives to limit destabilizing arms sales, a more visible role in the Middle East peace process, and support for the reconstruction needs of Kuwait and others. Washington welcomed such initiatives, and they helped salve some of the wounds the U.S.-Japan relationship had sustained during the Gulf conflict.

Postmortem

However frayed the relationship with Tokyo became at times, U.S.-Japanese collaboration during the Gulf war provided benefits to both nations. U.S. actions to protect Saudi oil fields, to force Iraq out of

Kuwait, to curb Saddam Hussein's nuclear weapons program, and to get the Arab-Israeli peace talks back on track served a variety of Japanese objectives. They kept the lid on oil prices, fostered stability in an area of acute Japanese commercial interest, and forestalled the spread of weapons of mass destruction. At the same time, Japan's support of the UN embargo, its generous financial support for the multilateral coalition, its assistance to frontline states and support for refugees, its help in repairing the damage done by the war, and its postwar agreement to participate in regional aspects of the Middle East peace talks helped advance a number of U.S. aims.

To be sure, the experience also left scars on both sides. The hesitancy of Japan's initial response, the multitude of conditions imposed on its financial contribution, its reluctance to share the risks as well as the costs of a major multilateral venture, and its tendency to reach tough decisions only under the most intense international pressure prompted questions among many Americans about its reliability as an ally and global diplomatic partner. At the same time, many Japanese were irritated by the intensity of U.S. criticism and resented the fact that their financial support for Desert Storm was all too often ignored in Western celebrations of the coalition's victory.

What, one might ask, brought the Japanese around and prompted them to provide such substantial financial and political support for Desert Shield and Desert Storm despite their initial, deep-seated reservations? The simple answer, I believe, is foreign pressure, principally from the United States. This pressure was sharply focused, and it was sustained. It was broadly based, embracing key elements of both the executive and legislative branches of the U.S. government. And it was fueled by strong emotional support from the American people. While the consequences of a lame response were difficult to calculate, Tokyo could not rule out profound changes in U.S. attitudes and policies toward Japan, including our future readiness to maintain the alliance. Nor was pressure confined to the United States. Some Europeans joined in the requests for substantial Japanese assistance. So, too, did the moderate Arabs, some of whom—most notably the Kuwaitis and Saudis—were important suppliers of oil to Japan.

Within the Japanese government, moreover, there were important players—particularly senior officials in the Foreign Ministry and powerful politicians in the LDP—who recognized the importance of demonstrating Japan's solidarity with the multilateral coalition, or feared the consequences of ignoring U.S. requests, or saw opportunities to stake out a larger international role for their country. In any case, while the United States insistently demanded generous financial and political support from Tokyo, requests for personnel contributions were sufficiently lacking in specificity that Japan was able to find means of responding that required neither a revision of the constitution nor a fundamental reordering of the postwar political consensus. Thus they managed to defer a decision on PKO legislation, placed conditions on the uses of Japanese cash contributions, and were able to avoid direct involvement by Self-Defense Force units—e.g., minesweeping—until hostilities had ended.

One could argue that Japanese policy during the Gulf war was not a radical departure from long-established policy lines and was notably successful in traditional terms. After all, Japan placed no Japanese citizens in harm's way. Its contributions were mainly hortatory support and cash. It suffered no disruption of its oil supplies; indeed, the price of petroleum fell. Its hostages were returned unharmed. Its relationship with the United States survived. No irretrievable decisions to abandon the Yoshida tradition were reached. And while its $13 billion subvention to the multilateral coalition was far from trivial, it paled in significance to the price the Japanese government and industry would have paid had there been an disruption in the oil supply or a major price increase.

The coalition's triumph in the Gulf war brought few tributes to the solidarity of the U.S.-Japan alliance. But the prompt and decisive outcome did have a variety of salutary results. It tempered the tendency of many Japanese to ruminate darkly about the United States' decline. It generated in Japan renewed respect for U.S. military capabilities and the dexterity with which the Bush administration had integrated its military strategy and coalition diplomacy. It reminded Washington that, for all its military prowess, the coalition's victory was financed by others. No nation outside the Gulf area had contributed greater financial support than Japan, and Tokyo paid its bills fully and on time.

The Gulf crisis also precipitated much Japanese soul-searching about its international responsibilities. Gradually, foreign criticisms that Japan should not confine its contributions to financial support alone were taken over by the Japanese themselves. One result was the PKO bill, which eventually passed the Diet in June 1992, thereby creating a legal foundation for Japan's subsequent personnel contributions to UN-sponsored peacekeeping in Cambodia, Mozambique, and Rwanda. Naturally, the effort to enlarge Japan's international role was accompanied by efforts to assure that new activities would be tailored to Japan's own definition of its interests. Thus postmortems of the Gulf crisis in Japan prompted self-criticism—and ultimately remedial measures—regarding the quality of the government's intelligence, the adequacy of its crisis management arrangements, and the sufficiency of its logistic capabilities to support disaster relief or peacekeeping activities far from Japan's shores.

Ultimately, the Gulf war—like the GATT negotiations—challenged Japan's readiness to participate fully in defining the rules for managing post–cold war international security and trade issues. The transition from consumer to provider of international security was not easy: as the Gulf war experience demonstrated, Japan was hardly poised to break into the ranks of the world's major military powers. In addition, the criticism Japan took from the U.S. media and Congress fueled resentment and even prompted some Japanese to express the concern that in a unipolar world the United States, unconstrained by the need to preserve its alliances to deter Moscow, might turn its ire on erstwhile allies like Japan and Germany. Thus the experience of the Gulf war cast some doubt on the efficacy of a global diplomatic partnership between Tokyo and Washington. Still, the host of novel challenges of the post–cold war world forced both capitals to persevere in the search for new patterns of diplomatic cooperation.

5

Forging a Global Partnership

Whether Secretary of State Jim Baker coined the term *global partnership* or not, he was, I believe, the first prominent member of the Bush administration to use it to describe the purpose and spirit of our relationship with Japan. It was an apt and meaningful description. Less a dramatic departure than a shift of emphasis, it signified a desire to enlarge the scope of our bilateral cooperation and to achieve greater equity in the distribution of our respective global responsibilities. During the Reagan years, Ambassador Michael Mansfield had tirelessly underlined the unique importance of the U.S.-Japan bilateral relationship; now the Bush administration sought to harness Japan's growing power to the achievement of those international objectives we shared. Broadly speaking, both Tokyo and Washington desired a more equal partnership. But Tokyo was more interested in augmenting its influence in formulating the terms of this partnership; Washington in assuring that Japan shouldered a larger share of the burden of implementing it.

The Concept

Both governments recognized that the relationship needed to be adapted to the changed requirements of a post–cold war world. Both acknowledged that Japan needed to translate its growing economic power into a more ambitious international role. Both realized that since our countries represented roughly 40 percent of the world's economic output, few international issues could be resolved without effective bilateral collaboration. Washington policy makers understood that its growing fiscal deficit made the United States' global leadership more and more dependent on Japan's financial support. Japanese policy makers feared that, in a post–cold war environment, the USA might retreat into isolation if its allies withheld diplomatic cooperation. And leaders in both countries, aware that public support for the U.S.-Japan alliance could decline as the Soviet threat receded, knew they needed to find new ways of demonstrating the practical benefits of an active partnership.

These then were the premises on which the Bush administration set out to enlarge the scope and enrich the content of diplomatic cooperation with Japan. The policy was never formalized in any National Security Council document. It was not conceptualized in great detail. No new institutional infrastructure emerged to guide its development. Yet the idea did focus the activities of both governments, and the term *global partnership* became a slogan for officials on both sides of the Pacific.

The agenda for the partnership was ambitious. The Bush administration hoped to enlist Japan's cooperation in providing economic support for fledgling democratic countries in Eastern Europe and Central America, defining new global rules for trade and collective security arrangements for the post–cold war era, and arranging solutions for pressing transnational challenges, from protecting the environment to exploring outer space. In Washington's view, such a partnership required active U.S. leadership. But administration leaders understood that Japan would resist "taxation without representation" and conceded that increased Japanese support would require more recognition of its status and power in various international organizations and a readiness to adapt our global agenda to Japanese perspectives and purposes.

The Agenda

For purposes of exposition, I have grouped the issues on our cooperative agenda into these broad categories: dealing with the other major Asian powers; resolving regional conflicts; strengthening the economic underpinnings of fledgling democracies; creating an Asia/Pacific framework for economic cooperation; encouraging closer scientific and technological cooperation; fostering trilateral consultations among the industrialized democracies; and accommodating Japan's desire for a seat in the UN Security Council. The process of policy coordination was never terribly orderly, not least because virtually all these matters were constantly in play, yet each question had its own unique constituencies, deadlines, and rhythm in accordance with events.

Managing Relations with the Other Major Powers in Asia

No challenge taxed the ingenuity of Washington and Tokyo more than avoiding divergent approaches toward Moscow and Beijing. Our policy reflexes toward these nations reflected distinctive historical memories, and our interests did not always converge. Nonetheless, an impressive degree of policy coordination was achieved.

Moscow.   Relations with the former Soviet Union enjoyed a high priority in both capitals, though for different reasons. Having contained the Soviets for a generation, the United States was eager to nurture political and economic reforms in Moscow, cooperate in resolving problems left over from a generation of East-West struggle, and integrate the old Soviet Union and its former satellites into the international economy. Japanese leaders recognized the importance of these challenges yet tended to focus more attention on a narrower and more specific aim: recovering the Northern Territories—four small island groups (Habomai, Shikotan, Kunashiri, and Etorufu) off the coast of Hokkaido that Stalin had seized at the end of World War II.

Washington regularly sought Tokyo's help in defining a more cooperative relationship between Moscow and the West. This entailed the provision of humanitarian aid, technical assistance, and financial support; promoting the dismantling of nuclear weapons; encouraging the conversion of defense plants to peacetime uses; and a host of other tasks. Tokyo wanted a voice in Western policy toward the Soviet Union, and it periodically requested U.S. help in urging Moscow to apply its much advertised "new thinking" on foreign policy to its approach to Asian issues. In practical terms, this meant putting the Northern Territories issue on the Soviet policy agenda and augmenting Tokyo's leverage in seeking the prompt return of the islands.

Policy coordination was complicated by the fact that the end of the cold war exposed decidedly different policy reflexes in the two capitals. Having spent trillions defending against the Russians, Americans were in principle prepared to offer significant support to a nation evidently seeking to implement political and economic reforms (in reality, these generous instincts were not readily translated into financial support, because of both the U.S. fiscal deficit and a parsimonious public mood). Recalling the debates about who lost China, moreover, U.S. politicians were wary of being accused of turning a blind eye to Russian needs, lest the demise of the reform movement in the USSR invite similar attacks. And U.S. support, urged even by hard-nosed conservatives such as former presidents Richard Nixon and Ronald Reagan, appeared warranted by the dramatic changes in military/security conditions on the Continent: Eastern Europe was liberated; the Warsaw Pact had disappeared; and the Soviet military threat to Western Europe was at least temporarily eviscerated.

Tokyo, on the other hand, possessed little generosity of spirit toward Moscow. Japanese relations with both imperial Russia and the Bolshevik empire had been at best correct, never cordial. Japanese leaders tended to assume that whatever political shape the former Soviet Union took, Moscow would remain a rival. And vis-à-vis Moscow, the Japanese felt themselves the aggrieved party. After all, Moscow, in their view, had broken a nonaggression pact, entered World War II at the last minute, stolen the Northern Territories, and packed hundreds of thousands of Japanese prisoners off to Siberia. Thus Tokyo, far from sensing any obligation to shower money on even a reformist government in the Soviet Union, felt it was entitled to conciliatory gestures from Moscow.

In any event, few Japanese officials anticipated that aid would have a decisive effect on internal developments in the former USSR, and no major domestic political constituency pressed Tokyo for a more forthcoming policy. The LDP was inclined to drive a hard bargain with Moscow; the business establishment betrayed little interest in Russia; foreign policy professionals accorded priority to Japan's ties with the West and Asia; armchair strategists tended to prefer a weak, even chaotic Russia to a stronger, albeit more liberal country across the Japan Sea; and the Finance Ministry had little interest in writing generous checks to finance aid programs for the Russians—most particularly plans conceived essentially by others.

Nor did the end of the cold war bring as immediate or dramatic changes in Asia as it did in Europe. Russian military forces in the Far East were not immediately drawn down. The Northern Territories dispute remained unresolved. Worse yet, Gorbachev moved swiftly to relax tensions with the Chinese, while displaying only modest interest in transforming relations with Japan. When Foreign Minister Sousuke Uno visited Moscow in the summer of 1989, Gorbachev, instead of offering to tackle the Northern Territories issue, proposed that the matter be placed on the shelf. Tokyo's apprehension was that Japanese concerns would be neglected as East-West tensions dissipated—an anxiety that was reinforced when U.S.-Russian discussions at the Malta summit in October 1989 scarcely touched on Asia, let alone the Northern Territories issue.

These differences notwithstanding, Washington and Tokyo were generally sensitive to each other's dominant concerns. During the cold war, Washington's support for Japan's territorial claims on the Northern Territories had put Moscow on the spot and kept Japanese policy in line with our own; after 1989 the chances of resolving this long-stalemated issue appeared to improve, and facilitating that result could help elicit Japan's support for positive initiatives aimed at Moscow. Thus the United States readily reaffirmed its support for Japanese claims to the Northern Territories.

We reminded the Russians how our return of Okinawa in 1972 had buttressed our relations with Japan. We echoed Tokyo's assertion that the seizure of the islands had been an expression of Stalinist excess rather than the appropriation of legitimate spoils of war. We accommodated Japanese requests to internationalize the issue by including references to it in G-7 summit communiqués; for example, at the Houston summit in 1990, the political declaration included this statement: "We support the early resolution of the Northern Territories issue as an essential step leading to the normalization of Russian-Japanese relations." The president, secretary of state, and other senior U.S. officials regularly urged Moscow to resolve the issue promptly in a forthcoming way. And key State Department officials—among them Counselor Bob Zoellick, Policy Planning Director Dennis Ross, and Undersecretary for Political Affairs Arnold Kanter—signaled a willingness to tackle the problem in an even more active way. There was at least one informal offer to serve as an intermediary.

The Japanese obviously welcomed our help in putting the issue on Moscow's agenda. They solicited our appraisal of the roles and attitudes of key Russian players on the Northern Territories question. And they appreciated our readiness to explain to Russian constituencies to which they had little access—the military, for example—the potential benefits of an early resolution of the issue. Yet senior Foreign Ministry officials had no evident desire for Washington to take on a more direct role. They presumably did not wish to lose control of the issue and may have feared that Washington would provide unwelcome advice if it assumed the role of intermediary. I once asked senior ministry officials informally whether they had considered submitting the Northern Territories issue to the International Court of Justice. They had a solid legal case; and given the pressures of nationalism in Russia, it would have been easier for Moscow to accept the verdict of an impartial third party than to submit to Japan's claim in a bilateral negotiation. My interlocutors gave the suggestion short shrift, citing the unpredictability of the court's decisions. In any event, they noted, resolution of the issue was properly a test of Moscow's political will and should not be left to the judgment of third parties.

While understandably eager to retain control over the issue, the Japanese were far from passive on the matter. They intensified bilateral contacts with the Russians. Foreign minister–level contacts became routine; vice ministerial–level discussions of a Russian-Japanese peace treaty were commenced. Leading LDP politicians traveled with greater regularity to Moscow. Two major LDP figures—Shintaro Abe and Ichiro Ozawa—undertook missions to Moscow in 1990 and 1991, respectively, to explore possibilities for expanding relations and making a deal on the islands. And Tokyo sought to build pressure on the Russians, as noted, by soliciting the support of their G-7 associates.

The Japanese also injected greater flexibility into their policy. Stung perhaps by Foreign Minister Edvard Shevardnadze's criticism of their insistence on the indivisibility of economics and politics—an interesting reversal of Japan's traditional tendency to separate politics from economics—in the fall of 1989 the Japanese developed a new formula that they called the "balanced expansion of relations." It was designed to permit them the flexibility to provide modest amounts of aid to the former Soviet Union even before a resolution of the territorial issue. The Defense Agency removed language referring to the Russian threat from its annual white paper. The Foreign Ministry resigned itself to the staged reversion of the islands. And despite the Russians' intransigence on the question, the Japanese undertook a variety of conciliatory gestures toward Moscow, such as aid to the victims of the Chernobyl nuclear disaster, the provision of emergency food and medical aid to residents of the former Soviet Far East, the dispatch of technical assistance missions to instruct Russian reformers about Japan's unique brand of capitalism, and a decision not to suspend their aid program when Russian troops sought to suppress local independence movements in the Baltic states.

The high-water mark of Japan's exploration of a deal on the territories came during the spring of 1991. Visiting Moscow in March to prepare the ground for President Gorbachev's visit in April, Ichiro Ozawa sought to determine whether there was any flexibility in Moscow's position and reportedly dangled a sizable aid package as a lure. Some press reports suggested Ozawa sounded out Moscow on an "Okinawan reversion" formula in which Russia would acknowledge up front Japanese sovereignty over all four Northern Territories islands. Subsequently, a peace treaty was to be concluded, whereupon Habomai and Shikotan would revert to Japan. As for the larger islands—Kunashiri and Etorufu—administrative rights would be restored to Japan ten years after the conclusion of a peace treaty. Whatever Ozawa's proposal, however, no breakthrough emerged.

Gorbachev's visit to Tokyo in April 1991—about which Prime Minister Kaifu consulted President Bush in Newport Beach, California, some weeks in advance—proved anticlimactic. There were prolonged talks and a lengthy communiqué. A number of bilateral agreements were signed—none of them earthshaking. But neither leader possessed the political strength to make significant concessions on the Northern Territories issue. The result was ambiguous. All four islands were mentioned by name in the communiqué, and the Russians promised a partial withdrawal of military forces from the territories. Yet Gorbachev refused even to acknowledge Japan's right to Habomai and Shikotan—a concession Moscow had offered as early as 1956. Kaifu promised no new aid to Russian resource development, and no long-term economic cooperation agreement was signed.

Following Gorbachev's ouster in September 1991, the Japanese thought Yeltsin's administration might adopt a more forthcoming posture on the issue. And initially Foreign Minister Andrei Kozyrev and Deputy Foreign Minister Genady Kunadze did imply a readiness to address the issue with greater flexibility. But Boris Yeltsin lacked the political capability—and perhaps the desire—to do so. This became crystal clear in September 1992, when Yeltsin canceled a scheduled visit to Tokyo at the last minute. When he sought to lay part of the blame for the decision at Tokyo's door, Prime Minister Kiichi Miyazawa rejected Yeltsin's innuendos sternly, and the relationship seemed back at square one.

With regard to aid for Moscow, Tokyo and Washington managed generally to synchronize their approaches. Technical assistance was easy; the costs were modest, and each government recognized an interest in helping the Russians acquire greater familiarity with the institutions of a market economy. We shared an obvious stake in dismantling Soviet nuclear weapons, and both capitals contributed sizable funds to facilitate that expensive yet necessary task. Humanitarian aid presented somewhat greater difficulties, if only because the needs appeared more substantial. The prospect of a major food crisis during the winter of 1991 spurred international efforts to provide food and medicine and to help with their distribution. Tokyo pledged $100 million in supplies, but bureaucratic snafus stalled deliveries for several years. Moscow and Tokyo each blamed the other for the delays. Tokyo claimed credit for its pledged assistance; Moscow criticized Japan's failure to disburse it swiftly.

By 1992 U.S. interest in furnishing more substantial economic assistance grew as the fate of Yeltsin's reforms appeared increasingly in jeopardy. Former president Nixon prodded the Bush administration to adopt a more forthcoming stance and chided Tokyo for its alleged parsimony. The G-7 nations put together a $24 billion aid package and in the process pressed Tokyo hard to make a generous contribution. The Japanese complied, though perhaps less out of conviction about the program's merits than from a desire to avoid diplomatic isolation. The gesture required a further modification of Tokyo's stance on the Northern Territories issue: rationalizing this display of economic cooperation as its contribution to a multilateral effort, Japan reaffirmed its resolve to use bilateral economic assistance as a residual lever for negotiating the return of the islands.

Thus a fair amount of parallelism was preserved in our approaches to Moscow. The territorial issue remained unresolved, but Washington demonstrated a genuine readiness to put some diplomatic capital on the line to assist Japan's diplomatic efforts. As for aid, Western promises to Moscow exceeded actual deliveries, and on this score, both Washington and Tokyo talked a better game than they played.

Washington kept the Japanese reasonably well informed about its interactions with the Russians. But there were occasions when the apparent intimacy of U.S.-Russia ties struck a jarring note in Tokyo. Washington's references to its "partnership" with Moscow puzzled the Japanese. With the resolution of long-standing contradictions between East and West, there was an unspoken fear that a new constellation of forces, extending from Vancouver to Vladivostok and embracing North America and all of Europe, might be taking shape. This upset many Japanese, triggering their primordial anxiety about diplomatic isolation—a worry reinforced by the fact that the thaw in Moscow's relations with Washington and the unification of Germany left Japan as the only G-7 country with a major unresolved dispute with the Russians. But in 1992–93 the rising tide of nationalism in Russia began to impose limits on Moscow's connection with Washington as well as with Tokyo, and this development in turn eased the coordination of U.S.-Japanese approaches to Moscow while highlighting the critical importance of our respective relations with Beijing.

China   Managing our links with China posed a quite different policy problem. Following the Tiananmen Square incident in the spring of 1989, political forces in Washington—above all the Democratic majority in Congress—sought to place the promotion of democracy and human rights at the center of U.S. policy toward Beijing even if that risked putting American relations with China into the deep freeze. Japan, while prepared to concur in G-7 slaps on Beijing's wrists, was unwilling to countenance enduring restrictions on its ties with China. Thus a disconnect between the United States and Japan became a serious possibility.

President Bush knew China well and valued the relationship with Beijing. While acknowledging the importance of respect for human rights, the administration believed that a constructive relationship with Beijing served U.S. interests by contributing to a stable Asia, a global equilibrium, and the expansion of U.S. commercial opportunities. Still, the administration had to take domestic political realities into account, and these were dramatically affected by the vivid television images in June 1989 of Chinese dissidents defying PLA tanks in Tiananmen Square. With the end of the cold war, moreover, many Americans believed that Beijing's strategic value to the United States had declined and that the power of information age technology—computers, fax machines, and telecommunication devices—would in time sweep away China's autocratic leadership as it had undermined the authority of Russian Leninists. An array of special-interest groups—e.g., pro-lifers offended by China's widespread practice of abortion, labor unions fearing the competitive power of its low-wage production base, and environmentalists anxious about the environmental consequences of China's polluting industries—joined the chorus of anti-China sentiment. Democratic leaders on the Hill, moreover, recognized a political opportunity, and at least some played a rather transparent political game. Lecturing the Chinese on human rights and proposing legislative conditions on trade and other interactions with China enabled congressional Democrats to score points with voters at home without having to worry about the foreign policy consequences, since they expected President Bush to veto their bills.

The Japanese approached China from a different perspective. Broadly speaking, their strategic concerns were consistent with ours: they shared an interest in seeing that China was neither dominated by, nor aligned closely with, the Russians. They likewise shared our interest in China's embrace of market principles and its opening to the world. A growing China provided an attractive source of raw materials as well as a promising market for Japan's manufactured exports. Japan's political concerns were oriented toward China's stability rather than its democratic evolution. Not that Tokyo was indifferent to the growth of political pluralism in China. On the contrary, sophisticated Japanese analysts expected continuing rapid economic growth to move China over time in directions observable in Taiwan and Korea, where economic development had generated pressures for democratic reforms.

But Japan's government was accustomed to separating economics from politics. Neither its politicians nor its bureaucracy exhibited an inclination to export "their 'gods' to other countries," in Kazuo Ogura's pithy phrase.[1] The thought never crossed their minds. They were accustomed to thinking of Japan as unique; its institutions, consequently, were not exportable. Rather than proselytizing on behalf of

---

1. Kazuo Ogura, "The Crevice Between 'the Empire of Ideas' and 'the Lost People,'" *Gaiko Forum* (June 1991): 4–11, quoted in Chalmers Johnson, *Japan: Who Governs? The Rise of the Developmental State* (New York: Norton, 1995), p. 317.

abstract values, they pursued practical aims while seeking enhanced respect and status. And they recognized that public support for China's political dissidents would merely provoke Chinese lectures about Tokyo's misconduct in the 1930s and 1940s.

Sino-Japanese relations during the years of the Bush administration were by no means trouble free. Beijing regularly complained about the terms of Sino-Japanese trade, Japan's reluctance to transfer technology, its Ministry of Education's treatment of the "Asian Continental war" in Japanese school texts, alleged signs of revived militarism, Tokyo's quasi-official relations with Taiwan, and its claims on the Senkaku Islands. For their part, the Japanese worried, among other things, about the incipient growth of China's defense budget, its purchase of sophisticated military equipment from the Russians, its export of defense technology to North Korea, and the assertiveness of its claims to islands in the South China Sea. Despite these differences, Tokyo and Beijing concentrated mainly on expanding the benefits of cooperation.

Had the Bush administration been allowed to pursue its own instincts regarding China, policy coordination with Tokyo would have been a breeze. Despite congressional pressures, collaboration generally prevailed. The president and his senior advisers agreed with the Japanese that isolating China was undesirable. But the White House needed cooperative gestures from Beijing to preserve some political running room at home. With these considerations in mind, Washington did not object to Tokyo's leaning farther forward in its relations with China and nudging the consensus within the G-7 toward the modification of sanctions. In the meantime, we encouraged Japan to utilize its political capital in Beijing to urge on the Chinese such steps as the termination of martial law and the release of political dissidents. Because of political considerations, however, although our bilateral consultations on China were generally candid and constructive, on occasion we kept the Japanese in the dark about our activities. It was not lost on Tokyo, for example, that they were informed only about the *second* Scrowcroft-Eagleburger mission to Beijing—an omission that may have prompted them to withhold some details of their own policy efforts vis-à-vis Beijing.

Periodically I was instructed to request Japanese intercession with the Chinese leadership on human rights issues. I generally encountered little resistance, and I have no doubt that our Japanese friends raised these matters as requested. Whether they did so in a deter-mined manner, intending to achieve results, or in a perfunctory way, merely to mollify Washington, I cannot say. But neither my political nor bureaucratic interlocutors in Japan concealed their doubts about the effectiveness of our own diplomatic methodology on human rights issues. Japan's foreign policy professionals criticized the West for overreacting to the events at Tiananmen, privately characterized our human rights diplomacy as bordering on meddlesome interfer-ence, and expressed sympathy for Chinese concerns about the poten-tial implications of growing domestic disorder. Foreign Minister Michio Watanabe was particularly forthright in his criticisms of our style. And whereas the United States' forty thousand Chinese exchange students took a leading role in urging sanctions against Beijing, the sixty thousand or more Chinese students in Japan remained curiously mute.

Yet the broad contours of Japanese policy toward China were clear. As the director general of Asian Affairs at the Foreign Ministry, Sakutaro Tanino, put it at the time, "We should remember that a more stable, affluent China will benefit not just itself but all of Asia and in fact the world. We need to avoid reacting emotionally and applying only West-ern values to each new set of political and social phenomena as it unfolds in China. Instead we should direct our efforts to bringing China into the framework of Asian peace, development, and prosperity."[2]

Japan's calculus was informed by its judgment that China's influ-ence and weight in world affairs were growing. In a period when trade frictions with the United States were increasing, China offered a huge market and an opportunity to diversify Japan's external trade links; at a moment when bargaining with Russia over the Northern Territo-ries appeared to enter a new phase, Tokyo saw its relations with Bei-jing as a source of leverage and a hedge against the failure of those negotiations; and at a time when Tokyo was contemplating a more ambitious and independent policy in Asia, Japanese policy makers rec-ognized its regional policy would not amount to much without sub-stantial links with China.

As noted above, the Tiananmen incident provoked a unified G-7 response—i.e., reduced high-level contacts and the suspension of

2. Sakutaro Tanino, "The Recent Situation in China and Sino-Japanese Rela-tions," *Japan Review of International Affairs* 4, no. 1 (spring/summer 1990): 30.

major concessional assistance. While Japan went along with the consensus at the 1989 G-7 summit meeting in Paris, it did so without enthusiasm and enforced the agreed-on restrictions without much rigor. Japanese private-sector activity in China was not curtailed. Disbursements of foreign assistance under existing programs were promptly resumed. Indeed, technical assistance personnel had been sent back to China by the end of August 1989. High-level political contacts resumed within several months, and senior business leaders scarcely interrupted their travels to the Chinese capital. Shortly after Brent Scowcroft's trip to Beijing in December 1989, the Japanese government began discussing technical details associated with the resumption of their third yen loan program to China, though they deferred formal resumption of such assistance until they had secured U.S. acquiescence to the decision at the Houston summit the following summer. Prime Minister Kaifu's display of independence on the China issue at Houston enhanced his political standing back home.

When loans were disbursed under the new program, they were described as "humanitarian." But the definition proved flexible enough to include hydroelectric power dams and chemical fertilizer plants. The overall level of Japan's aid disbursements increased rapidly. And when Tokyo announced new aid guidelines in the spring of 1991 indicating that Japan would look carefully at recipient countries' military budgets, arms exports, and human rights records, China appeared exempt from their application. Prime Minister Kaifu subsequently visited Beijing in August 1991—the first G-7 leader to do so since Tiananmen Square. He used the occasion to announce a further expansion of aid without limiting it to humanitarian projects. For his troubles he was rewarded with China's pledge to join the Nuclear Nonproliferation Treaty (NPT)—a not inconsiderable gesture with which Washington was duly impressed.

Thus Japan, without formally breaking the G-7 consensus, pursued its own agenda with Beijing. Tokyo kept us reasonably well informed, and few of Japan's specific policy measures gave Washington heartburn. Yet they clearly set the pace for Western policy toward Beijing, protecting Japan's major foreign policy and commercial equities without breaching solidarity with Washington and other Western capitals. This was in keeping with past practice: Japan had always sought in its policy toward China the maximum autonomy it felt Washington would tolerate.

Resolving Regional Conflicts

As the cold war ended, Japan and the United States shared an interest
in cleaning up some of the problems it left behind. Our collaboration
was naturally most intense in Asia. Washington continued to shoulder
major military burdens in Korea and diplomatic responsibilities for
promoting a settlement of the Cambodian problem. Japan was eager
to tackle a more substantial role in its own backyard. A familiar pattern
appeared. Washington attempted to enlist Tokyo's support in its quest
for political settlements in Korea and Cambodia; Tokyo sought to ini-
tiate autonomous actions with which to influence events in both areas.
This presented opportunities for cooperative action as well as occasional misunderstandings.

Cambodia   Throughout the 1980s Japan's diplomacy in Southeast
Asia was generally guided by commercial considerations. Its approach
to Indochina was largely shaped by its sensitivity to the priorities of
ASEAN nations and to U.S. policy guidelines. Thus when Hanoi
invaded Cambodia in 1978, Tokyo condemned Hanoi's action,
demanded its withdrawal, froze its assistance to Vietnam, refused recognition to Heng Sam Ren's government, and augmented its aid to Thailand as a frontline state. Yet Asian specialists within the Foreign Ministry perceived a strategic interest in promoting a cohesive Indochina
that could serve as a check on China's influence in Southeast Asia. So
long as ASEAN retained a united front on Indochina issues and the
United States regarded Heng Sam Ren as a puppet of Hanoi, Tokyo
clung to its low-profile policy in the area.

In the late 1980s, however, Tokyo began to formulate a more independent assessment of the politico-military situation in Cambodia and
to contemplate political initiatives of its own. It was encouraged in this
regard by adjustments in Thai diplomacy and divisions within ASEAN
that provided Japan with greater room for maneuver and, arguably,
more persuasive evidence for the necessity of some choice. The Foreign Ministry's long-term objective was to nurture the gradual integration of Indochina into ASEAN. In this connection, the peaceful evolution of Cambodia was a necessary precondition.

Tokyo's heightened diplomatic interest in Cambodia coincided with
an increase in the tempo of negotiations for a peaceful settlement in
Cambodia—a by-product, among other things, of Moscow's more

accommodating diplomacy. Encouraged by the Thai, the Japanese had invited Prince Sihanouk to Tokyo in August 1988 to convince him that Japan had a serious role to play in promoting a settlement. Senior Foreign Ministry officials concluded from those conversations that Sihanouk planned to break away from the Khmer Rouge and move closer to the authorities in Phnom Penh. In the first meeting of the International Conference on Cambodia in Paris the following summer, Japan was asked to cochair a committee on reconstruction and refugee relief. Tokyo was prepared to shoulder responsibilities for Cambodia's future development, but it had no intention of bankrolling the results of diplomatic efforts in which it was accorded no role. This was an entirely reasonable proposition, which Washington accepted in principle, without necessarily welcoming all of its practical consequences.

The Japanese embarked on a more active phase of diplomacy in early 1990, sending representatives to Phnom Penh in mid-February to reconnoiter the situation and meet with leaders of the Heng Sam Ren government. They concluded that the regime in Phnom Penh was more resilient and possessed more staying power than they had previously thought. They also judged that Phnom Penh authorities genuinely wished to open their economy and limit Vietnam's influence in Cambodia. Equally important, they sensed the widespread fear and hatred of the Khmer Rouge among the Cambodian populace and determined that stronger efforts were required to cut it down to size. The practical result of this review was Tokyo's decision to invite representatives from the four Cambodian factions to a conference on Cambodia in Japan on June 4–5, 1990.

In this conference, organized with the help of the Thai, Japan sought to enhance the position of Sihanouk, diminish the clout of the Khmer Rouge, and encourage support for a supreme national council of Cambodia that would have two rather than four parties. Khieu Sampong, the Khmer Rouge leader, traveled to Tokyo but boycotted the proceedings, leaving Sihanouk and Heng Sam Ren to shape the joint communiqué.

The Chinese were unhappy, and Beijing persuaded Sihanouk subsequently to express second thoughts about the outcome of the Tokyo conference. Washington's reaction to the meeting was tepid; it held no brief for the Khmer Rouge but doubted the efficacy of securing an agreement on Cambodia without Beijing's active collaboration. The reaction among ASEAN countries was mixed; the Thai were understandably satisfied with Tokyo's efforts, while others expressed mild irritation that Tokyo was horning in on an ASEAN preserve. All in all, though, Tokyo, was content with the results of its foray into more active diplomacy in Indochina.

The process by which the Cambodian agreement was negotiated, however, irritated the Japanese. The locus of much of the action rested with the so-called P-5 (the permanent members of the Security Council). Japan was not included, and this rankled. Washington regularly invited the Japanese to send representatives wherever P-5 meetings were held and endeavored to consult the Japanese before and debrief them after the negotiations. In fact, Washington would have been happy to have the Japanese participate directly, but others—most notably the French—resisted.

Relegated to the periphery of the negotiations, Tokyo was less inhibited about raising questions about the results achieved and made no effort to conceal its belief that there were ways in which the P-5 draft accord on Cambodia, released in November 1990, could be improved. It promptly sent representatives to Cambodia to engage in shuttle diplomacy, lobbying directly with the Cambodian factions for various changes in the text. In essence, Tokyo wanted tougher measures to prevent recurrence of the Khmer Rouge's genocidal policies, stronger methods for verifying the disarmament of the Khmer Rouge during each stage of the cease-fire, stronger sanctions against groups that were found to have violated the disarmament procedures, and the establishment of a UN body to monitor the activities of the Khmer Rouge. Substantively, I thought the Japanese reservations about the text were justified, and they found some resonance in Congress and the press. Yet they caused some pique in the State Department. Achieving an agreement among so many parties had been a painstaking business, and the negotiators did not relish reopening tough issues—even when, as most conceded, the Japanese had a point. Ultimately, Tokyo's effort came to naught as a result of the unremitting opposition of the Khmer Rouge and the Sonn Sann faction.

In the end, it was the relaxation of tensions between Beijing and Hanoi that opened the door to the Cambodian settlement in June 1991. Nevertheless, Japan took pride in having played a more energetic and visible role. It had highlighted key issues through the Tokyo conference; its promotion of a two-party supreme national council had borne fruit (although it was, of course, neither the only nor the most influential proponent of this arrangement); it had encouraged the alliance between Sihanouk and Hung Sen. And these contributions enhanced Japan's readiness to take the lead in mobilizing resources for Cambodia's future reconstruction and development needs and to support the UN transitional authority by dispatching election monitors and an engineering battalion.

From the United States' standpoint, Tokyo's contributions were a net plus. Japanese diplomatic initiatives did not always coincide perfectly with Washington's perspectives and tactical judgments, but its efforts generally complemented ours, helped nudge the process to a successful conclusion, and laid the political groundwork for Japan's leadership in pulling together the necessary financial support for Cambodia's reconstruction.

As peace returned to Cambodia, a principal obstacle to more normal relations with Vietnam was removed, and, for both political and economic reasons, the Japanese were eager to move ahead with the resumption of their aid program. Washington, ever sensitive to Vietnamese cooperation on the POW/MIA issue, embarked on a more leisurely course that, it hoped, would lead to eventual normalization. We consequently urged delay of Japanese initiatives directed toward Hanoi in order to avoid political problems in the United States. The Japanese were reasonably acquiescent, repeatedly delaying the resumption of aid in response to our pleas—right up to and through the presidential election campaign in 1992. Of course, their trading companies were much in evidence in Vietnam, much of the preparatory work for resuming Japanese aid was being laid, and the Japanese kept prodding Washington to move forward steadily in order to accord greater recognition to Hanoi's reform efforts.

Korea   The Korean Peninsula was an even more natural focal point for U.S.-Japanese diplomatic cooperation. While relations between Pyongyang and Seoul remained largely frozen in the late 1980s, in other respects the diplomatic setting for tackling the Korean problem was changing dramatically. Moscow and Beijing were constructing new commercial and diplomatic ties with South Korea. As host of the Seoul Olympics in 1988, South Korea had enhanced its international standing at the same that North Korea's economy went into a tailspin. And South Korea, buoyed by its economic success, had embarked on an active "Nordpolitik" and appeared for the first time to welcome efforts by others to draw Pyongyang out of its diplomatic isolation.

Japan generally approached Korean issues cautiously and pragmatically. Its ties with South Korea were official and substantial. With the North, quasi-official relations were managed principally through LDP Diet delegations, supplemented by warm party-to-party links between the Socialists and the North Korea Workers Party. Some Japanese described this as a "one-and-a-half Korea policy."

With the changing circumstances in Northeast Asia, however, Japanese leaders wanted further to fortify their connection with Pyongyang. Their motives went beyond merely emulating Russia's and China's diversification of relations on the Korean Peninsula. Moscow was entering a period of intense internal reform. In a post–cold war environment, the Japanese anticipated growing pressures on the United States to scale back its security responsibilities in Asia. This could have left China in a position to exert substantially greater influence on the Korean Peninsula. Strategic thinkers in Japan felt this warranted some effort by Tokyo to balance China's influence in Pyongyang as well as in Seoul.

Of course, there were also immediate and practical reasons for upgrading links with the North. The Japanese hoped that an improvement in relations would moderate Pyongyang's vitriolic propaganda attacks on Japan's growing influence in the Asian region. This in turn could relieve Tokyo's problems with the polarized community of Korean nationals in Japan. Commercial benefits also beckoned: North Korea possessed valuable minerals and an ample supply of labor, while it needed the manufacturing skills and technology that Japan possessed in abundance. Finally, the government felt continuing pressure from the public and press to secure the release of Japanese crew members of the fishing vessel *Fujisanmaru*, which had been seized by the North Koreans in 1983.

North Korea had its own incentives for expanding its dialogue with Tokyo. It was groping for ways to escape its diplomatic isolation and to counter Seoul's regional diplomacy. It coveted the benefits of economic cooperation with Japan. It probably expected that an opening to Tokyo might soften U.S. resistance to a more normal relationship. And, recognizing that the cultivation of special ties with the Japanese Socialists had brought few benefits over the years, Pyongyang decided to direct its overtures to the Liberal Democrats.

In the spring of 1989 the Takeshita cabinet put out feelers to North

Korean authorities through a Socialist delegation that was visiting
Pyongyang. A year later, Prime Minister Kaifu sent word that Japan
was ready to apologize for its colonial rule and to open a dialogue with
the North without preconditions. Pyongyang responded by sending
word through Socialist leader Makoto Tanabe that they would welcome a visit by a delegation led by a prominent member of the LDP.
They hinted that the delegation should be prepared not only to apologize for Japan's past conduct but to discuss compensation and economic assistance. Shin Kanemaru, leader of the LDP's most powerful
faction and a personal friend of Tanabe's, was chosen to lead the delegation. The trip was set for late September 1990.

Kanemaru and his entourage, which included a representative from
the Ministry of Foreign Affairs, was accorded a warm welcome in
Pyongyang. The delegations got right down to business—which
turned out to be more far-reaching than anyone had anticipated.
Kanemaru expressed profuse apologies for Japan's past conduct and
intimated a readiness to extend reparations not only for the colonial
period but for losses suffered by the Korean people in the forty-five
years following the end of the war. Indeed he implied that Japan might
even make a down payment on reparations before a normalization of
relations was achieved. In addition, he agreed to remove the North
Korean exclusion clause from Japanese passports and to move toward
the establishment of diplomatic relations. In return, Pyongyang agreed
to release the Japanese fishermen under detention, to allow the establishment of direct air service from North Korea to Japan, and to set up
a bilateral communications network.

Kanemaru's diplomatic venture jolted Seoul and Washington. It was
unprecedented for the Japanese to undertake such a wide-ranging initiative in Korea without consulting the countries that bore the principal responsibilities for maintaining peace and stability on the peninsula.
Kanemaru's evident readiness to discuss compensation for unspecified
sins of commission or omission in the postwar period was even more
astonishing. The offer went far beyond Tokyo's reparations agreement
with South Korea and overlooked the fact that North Korea's initiation
of the Korean conflict had caused unspeakable suffering for South
Koreans, Americans, and others. Moreover, reparations in the absence
of IAEA safeguards on nuclear activities and military force reductions—
not mentioned in the communiqué—could be regarded as indirectly
supporting North Korea's threatening military posture.

The Japanese government recognized that the Kanemaru mission had been badly mishandled and moved promptly to make amends. The Foreign Ministry, embarrassed by the sloppy communiqué and irritated over the expropriation of its role by politicians, sought to distance itself from the communiqué's language without repudiating the mission's central objective: initiation of a dialogue with North Korea. The LDP leadership—stung by a chorus of criticism from within its own ranks—scrambled to find prudent policy guidelines for handling the fallout without provoking an open break with the party's most powerful faction leader. LDP leaders evidently agreed to proceed cautiously with normalization talks in order to avoid upstaging or undermining a north-south dialogue in Korea and decided to apply the same principle with respect to reparations as they had utilized with the South—i.e., for the colonial period only. They also reportedly agreed, however, that Japan should give some consideration "in a spiritual sense" to North Korea for the delay in compensating it for the colonial era. This last desiderata was designed to keep Kanemaru on board.

Although Kanemaru had implied to the North Koreans that the initiative had been a party matter, fully authorized by the Japanese government (the North Koreans continue to regard his pledges as official, and this remains one of the issues holding up Japanese–North Korean normalization talks), he flew to Seoul to express his regrets to President Ro Tae U for blindsiding the South Koreans. And on October 9, 1990, he visited my office to apologize for going over our heads. He emphasized that his visit was a party-to-party undertaking designed to pave the way for government-to-government talks by establishing an atmosphere of mutual trust. It was in this context, he said, that he had agreed to a positive reference in the communiqué about compensation for postwar losses. If he had refused, the mission would have collapsed, Japanese crewmen would continue to languish in prison, and normalization talks would have remained an idle hope. I observed that Pyongyang had caused a war that claimed thousands of American lives and had forced us to bear a heavy security burden on the Korean Peninsula for more than forty years. Americans would neither understand nor accept post–World War II compensation to North Korea. Kanemaru acknowledged my point and then informed me that Ichiro Ozawa and Takako Doi would be visiting Pyongyang on the following day to pick up the *Fujisanmaru* crewmen.

Kanemaru made several comments to me regarding North Korea's nuclear activities that betrayed a rather naive confidence in the veracity of Kim Il Sung, who, he said, had told him that North Korea had no nuclear facilities whatsoever, aside from an antiquated and virtually abandoned Russian research reactor—a claim belied by much hard evidence in the hands of U.S. intelligence. I offered to bring experts from Washington to brief him. He readily agreed. All in all, the conversation left me—along with many Foreign Ministry professionals and not a few LDP Diet members—anxious about diplomatic freelancing by politicians.

Once the Japanese crewmen were safely back in Japan, some of the fire went out of this issue. While the government made clear that it would persevere with the effort to establish diplomatic relations with Pyongyang, responsibility for the negotiations was handed off to the Foreign Ministry professionals who undertook to consult closely with Seoul and Washington as the talks proceeded. The negotiations commenced in January 1991 and were scheduled to address four issues: a Japanese apology, North Korea's claims, nuclear inspection arrangements, and the status of Koreans in Japan. By June 1992 seven rounds of talks had been held. Some progress was registered, but no breakthroughs were achieved.

Throughout the negotiations, Washington and Seoul urged Japan to press North Korea to place its nuclear energy programs under full IAEA inspection. This was a little like leaning on an open door, for Tokyo officials were as distressed by North Korea's nuclear activities as anyone. North Korea's acceptance of such inspection arrangements was made an essential condition for Japanese diplomatic recognition and the economic cooperation that might flow from it. North Korea adamantly refused inspections until January 1992, arguing that the issue was inappropriate for bilateral discussion.

A U.S. initiative provided a means of escaping this impasse. In September 1991 President Bush announced a decision to return all tactical nuclear weapons to U.S. territory and to remove such weapons from American ships and naval aircraft. The inference was clear: any nuclear weapons that might have been deployed in South Korea would be removed. North Korea subsequently agreed in January 1992 to sign a safeguards agreement with the IAEA—which was subsequently ratified by its parliament in March—and to allow the IAEA's director, Hans Blix, to visit North Korean nuclear facilities. For at least a few months it appeared the nuclear issue was on the road to resolution. This hope was subsequently dashed, and bilateral talks were suspended in June 1992, as a result of Pyongyang's unequivocal refusal to address issues related to its involvement in terrorist activities.

During this same period Tokyo had undertaken active measures to put its relations with Seoul on firmer ground. Official visits were exchanged, and consultations increased. Japan made progress in regularizing the status of Korean nationals within its borders and offered official apologies for past conduct in Korea. These efforts were welcomed in Washington, and trilateral consultations among Seoul, Washington, and Tokyo were initiated to ensure closer coordination of our respective approaches to the nuclear issue and the promotion of a more significant dialogue between North and South Korea.

In the end, the Kanemaru initiative proved to be an aberration of sorts. I believe that he went with the approval of the government and that his mission was designed to advance a long-standing objective: diversification of Japan's relations on the peninsula. Kanemaru, however, was a powerful politician who felt no compelling need to reveal every detail of his intentions to a new and reputedly weak prime minister. He and his associates evidently exceeded their brief in Pyongyang, caught up in the ostentatious warmth of the North Koreans' reception. Recognizing the dangers of a reputation for improvisation on delicate issues affecting the United States and South Korea, Tokyo swiftly backtracked and, without altering its purpose, placed the implementation of policy in the hands of those who were accustomed to coordinating Korean policy issues more closely with key allies.

Strengthening the Economic Underpinnings of Fledgling Democracies

Since the mid-1980s Washington and Tokyo have consulted regularly in an effort to coordinate our respective aid programs. As undersecretary of state, I had initiated these consultations in 1985. Our objective was to encourage Japan to direct more of its economic assistance to countries of strategic consequence to the West, such as the Philippines, Thailand, Egypt, Turkey, and Pakistan. The discussions were straightforward, and a fair amount of parallelism in our aid efforts emerged. With the end of the cold war, the focus of U.S. assistance shifted to support for friendly governments confronted by acute security challenges and for nations turning away from communism and statist economic practices. The Japanese, whose aid program was expanding rapidly, possessed the capacity to help. And help they did—particularly in the Philippines, Eastern Europe, and Central America.

The Multilateral Assistance Initiative for the Philippines was conceived during the Reagan administration, and Japan's initial response was enthusiastic. The project was formally launched in July 1989 in Tokyo, with Secretary Baker participating in the ceremonies. The purpose was to mobilize financial support to help revive the Philippine economy, devastated by Marcos's crony capitalism. Tokyo and Washington recognized that the aid would be useful only insofar as it provided incentives for Philippine efforts to revitalize its private sector. Collaboration among Japanese, American, and Philippine officials and private-sector representatives was exemplary. The results were at best mixed—not least, because the Aquino administration displayed more zeal for democratization than for economic reform.

As Eastern Europe was liberated from communism, Washington recognized a need to help democratic leaders achieve economic results in order to buttress their legitimacy. This prompted U.S. requests in 1989 for Japanese contributions both to the European Bank for Reconstruction and Development and to bilateral assistance programs for Poland and Hungary. Tokyo responded affirmatively, despite the fact that Eastern Europe was a remote region about which they knew relatively little and in which they had limited commercial interest; some officials, moreover, were wary of undertaking significant responsibilities there for fear of stepping on Western European toes. Nevertheless, they came up with a pledge of $1.5 billion for Hungary and Poland, composed of humanitarian aid, export/import bank credits, and government guarantees to underwrite loans.

When enterprise funds were subsequently established for various Eastern European countries—e.g., Czechoslovakia, Bulgaria, Romania—Japan likewise contributed to those. Soliciting their cooperation for these funds proved somewhat more challenging, however, because senior officials in Tokyo doubted they had the expertise to appraise requests for small loans and because the Foreign and Finance Ministries tended to see their aid priorities elsewhere. Vice President Quayle pressed this issue vigorously during his visit in 1992 and managed to achieve some results. All in all, Japanese support for economic reform efforts in Eastern Europe, while modest in scope, was impressive, given their limited interest in the region.

A third area of special concern for Washington was Central America. Our interests were huge; Tokyo's were not. It had little strategic stake in Latin America, which was neither a primary market nor a major source of critical raw materials for Japan. But Latin America was an area where Japan could demonstrate its value as a partner to the United States while cultivating friends and mobilizing support for its objectives in wider multilateral forums. Thus Tokyo was surprisingly active in the region, allocating roughly 10 percent of its aid budget to Latin America.

The cessation of the Nicaraguan civil war, followed by Violeta Barrios de Chamorro's inauguration as president in 1991, set Managua on a more democratic political course and eased pressures on neighboring Central American governments. Financial stability was needed to underpin the democratic transition under way in the region. Japan recognized that modest assistance could help stabilize a troubled region while netting it political dividends in Washington. Specifically, the Japanese hosted an official visit by President Chamorro to Japan and helped finance bridge loans to Honduras, Nicaragua, and Panama that cleared their arrears to the IMF and World Bank and made them eligible for additional loans from international financial institutions. The Japanese understandably wanted the United States to remain out in front on Central American issues, but they proved consistently supportive.

Of even greater consequence, Japan joined in rescheduling Mexico's considerable debts. Japanese Finance Ministry officials collaborated closely with the Treasury Department in arranging the deal, and Japanese banks were among the leading underwriters of the scheme. This was critically important to President Salinas's ability to implement proposed economic reforms that brought renewed prosperity to Mexico. More broadly, the Japanese not only endorsed the Brady plan to tackle Third World debt problems, but they promised sizable monetary contributions to back it. This was somewhat ironic, as a similar plan put forward in 1988 by then–finance minister Kiichi Miyazawa had been openly attacked by Washington. That plan was withdrawn, and the Japanese graciously supported the United States' mildly amended version when it was proposed a few months later.

Japan also was persuaded to contribute to two multilateral efforts aimed at fortifying democratic reforms in the Caribbean and Central America: namely, the Enterprise for the Americas initiative and the Political Development and Democracy Program. In Peru, the Japanese needed little prodding to provide expanded economic support. Beyond the presence of a substantial Japanese immigrant community there, the election of Alberto Fujimori as president in 1990 caught the attention of Tokyo, because Fujimori was the first person of Japanese descent to become president of any country outside Japan. Cooperation was easily managed until 1992, when Fujimori assumed dictatorial powers in order to cope more effectively with the drug cartels and terrorist groups. Washington suspended its aid and pressed Tokyo to follow suit. The Japanese demurred but used their close contacts with Fujimori to encourage him to moderate his political course to accommodate U.S. political requirements. They issued no public exhortations but applied steady pressure, making it clear, for example, that refusal to provide the International Committee of the Red Cross with access to Peruvian prisons was a genuine impediment to the resumption of international support and the improvement of ties between Washington and Lima. Tokyo also reminded Washington of the need to take more fully into account the delicacy of President Fujimori's own political dilemmas.

Creating an Asia/Pacific Framework for Economic Cooperation

Pressures to institutionalize a framework for Asian regional economic cooperation grew in the late 1980s. Asian interest was stimulated by the emergence of more integrated markets in Europe and North America. U.S. interest was a by-product of the vibrant growth in the Pacific Basin economy. A sharply rising trade deficit with Asia increased Washington's stake in a regional forum in which to promote trade liberalization. The administration calculated that Asian/Pacific regional institutions could remind Europeans that if they cut their deals for regional integration at the expense of non-European trading partners, we could respond in kind. With the end of the cold war, moreover, some in Washington recognized the potential utility of an Asian regional dialogue on security matters. And with Japanese and Chinese power growing rapidly, a political framework in which to channel the restless energies of these dynamic countries exerted a growing appeal.

I had long been interested in promoting Asia/Pacific institutions, and regarded quasi-official fora like the Pacific Economic Cooperation Council—which included academic and business representatives alongside government officials—as useful but insufficient to meet the growing requirements for regional cooperation. During my preconfirmation calls, I was delighted to discover similar concerns among leading senators. More importantly, Jim Baker was personally interested in the concept, as was his counselor, Bob Zoellick.

The Asia Pacific Economic Cooperation (APEC) initiative thus appeared to be an idea whose time had come. By January 1989 the Australians were already busy proselytizing on behalf of a regional initiative that made no provision for U.S. participation, and the Japanese appeared poised to support it. The Bush administration recognized that it had to clarify its own intentions or leave the field to others by default.

The Japanese had exhibited interest in regional institutions since the late 1970s but were reticent to assert a strong lead because of their sensitivities to Asian—and particularly ASEAN—reactions. On top of this, the usual bureaucratic rivalries were in play, with MITI displaying somewhat greater enthusiasm initially than did the Foreign Ministry—arguably because they spotted a bureaucratic vacuum on the issue. Nonetheless, the Japanese government enthusiastically endorsed the establishment of APEC in October 1989 and consistently nurtured its evolution in the years that followed.

The principal challenge for U.S.-Japanese policy coordination arose some months later, when the Malaysian prime minister, Mahatir bin Mohamad, proposed an alternative to APEC: the East Asian Economic Group (EAEG), subsequently modified and renamed the East Asian Economic Caucus (EAEC). Whatever Mahatir's motives—and they were invariably complex—he rationalized his proposal as a regional reaction to the perceived failure of the Uruguay round of the GATT talks, to European and North American steps to form regional trading arrangements, and to the growing protectionist inclinations of the U.S. Congress. In practical terms, Mahatir invited Japan to assume leadership of an exclusively Asian forum for economic cooperation.

Washington perceived this proposal as an effort to mobilize Pan-Asian sentiments against the United States. In presenting the proposal, Mahatir's rhetoric was frequently laced with barbed references to the United States, and there were undertones of racism in his exclusion of Australia and New Zealand along with Canada and the United States.

In March 1991 I attended an Asia Society conference in Bali, and when key State Department officials dropped out at the last minute, I wound up as Washington's only senior official representative. In his keynote address to the conference, the Malaysian prime minister launched a blistering attack on Washington and argued that the EAEG was the most efficacious means of countering the United States' allegedly malign influence on global trade. I was instructed to respond to Mahatir on the following day. At that time, I affirmed U.S. support for regional cooperation but emphasized that we considered the Asia/Pacific region as the logical geographic framework for such cooperation, since the United States remained the prime export market for virtually every East Asian country. I suggested that Asian nations might better devote their energies to assuring the GATT round's success than to adjusting preemptively to its presumed failure. I noted that since the declared objectives of the EAEG were essentially identical to APEC's, their achievement was more likely in a more inclusive forum. I challenged Mahatir's assertion that NAFTA was likely to discriminate against Asians, noting that the United States traded three times as much with East Asia as it did with Latin America. And while acknowledging that the Malaysian proposal had not been a significant feature of our dialogue with the Japanese, I expressed doubt that ASEAN would be well served by an arrangement that might, even inadvertently, encourage more intense economic rivalry between Tokyo and Washington.

Needless to add, I and others registered these concerns on numerous occasions with Japanese friends in the months to come. The Malaysian proposal clearly put the Japanese on the spot. As a global trading nation, they were loathe to encourage regional blocs. Economic ties with the United States counted for much, and in the wake of the political difficulties that had surfaced during the Gulf war, the Japanese were not eager to risk Washington's ire on another issue. Several key ASEAN countries, moreover, had their own misgivings about the Malaysian initiative, and Tokyo preferred not to choose among them. These considerations notwithstanding, the offer of leadership in an Asian regional arrangement exerted an undeniable attraction for many Japanese. Tokyo consequently decided to defer a formal response to Mahatir's proposal until ASEAN had developed a unified response.

By altering his proposal to suggest that the EAEG serve as a caucus within APEC, Mahatir attempted to soften up Asian resistance to his idea and to finesse Washington's outright opposition. But the consultative process within ASEAN and between it and other Asians, ground slowly.

And through the balance of my tenure in Tokyo, the Japanese remained firmly ensconced on the fence. They never said no, but neither did they endorse the Malaysian proposal. But they did find ways to augment their own consultations with Asian nations across the board.

Encouraging Cooperation in Science and Technology

The United States and Japan have long benefited from collaboration in science and technology. Government efforts to encourage such cooperation date back to the 1960s, and over the years Japan has become one of our most valued partners in the fields of space exploration, oceanography, atmospheric sciences, earthquake engineering and prediction, and nuclear energy. Since a comprehensive science and technology agreement had been concluded in 1988, our efforts were concentrated on implementing this agreement and facilitating new forms of collaboration.

The highest profile quest was for Japanese support for the superconducting supercollider (SCC). This ambitious scientific project—whose fundamental aim was to comprehend more fully the nature of matter—had become extraordinarily expensive. Congressional support for the necessary appropriations had consequently become increasingly dependent on the administration's success in securing financial assistance from abroad. Japan was at the top of every fundraiser's list, with Washington visitors highlighting the importance of the project to the future of science, to our political partnership, and to the administration—several of whose most influential members came from Texas.

Enthusiasm for the supercollider within Japanese scientific circles was decidedly limited. The Japanese were just awakening to the deficiencies in their own basic scientific research efforts. University research facilities were primitive and underfunded. Dr. Akito Arima, the president of Tokyo University, had launched a major effort to secure substantially greater Japanese government support for renovating these facilities. Many Japanese scientists consequently saw our request as a threat to their priorities.

Some in Washington expressed the hope that the Japanese might pledge as much as one billion dollars to the supercollider. I considered that quite unrealistic but did not rule out a substantial contribution of cash plus technical support for some of the project's key components.

During President Bush's trip to Tokyo, the SCC was accorded less attention than it had received in some of the advance work for the trip.
Nonetheless, in a late-night session during the visit, Brent Scowcroft
kept the possibility of a contribution alive by persuading the Japanese
government to establish a joint working group to assess the issue of
Japan's participation in the project. Senior Japanese officials had complained to me, not unreasonably, that they were being asked to help
finance a project without guarantees that they would be assured a substantial voice in its management. The joint working group was, inter
alia, to look into methods of assuring donors an appropriate role in
managing the project. In the ensuing months, Japanese scientists and
officials played an active role in the committee, occasionally even displaying some enthusiasm for it. But whatever slight hope there may
have been for Japanese participation faded when the House of Representatives voted down the appropriation for the SCC in June 1992.
Though the vote was later reversed, the damage was done, and Congress later killed the project again—this time, for good.

Another of our aims was to encourage through bilateral exchanges
the wider internationalization of Japanese science and technology
activities. Getting more Americans into Japanese research laboratories
was a high priority. The annual reception I hosted for the National Science Foundation's Summer Fellows turned up fifty to seventy-five
young American graduate students and post-doctoral candidates who
were spending several months in Japanese university, government, and
corporate labs. In addition, Vice President Quayle took the lead in urging the creation of manufacturing technology fellowships, which
eventually were to bring U.S. engineers and technicians to Japan for
firsthand exposure to manufacturing techniques on the shop floors of
some of Japan's leading production facilities. We also successfully
encouraged MITI, beginning in 1990, to open all of its new industrial
research projects to foreign participation. The response of many U.S.
companies was understandably guarded in the light of complicated
application processes and intellectual property rights provisions. On
one such project—the New World Computing Project—the administration even requested that U.S. universities not join until an inter-
governmental structure could be established to ensure an equitable
balance of benefits. This effort bore fruit, and U.S. and Japanese scientists subsequently collaborated on opto-electronic research.

On at least one project, the Japanese sought our financial support for their initiative. During Prime Minister Nakasone's tenure, the Japanese launched the Human Frontiers Science Program to support research in molecular biology and explore the functioning of the human brain. By the late 1980s a modest international research program was under way, and it had earned high marks within scientific circles. Key European countries were providing support; we were not. In 1991, however, Dr. Allen Bromley, the White House scientific adviser, managed to cajole several U.S. agencies into putting up $3 million annually to support the program. Some saw it as a sweetener for our own requests that Japan provide much larger financial subventions to the supercollider—a not-inaccurate perception.

In the field of environmental policy, we found ourselves frequently at odds with Japan. On many conservation issues—whaling, driftnet fishing, hawksbill turtles, etc.—Japan's commercial interests brought it into conflict with environmentalists in the United States and elsewhere. But whereas the USA and Japan both initially objected to a proposed fifty-year moratorium on Antarctic mining, Japan subsequently softened its objection, leaving us as the only advanced country not endorsing the ban—a position President Bush subsequently abandoned in mid-1992.

In the run-up to the Rio Conference on the Environment, other differences surfaced. The Japanese, in their search for areas in which to exercise greater international leadership, zeroed in on the environment in the early 1990s. Former prime minister Takeshita—one of the wise men advising Maurice Strong, the secretary general of the Rio conference, was a driving force behind this search for a larger role.

At Rio, Japanese policy visibly diverged from our own on two major issues: (1) the attempt to include in the Climate Change Convention explicit commitments to stabilize CO_2 emission levels; and (2) support for the Biodiversity Convention. On the first, the Japanese were prepared to commit to stabilizing emission levels at 1990 levels by the year 2000, while we ducked that commitment; on the second, they supported ratification of the convention, and we did not. Ultimately, however, neither the United States nor Japan played very prominent roles in Rio, which may have muffled the effects of these disagreements. President Bush made a brief appearance; Prime Minister Miyazawa felt unable to absent himself from the Diet debate on a revised UN peacekeeping bill. The United States was a target of much criticism at the conference; Japan was not a visible presence.

Fostering Trilateralism

The summit meetings of the G-7 nations provided a key forum for policy coordination between the United States and Japan, and the Japanese became more assertive on political as well as economic issues in these gatherings. As noted, they used the summits to internationalize their territorial issue with the Russians and to press for the modification of sanctions against China. But the summit meetings became progressively more routinized and bureaucratized—occasions for signing communiqués laboriously negotiated by "sherpas." There was an evident need for ongoing consultations among senior officials that went beyond the occasional meetings that brought them together each spring to prepare the political declarations issued annually by the heads at the summit.

Undersecretary for Political Affairs Bob Kimmitt was eager to regularize the contacts among political directors of G-7 countries into an continuing consultative process. I encouraged him, thinking this would help incorporate our dialogue with the Japanese more deeply into the institutional framework of the West. Senior Foreign Ministry officials appeared enthusiastic. Yet in the end the effort to create such a U.S.-Japan-Europe forum fizzled, mainly because of resistance from the French.

Of course, the Japanese were not interested in having their relations with Europe confined to multilateral institutions in which we played a dominant role. On the contrary, they undertook successful efforts to diversify their trade with Europe; they bolstered their links with the European Community, negotiating a declaration of principles to guide their relationship; and they intensified bilateral ties with key European countries. Still, the Japan-Europe nexus remained tenuous, and genuine trilateralism continued to be more of a hope than a reality.

Accommodating Japan's Desire for Permanent Membership in the UN Security Council

As East-West tensions faded, the United Nations promised to become the powerful force in world affairs that its founders had envisaged. For Japan to be a genuine global partner, it was essential that its voice in international organizations reflect more accurately its growing power. And it was only natural that Japan would seek a larger role in a revitalized UN. As economic concerns appeared likely to supplant military anxieties, Japan's claims to more substantial representation in the Security Council appeared all the more justified; its financial subventions to the United Nations already exceeded the combined contributions of China, the UK, and France.

The United States had been on record in support of Japan's permanent membership on the Security Council since 1972. I had collaborated on papers promoting that policy as a member of the State Department planning staff and felt that enhanced Japanese involvement in the UN would both accommodate a legitimate Japanese claim and encourage Tokyo to assume larger international responsibilities. In the late 1980s and early 1990s the question was whether the USA would move from rhetorical to operational support for Japan's aspirations. To me, this seemed a natural and appropriate trade-off for the expanded help we sought from Tokyo on a wide variety of substantive issues.

Over the years, the Japanese government had expressed its interest in a seat on the Security Council in a somewhat sporadic and diffident manner. During and immediately following the Gulf war, it was inclined to lie low, doubtful that it could secure the requisite support in light of its hesitant performance. The Tokyo political establishment appeared divided over the wisdom and efficacy of an active campaign for a permanent seat. Some felt Japan's credentials spoke for themselves and that an overt quest for the seat would be unseemly. Others feared such a campaign might inadvertently accelerate the dismantling of constraints on Japan's military role while exposing it to new pressures to tackle jobs where sweat and blood were needed along with cash.

Ambassador Yoshio Hatano, Japan's permanent representative to the United Nations, harbored no such reservations. He embarked on an energetic campaign in New York to promote the reform of UN institutions, including the removal of the so-called enemy clauses in the charter and an expansion of the Security Council to democratize its membership. Whether Hatano's activism was encouraged by Tokyo or he took the lead to overcome Tokyo's inertia, I do not know. But his activities made Tom Pickering, the U.S. permanent representative to the UN, nervous and attracted Washington's attention. Pickering feared that Hatano would generate pressure for wholesale change in the membership of the Security Council before we had discussed a game plan for managing Japan's entry.

I was asked to remind the Foreign Ministry that while we supported Japan's claim to a permanent seat on the council, we expected the Japanese to develop a plausible strategy for achieving their objective without inadvertently undermining the council's usefulness—an interest the Japanese were presumed to share. The ministry readily acknowledged the need for a thoughtful strategy and agreed to consult with us before attempting to implement it. Tom Pickering visited Tokyo to review his assessment of the situation in New York and to urge an approach in which the Japanese would concentrate on making the case for their own entry without opening the door to unrestrained logrolling among the many other countries that coveted a permanent seat.

While the Japanese worked to develop a strategy, a related question reared its head: whether Japan's highest-ranking executive within the UN system, Dr. Hiroshi Nakajima (director general of the World Health Organization), would enjoy the United States' backing for a second five-year term. Somewhere along the line Dr. Nakajima had provoked the ire of many representatives to the WHO. He was criticized, among other things, for his management style and his approach to certain international public health questions (e.g., AIDS). The U.S. ambassador accredited to UN organizations in Geneva, Morris Abram, was clearly sympathetic to those who sought to mobilize support for another candidate—an Algerian who had previously served as Dr. Nakajima's deputy.

The Japanese regarded a second term for Nakajima as a matter of face. Few Foreign Ministry officials energetically defended Nakajima's performance, but they argued that since all previous directors general had served two terms, their man deserved comparable treatment. They promised to persuade Nakajima to shake up his staff and improve his management style. They also indicated clearly their determination to call in all the chits to assure Nakajima's reelection.

I had known Dr. Nakajima in the Philippines in the early 1980s and had seen him from time to time during my stint as undersecretary. I had no means of judging his effectiveness at the WHO, and the reports about his performance were troubling. Yet a highly visible U.S. role in a campaign to oust Nakajima was destined to offend Tokyo; I doubted Geneva's estimates of the vote count; and it struck me as a poor issue on which to pick a fight with a government whose support we routinely requested on matters of far greater consequence. I worried especially about the signal our opposition to Nakajima would convey to Tokyo about the larger issue of Japan's membership in the Security Council.

I expressed these reservations on a number of occasions. But persuading Washington proved to be an uphill task. In the end, Larry Eagleburger, who saw Nakajima in action at the Tokyo Cambodian Donor's Conference in the spring of 1992 made the call and committed the United States to supporting Nakajima's rival. The Japanese were resentful. They pulled out all the stops for Nakajima's reelection, and, as I expected, their campaign succeeded.

President Bush's Trip to Tokyo

President Bush's decision to attend Emperor Hirohito's funeral in February 1989 was genuinely appreciated by the Japanese, and this thoughtful gesture relieved pressure for an early official visit to Tokyo. But the Japanese remained eager to arrange a state visit, which had last occurred when President Reagan had visited Tokyo in 1983. The president repeatedly was invited to visit Japan, and he displayed an evident interest in doing so. Momentous events in the Soviet Union, Eastern Europe, and the Gulf, however, kept it off the schedule. When the Gulf war ended, the Japanese reconfirmed their invitation and urged an early trip. The president seemed agreeable. Through the summer of 1991, dates were discussed, and eventually it was agreed the trip would take place in late November.

This pleased me greatly, because a state visit offered a chance to affirm the interests the United States and Japan shared after several years of tumult and friction. I shared with members of the embassy and Washington officials who paid close day-to-day attention to Japan the belief that such a visit would provide an appropriate occasion on which to issue a joint declaration outlining the conceptual underpinnings of the global partnership we had been seeking to forge—an occasion for celebrating the collaboration we had achieved while adding new content to it. As plans for the trip took shape through the summer and early fall, no major bilateral issues surfaced that appeared to demand resolution at the summit. The SII talks were by this time on the back burner. An extension of our bilateral agreement on semiconductors appeared achievable without engaging the president and prime minister directly. Discussions between our respective industries and governments appeared to be generating some movement on Japanese procurement of auto parts.

With a summit in prospect, the number of Washington visitors to Tokyo increased perceptibly. At no time during my tour, in fact, did cabinet members display a greater interest in stopping there. Among those visiting in the fall of 1991 were Vice President Quayle, Secretary of State Baker, U.S. Trade Representative Carla Hills, Secretary of Defense Cheney, Secretary of Commerce Mosbacher, Secretary of Energy James Watkins, and Chairman of the Joint Chiefs of Staff Colin Powell.

Before the discussions regarding the visit reached a point of decision, however, President Bush's trip was postponed. At first I thought it had been canceled. I heard that surprising news while en route from Kumamoto to Fukuoka in early November. I got the word by phone from my deputy, Bill Breer. Agitated, he told me that the White House had just informed him that the trip was being canceled. I asked why. He said the decision appeared to be a knee-jerk reaction to the results of the Pennsylvania Senatorial election, in which the Republican candidate, former attorney general Dick Thornburg, had been beaten by Harris Wofford in a campaign that included generous criticism of the president's alleged neglect of domestic matters. I asked whether the decision had been publicly announced. Bill said that it had not, but because the television networks evidently had gotten wind of it, the White House planned to go public with their decision shortly. I asked whether the Japanese government had been informed. He said it had not but that he had been instructed to do so by the NSC. He volunteered to call the director general of North American Affairs, Koichiro Matsuura. Since there appeared insufficient time to request reconsideration of the basic decision before it was announced, I told him to call Matsuura immediately.

The decision was publicly characterized as a postponement rather than a cancellation. I assumed this was for the sake of appearances, since a trip postponed for domestic political reasons seemed unlikely to be rescheduled even closer to the election season. I was distressed that a decision of this importance had been made without consulting those on the spot and announced without the courtesy of a presidential telephone call to the prime minister. We reported the disappointment that was evident throughout the Japanese government, but I did not undertake a major effort to reverse the decision, fearing that a presidential trip driven heavily by domestic political considerations was unlikely to produce a salutary result. I do not claim any prescience about the misfortunes that were about to befall the president.

In any case, within a short time, the president's own second thoughts produced a decision to put the trip back on the schedule. This surprised me as much as it seemed to please my hosts. They would have reason to reconsider before the fourth of January, the newly decided date for the president's arrival.

I got a taste of the changing political realities at home in early December, on a trip to Honolulu where an Asian Chief of Missions meeting was scheduled to coincide with a presidential visit to Honolulu to commemorate the fiftieth anniversary of the attack on Pearl Harbor. I was delighted to attend the ceremonies and was impressed by the statesmanlike tone and content of the president's address. In defending to an audience of veterans the U.S.-Japan relationship on such an occasion, he displayed political courage as well as unusual sensitivity to the feelings of both Americans and Japanese.

Following the president's address, the assembled ambassadors met with him for about an hour and a half. Representatives to the countries he was planning to visit—Australia, Singapore, South Korea, and Japan—were asked to summarize their expectations for his visit. When I observed that most of the planning in Washington and Tokyo for his earlier visit had focused on a joint declaration regarding our global partnership, the president asked pointedly, "What do we get out of it?" This took me slightly aback, for, aside from the supercollider project, none of the recent cabinet-level visitors to Tokyo had pressed for specific results at the summit on the bilateral economic and trade issues to which the president now referred. Obviously there was an urgent need to make swift adjustments in our discussions with the Japanese about the visit. To Brent Scowcroft and others I expressed the hope that a senior official sensitive to the changing political climate in Washington could be sent to Tokyo to provide help on the substantive preparations. Happily, Bob Zoellick took on that task and announced his intention to visit Tokyo with a team of senior people from the U.S. trade representative's office and the Departments of Commerce and State on the twentieth of December.

This was rather late to engage the Japanese on what amounted to a new agenda for the visit. Since New Year's holidays are sacred to Japanese officials, by the time Bob arrived in Tokyo, there were only seven working days left before the president arrived in Kyoto. Bob was extremely businesslike, and when asked what the president's priorities were, he announced, "Auto, autos, autos." The supercollider, if not forgotten, was relegated to secondary status.

Zoellick's arrival was heralded by another unanticipated announcement from Washington: namely, that the president would be accompanied to Tokyo by a group of senior business executives including Lee Iacocca, "Red" Poling, and Robert Stempel from Chrysler, Ford, and GM respectively. I never knew precisely where this suggestion had come from; news reports attributed it to Bob Mosbacher.

Vice President Quayle had been accompanied by three representatives from the private sector during a visit several months before. On that occasion, the business community representatives had maintained a low profile, and their presence had attracted little notice. I was not opposed to the idea of an accompanying business delegation to underline the importance of export promotion. But I doubted the advisability of giving the automobile executives such prominence, since they had not undertaken very impressive steps to crack the Japanese market: for example, none had fielded a right-hand steering wheel model aimed at a mass market, and only Ford had begun to establish its own distribution system.

In light of the inclusion of these CEOs from Chrysler, Ford, and GM, however, Bob Zoellick's emphasis on the importance of expanding sales of autos and auto parts was quite understandable. At his opening meeting with Japanese officials, he comprehensively described the political situation in Washington and the reasons Japan's interests should impel it to help the president achieve tangible and significant results during his visit. His interlocutors appeared shaken by the request virtually to start from scratch in preparing for the visit. Fortunately, the senior Japanese government representatives—Koji Watanabe, deputy minister of foreign affairs; Yuji Tanahashi, vice minister of MITI; and Tadahiro Chino, vice minister of finance—were seasoned professionals who were prepared, despite the short time available and the impending holiday period, to see what could be done.

We swiftly organized a process in which simultaneous efforts were undertaken to complete the so-called Tokyo Declaration and to supplement it with an action program that had both a political and an economic component. The latter was the focus of intense negotiations over the next two weeks. The auto issue was the most important—and the most difficult. Before the scheduled visit of the president in early

November, Japanese auto executives had volunteered announcements of their plans to increase significantly their purchases of American auto parts for their transplants in the United States. Now they were being asked to go back to the well, and they didn't like it.

MITI and the Ministry of Transportation were asked to broker arrangements for streamlining the certification of U.S. cars for Japan's market. It stuck in Detroit's craw that Japanese companies certified the safety of cars they manufactured for export to the United States yet insisted on carrying out inspections on American exports in Japan. The Japanese rationalized this imbalance on grounds that Japan manufactured hundreds of thousands of cars to meet the regulatory requirements of our market and no one doubted that the cars they produced met our standards. Detroit, on the other hand, accorded a much lower priority to exports and sought to sell cars in Japan that had been designed essentially for other markets. The Japanese consequently insisted on overseeing the so-called homologation process through which these cars were adapted to Japan's demanding safety requirements.

Whatever the logic of the arrangement, there can be no doubt that the Japanese had long utilized this system to increase the costs and complicate the problems of market entry for every would-be importer of automobiles. The lack of reciprocity was galling, particularly since Japan sold more cars in the United States in a week than we sold in Japan in a year. But the Transportation Ministry controlled Japan's standards, and it seemed indifferent to these political concerns. It was in charge of the regulations and exhibited little interest in sharing, let alone giving up, its prerogatives.

Washington also wanted help in gaining access to automobile distributors to facilitate sales of finished automobiles in Japan—a point registered strongly by Vice President Quayle during his visit to Tokyo. Since only Ford had the rudiments of an effective distribution system in Japan, this meant leaning on Japanese car companies to open up their own distribution channels. The Japanese had clearly benefited from the readiness of American independent distributors to handle their products alongside Detroit's. In Japan, by contrast, each maker maintained exclusive distribution channels, and each company's sales force was extraordinarily loyal; none of their companies was interested in easing the entree of additional competitors. Relying on them to market U.S. products struck me as akin to McDonald's expecting Burger King to help it increase its market share. It was a manifestation of Detroit's desperation. Yet the imbalance in market access arrangements was outrageous, and we needed all the help we could get.

I had learned something about the Japanese auto distribution system from an anonymous source in the early months of my tenure. A graduate student from Johns Hopkins University who was spending some time working for Mitsui Bussan sent me a blind copy of the conclusions he had reached in his research on the auto industry. He had wandered around Tokyo asking lots of thoughtful questions about how U.S. auto manufacturers were faring in marketing their products in Japan and had spent considerable time at the Autorama distribution centers where Ford's cars were on display. Though Autorama was a joint venture with Mazda in which Ford owned roughly a 33 percent equity share, the sales force was thoroughly committed to Mazda. When my anonymous friend inquired about Ford products, he was astonished to hear the salesmen repeatedly express utter contempt for Ford products. I sent a copy of his paper to Ben Lever, Ford's resident manager, with the comment that if this was an indication of the enthusiasm of Autorama distributors for Ford's products, he had a more serious problem than I had been led to expect.

There were other issues as well: the conclusion of an agreement on government procurement of computers, understandings regarding the opening of market access for glass and paper products, the right of each side to raise new issues in the ongoing SII talks, and of course, the supercollider. By the time the president arrived, the action plan concerning economic and trade relations had acquired substantial content. Unfortunately, it was to attract little favorable attention during the visit, because the press soon became preoccupied with the president's unexpected illness and the complaints of various members of his business delegation.

The president's arrival in Kyoto was marked by extraordinarily beautiful weather. The city glistened in the winter sunlight, and the initial events—a visit to a famous temple and a luncheon at a traditional Japanese inn—got the visit off to an amiable start.

The first business was the opening of a new Toys R Us outlet near Osaka. In the helicopter en route, the president pulled out remarks that had been drafted for the occasion. He looked distressed and asked Brent Scowcroft and me to take a look. The reasons for his unhappiness were immediately clear. The remarks had been drafted as if prepared for a domestic American audience; they were lacking in grace and seemed scarcely presidential. Unfortunately, the helicopter ride was brief, and there was no chance to redraft them. The president improved the remarks in the delivery, but the tone still seemed off.

Things got worse. The visit to Tokyo started well enough. Consultations with Prime Minister Miyazawa went smoothly. The two leaders had enjoyed cordial relations for a long time, and they both were comfortable with the nuances of all the crucial foreign policy issues. At a luncheon banquet hosted by the prime minister on January 5, I detected nothing untoward other than the fact that the president did not eat everything put before him. I assumed that this was perhaps because he and I were scheduled to play tennis with the emperor and the crown prince immediately after lunch. I was unaware that the president was feeling under the weather, and he appeared eager for some exercise. Before the game, the crown prince asked me how we should divide up. I left it up to him, and he paired up with his father. They beat us rather convincingly. After a set, the emperor invited us to have tea, but the president insisted on a chance to even the score. We lost again. After snacks and a pleasant chat with the emperor, empress, and other members of the family, we returned to Akasaka Palace. The president had good color, and again I had no inkling of anything amiss.

When I returned to accompany the president to the prime minister's official residence for dinner, I overheard a White House staff member comment that Mr. Bush was feeling "only about seven on a scale of ten." Yet as Bonny and I went through the reception line, he looked fine. I was consequently surprised when Brent Scrowcroft sought me out a few moments later to say that the president had been forced to leave the receiving line, was feeling poorly, and, though he did not wish to cancel the dinner, hoped it could be accelerated. I found the chief of protocol, explained the situation, and asked that the dinner be speeded up. He readily complied.

When the president entered the dining room, it was clear that he was under the weather. His color was gone, and so was the animation he customarily displayed. I kept a close eye on him from my seat at the table—no more than twenty or twenty-five feet away from him—and I noticed midway through dinner that he looked over his shoulder, as though seeking to locate a door. A beautiful Japanese screen extended from wall to wall behind the head table, however, and denied him any ready means of egress. As he turned back to the table, the awful scene reproduced hundreds of times on television unfolded: the president lost consciousness, expelled his dinner, and slid to the floor with his head in Prime Minister Miyazawa's lap. Though he regained consciousness swiftly, it did not seem so at the time. My most vivid memory is of Mrs. Bush, who rushed toward the president and then, displaying extraordinary composure, informed the crowd, "He's all right. He's all right. He's all right." She clearly knew more about his condition than anyone else and recognized the symptoms of the flu bug that had been circulating among members of the traveling party.

The president promptly regained his composure—to the extent one can under such circumstances—and was driven back to his quarters. Mrs. Bush remained, and the prime minister asked her to speak after Brent Scowcroft read the president's formal toast. With an eye to the audience back home, Mrs. Bush cocked her eye at me and extemporized, "It's all the ambassador's fault. He and the president played tennis with the emperor and the crown prince this afternoon. They were soundly defeated, and it just makes George sick to lose!" She looked at me rather severely as she spoke and then broke into a broad smile, to the amusement of the audience. I'm sure it was a source of reassurance to Americans back home to hear the First Lady making light of the spectacle captured on television.

Mrs. Bush's remarks were repeated scores of times on Japanese television over the next several days. Unfortunately the film clip had been edited to omit Mrs. Bush's smile, and many Japanese friends assumed my tenure in Tokyo was about to be drastically foreshortened. When I saw Mrs. Bush the next morning, she said, "Mike, you'll probably never forgive me for my remarks last night." "Well," I said, "what, after all, are ambassadors for?"

"The effect of the president's illness was devastating for the visit. Many commentators blamed the presence of the business delegation for the trip's bad publicity, but I believe his illness had a more profound effect. Since he had to cancel his schedule for the following day, the planned events lost their focus. A breakfast meeting that had been intended to bring the president into contact with Japanese and American business representatives turned into a gripe session, and the U.S. auto executives dominated the next day's headlines with their own press conference remarks. The president's speech, which was to have been delivered to a blue-ribbon audience of several hundred, was read by Treasury Secretary Nick Brady. It received scant coverage in the press. A visit to the Kodak Research and Design Center in Yokohama, which had been planned to demonstrate how U.S. companies that organized their business properly could achieve impressive results in Japan, became a nonevent. With the president unable to attend, the press bus to Yokahama was canceled. Thus, despite some useful progress on substantive matters, the trip was a public relations disaster that conveyed unfortunate images of the United States to the Japanese people and exacerbated the already sour undertones in the relationship.

In some respects, the 1992 Bush visit to Tokyo was a metaphor for the hope and shortcomings of the still incomplete partnership between the United States and Japan. The personal ties between President Bush and Prime Minister Miyazawa were exceptionally cordial. The joint declaration they issued captured the breadth of the interests our nations shared. The joint action program demonstrated the wide range of issues on which government-to-government collaboration had became routine. These cooperative links, while centered in Asia, had acquired truly global scope. And the alliance that provided the foundation of this partnership was alive and well. Yet the visit called attention to persisting tensions in the relationship, and in its aftermath, accusations and recriminations were hurled in both directions across the Pacific. Disdainful comments by Diet speaker Yoshio Sakarauchi and Prime Minister Miyazawa about the American work ethic provoked an outcry in the U.S. media and Congress. Senator Hollings responded with a crude and tasteless remark designed to remind the Japanese that some American products (for instance, the atomic bomb) worked perfectly well. Despite the range of shared interests between the United States and Japan, a genuine spirit of collaboration was frequently missing. For Americans, Japan was too often an afterthought—a convenient source of financial support for initiatives about which its views were solicited only after Washington had made up its mind. And too often Japan devoted its energies principally to the pursuit of its own narrow interests within the framework of an international system whose definition and defense it left largely to others.

The coordination of our respective interests was at times a bit ragged, but that was understandable. No new world order had replaced the familiar contours of cold war competition. Many in each country found the emerging terrain of the post–cold war world unfamiliar and unsettling. The resolution of contradictions within Europe and between Europe and North America appeared to open the door for a new international constellation of forces that was unsettling for Tokyo. Japan's experience during the Gulf war had provided an unpleasant reminder of how dependent Japan remained on the United States. Yet if the USA's performance in the Gulf reassured allies of its military power and political resolution, the L.A. riots in the spring of 1992 reawakened apprehensions that intractable domestic problems would redirect American attention and resources inward. All these concerns reinforced a natural Japanese inclination to hedge their bets; in this case, by provoking interest in a re-Asianization of Japanese policy.

On the U.S. side, questions persisted about Japan's willingness and ability to tackle a more ambitious global role. It possessed the resources for it—of that there was no question. But whether it could overcome the provincialism and passivity, the aversion to risk and the inclination to free riding, that had shaped its diplomatic reflexes for a generation remained uncertain. Doubts on this score prompted many in Washington to encourage a hard-nosed approach that highlighted the competitive more than the collaborative aspects of the relationship.

Thus, while the benefits of collaboration were clear, they could not entirely quell the tendencies in both Tokyo and Washington to regard the other as an incipient rival. These were among the reasons that explained why, when things went wrong, commentators on both sides of the Pacific too often concluded that the relationship was fundamentally in jeopardy. Objectively, the partnership paid large dividends to both sides. But the emotional and psychological underpinnings seemed fragile.

In some respects, the Japanese tackled the problem more forthrightly than we did. In a little noted speech in Atlanta during the summer of 1991, Prime Minister Kaifu proposed a "Communications Improvement Initiative," or CII, to match the SII initiative we had earlier launched. Its purpose was to reciprocate the generosity of the United States' postwar Fulbright and Garioa Programs with a comparably magnanimous gesture: the creation of a Center for Global Partnership, endowed with more than $300 million, to provide support for bilateral education and cultural exchange programs. In setting up the fund, precedence would be given to supporting projects that engaged Americans and Japanese in tackling regional and global problems. The intent was to build a wider human infrastructure to support our official relationship. Commemoration in 1990 of the thirtieth anniversary of the Treaty of Mutual Cooperation and Security and, in the spring

of 1992, of the twentieth anniversary of Okinawa's reversion were likewise undertaken as expressions of Japanese gratitude and efforts to create a less cantankerous atmosphere for our official dealings.

In the end, however, the benefits of collaboration that the global
partnership promised were not matched by the spirit of cooperation
both governments initially sought. And with the inauguration of President Clinton in January 1993, the concept of a global partnership quietly dropped out of sight.

6

The Clinton Administration's Japan Policy

Following President Bush's visit to Tokyo in January 1992, many Japanese feared that their country and the U.S.-Japan relationship would be drawn inexorably into our presidential election campaign. The Japanese government consequently made what appeared to be a conscious effort to avoid injecting itself into the political cross fire in the United States.

The Japanese were reassured to see Democratic contenders whom they considered protectionist—e.g., Tom Harkin and Jerry Brown—fade quickly. They were relieved when Bob Kerrey's experimental television spots featuring what the press in Tokyo characterized as "Japan bashing" backfired and were quickly canceled. And they were pleased as well as surprised when U.S.-Japan trade issues slipped onto the back burner in the general election campaign.

Throughout 1992 Bill Clinton's views of Japan remained largely a mystery to the average Japanese. To be sure, as governor he had made several visits to solicit trade and investment for Arkansas, and he had left a favorable impression among those he met. But the focus of his campaign was mainly on promoting change in the United States. His speeches on foreign and security policy fell broadly within the internationalist tradition of the Democratic Party. His equivocations on trade issues like NAFTA and GATT did not seem to excite special apprehensions. They did, however, confirm what most Japanese officials believed: Democrats were more inclined to economic nationalism than Republicans were.

Clinton's endorsement of an extension of Super 301 to prod Japan into opening its market further reinforced that impression. So did the fact that during the campaign the Democrats trashed the SII process in favor of what they characterized as results-oriented trade negotiations. His emphasis, moreover, on a more aggressive pursuit of human rights in China and the provision of larger subventions to reformers in Russia aroused concerns that a Clinton victory might put the United States and Japan at odds with respect to our relations both with Moscow and Beijing. Finally, memories of Jimmy Carter's plan to withdraw troops from Korea tended to reinforce doubts about the steadiness of a Democratic administration's approach to the Korean Peninsula.

By contrast, President Bush's views on foreign policy issues were well known. He played down the Japan issue during the campaign—presumably because of the unfortunate political fallout at home after his Tokyo visit. I was perhaps an inadvertent beneficiary of this. As a career foreign service officer, I expected my tenure in Tokyo to end after three years, in May 1992. I was exempted, however, from a routine transfer largely, I suspect, because the confirmation hearings for a new ambassador might have provoked a partisan struggle over Japan policy.

Most of my Japanese friends and acquaintances appeared to assume that President Bush would be reelected and gave the impression that such an outcome would suit them fine. I encountered openly acknowledged hopes for a Clinton victory only sporadically among a smattering of senior Japanese bureaucrats and journalists. This group reasoned that Republican control of the White House would guarantee further executive-legislative gridlock in the United States and that the consequent inability to tackle pressing domestic problems would fuel the search for foreign scapegoats—with Japan the leading candidate.

But if the Japanese establishment appeared to prefer President Bush's reelection, it did little to extend tangible help. There were opportunities. A more expansive budget to stimulate domestic demand could have increased U.S. export possibilities and helped to accelerate our economic recovery. Diplomatic assistance in bringing the GATT negotiations to a successful conclusion would have added luster to the Bush administration's foreign policy record. Announcement of Japan's intention to purchase the AWACS aircraft might have bolstered support for the president in states where Boeing and its suppliers had major production facilities.

In fact, initiatives were contemplated (for reasons related to Japanese interests rather than U.S. politics), but they were stymied by internal opposition. Prime Minister Miyazawa promised a stimulative budget; however, the Finance Ministry managed to block it. Some senior officials in the Foreign Ministry hinted at efforts to move the GATT negotiations along, but the Ministry of Agriculture and Fisheries squelched any movement in that direction. And the Japanese government eventually decided to purchase four AWACS aircraft, though the announcement came only after the 1992 election was over—scant consolation for the president.

Interregnum

In accordance with custom, I filed my resignation with President Bush some weeks before the election, expecting it to be accepted shortly thereafter. I did not covet another post either in Washington or overseas and planned to leave the Foreign Service when my assignment in Tokyo was finished. Naturally, the Japanese press immediately began speculating about my successor. Some of those mentioned—such as Governor Booth Gardner of Washington and Dick Holbrooke, a former assistant secretary of state for East Asian affairs—were well qualified candidates whom I knew were interested. Others—for example, Speaker of the House of Representatives Thomas Foley—were unlikely to be available, and rumors about their interest reflected the Tokyo media's inclination to indulge in wishful thinking. I swiftly learned what it was to be a lame duck.

As it turned out, the Clinton administration displayed little urgency in filling ambassadorial posts. And by the end of 1992, I had received informal word that I should plan to stay on in Tokyo for a few months while the administration made its choice. This was agreeable to me, for I had no desire to leave before a successor was designated. But I encouraged the new team at the State Department to have a new ambassador in place well before the G-7 summit convened in Tokyo in mid-July 1993. This would enable Washington's new representative to benefit from visible association with the president and gain a swift immersion in the bilateral and multilateral dimensions of our relationship. The top people in the department acknowledged these advantages but were unable to confirm that such a timetable was achievable.

During this period, I busied myself urging Japanese officials and politicians to take early action to preempt problems with the incoming administration. The bilateral trade imbalance had begun to surge upward again in 1992, and that trend was destined to continue as the United States entered a period of even stronger economic recovery in 1993. This guaranteed that the trade issue would be near the top of the new administration's agenda. I therefore counseled all who would listen to consider stronger measures to stimulate domestic demand in Japan as well as initiatives to facilitate an early conclusion of the GATT negotiations.

The response of Japanese officials and key Japanese politicians was surprisingly complacent. I encountered little soul-searching about Japan's rapidly accumulating global current account surplus and a diminished sense of urgency about reducing it. There were perhaps several explanations. U.S.-Japan trade issues had not been a central feature of the presidential campaign. Neither had Tokyo confronted concerted G-7 pressures for remedial action at the Bonn summit in July 1992. Besides, the Miyazawa cabinet had formulated, though not yet implemented, a sizable domestic demand stimulus package, which it could contend would result in a major expansion of imports in 1993.

The business community was receptive to the call for domestic demand stimulus. The major economic federations—Keidanren, Keizai Doyukai, Nikkeiren, the Chamber of Commerce—all encouraged corporate and personal tax cuts to stimulate demand. And the Policy Research Council of the LDP, led by Hiroshi Mitzuzuka, jumped aboard the bandwagon. Tax cuts also had an undeniable political appeal. The Miyazawa government was at the time working on a five-year budget proposal designed ostensibly to transform Japan into a "lifestyle" superpower. From 1988 to 1992 the percentage of the Japanese GDP that went to personal consumption had declined from 62 percent to roughly 58 percent. Merely restoring consumption to 1988 levels would have unleashed enormous demand, consistent with the structural changes heralded in the Maekawa Report of the mid-1980s.

The Ministry of Finance had a different agenda, however. It continued to assign priority to fiscal reconstruction, i.e., reducing the public debt incurred in the late 1970s and early 1980s. And once it articulated its opposition to tax cuts, it was amazing how quickly the business community and LDP dropped the issue. Indeed, many began parroting the ministry's arguments for why it was such a bad idea. On the trade issues, moreover, the Japanese preferred to play a waiting game. Why offer preemptive concessions before it knew what to expect from the new administration?

The Clinton Administration: Trade Policy

Eager to obtain a better feel for the new administration's thinking, I returned to Washington for consultations in mid-February 1993 and made the rounds of new cabinet members interested in the U.S.-Japan relationship. I met with Warren Christopher, Lloyd Bentsen, Laura Tyson, Ron Brown, Mickey Kantor, and Tony Lake. All expressed a determination to press for greater reciprocity on trade matters with the Japanese, and though none appeared firmly committed to a particular approach, all were clearly interested in differentiating the new team's negotiating strategy from that of the Bush administration.

I encountered much talk about a results-oriented approach but little evidence that a newly reconstructed interagency policy-making process would swiftly hammer out a new strategy. A process was planned, to be reconfigured through the creation of a new National Economic Council to coordinate the formulation of domestic and international economic policy. Whether trade policy toward Japan would fall principally under the NEC or NSC was resolved in favor of the former. But it took some time to get both councils up and running. Lengthy delays in getting key officials confirmed further slowed the process of policy formulation. The locus for policy making eventually came to rest with the interagency deputies committee, chaired by Bo Cutter, Bob Rubin's deputy at the NEC, and composed of senior officials from all relevant agencies. The subcabinet officials with responsibility for formulating policy toward Japan—Joan Spero (State), Roger Altman and Larry Summers (Treasury), Alan Blinder (CEA), Charleen Barshefsky (U.S. trade representative's office), Jeff Garten (Commerce), and Cutter—were all highly intelligent and pragmatic individuals. Each had some prior experience with Japan, mostly in the private sector, and several bore the scars of previous business negotiations with the Japanese.

In January 1992 my economic minister, Joe Winder, and I had collaborated on a cable to Washington expressing our views on trade policy. We warned that there was "no silver bullet, no quick fix." We observed that progress in reducing the imbalance was pick-and-shovel work. We urged the new administration to concentrate on coordinating macroeconomic policies, pursuing further sectoral agreements, attempting to remove more structural impediments to open trade, and improving multilateral rules for trade by wrapping up the Uruguay round.

During my February 1993 visit, I was pleased to note that the cable had been widely read, but the prevailing consensus in Washington seemed to be moving well beyond our suggestions. What I found particularly noteworthy was the widespread supposition—particularly at the U.S. trade representative's office and the White House—that the semiconductor agreements of 1986 and 1991 and the auto parts understandings of January 1992 were virtually the only bilateral trade agreements that had produced any noteworthy results. Since the Japanese trade bureaucracy repeatedly emphasized its resolve never again to replicate such agreements, it was clear that a major struggle loomed.

In fact, the administration got off to a favorable start on trade issues with the Japanese. The president's first authoritative remarks on the subject, during a speech at American University on February 26, 1993, urged an early conclusion of the Uruguay round and indicated that the administration would utilize the tools at its disposal—multilaterally where possible, bilaterally when necessary—to achieve a rough equality of trade and investment opportunities with Japan. The administration also introduced an important tactical adjustment in the U.S. approach to the GATT negotiations, giving priority to market access issues rather than agriculture. This permitted us to find some common ground with the Japanese, leaving the tough rice issue until other details of an agreement had been filled in. Beyond this, Secretary of the Treasury Lloyd Bentsen made it clear that he would utilize the G-7 finance ministers for discreet consultations rather than high-profile communiqués—a stylistic change the Japanese welcomed. Most important, the president accorded top priority to reducing the fiscal deficit. By the time he visited Tokyo, the broad outlines of his deficit reduction plan had taken shape, and this lent credibility to his requests to Japan and Europe to make their own contributions to global growth.

By midspring the broad outlines of the administration's trade strategy toward Japan began to surface. From the outset it was clear that it would not be an easy sell in Tokyo. First, it rejected a quest for piece-meal agreements in favor of a comprehensive negotiation to include macroeconomic coordination as well as bargaining over sectoral and structural issues. The extensive agenda foreshadowed detailed discussions on the following subjects: (1) government procurement of computers, satellites, medical technology, and communications equipment and services; (2) regulatory reform and competitiveness (including financial services and insurance, as well as the distribution system and administrative guidance); (3) "other major sectors" (a general heading that served as a euphemism for autos and auto parts); (4) economic harmonization (a category that would extend to such subjects as foreign direct investment, intellectual property rights, and buyer-supplier relationships); and (5) a review of how existing bilateral agreements were being implemented. The premise underlying this last proposal was that Japan routinely violated or ignored most of its trade commitments—a difficult basis on which to enlist the cooperation of a negotiating partner. In fact, the distrust was mutual. If U.S. negotiators assumed that Japanese trade pledges were worthless unless they were reduced to quantitative targets, the Japanese team believed that even the vaguest promises made to Americans would be transformed into explicit pledges to accomplish a specific result within a fixed time frame.

The strategy proposed to assure effective results by creating agreed, visible, and quantifiable standards against which progress could be measured. Specifically, we would seek Japanese commitments to reduce the size of its current account surplus and increase the volume of its manufactured imports to explicit percentages of its GNP. In the various sectoral negotiations, moreover, we proposed to identify numerical targets or objective criteria against which Japan's performance could be judged.

Finally, the president would commit himself to meeting the Japanese prime minister at frequent, periodic intervals to review progress. Such meetings, initially contemplated at roughly six-month intervals, were envisaged as action-forcing events and were to be preceded by detailed preparatory negotiations between U.S. and Japanese subcabinet-level officials.

The administration appeared determined to resist a process that allowed the Japanese to table their own complaints about U.S. policies, as they could in the SII talks. It also sought to minimize the focus on collaborative activities, evidently fearing that these would divert attention from Washington's central concerns. The Clinton economic team also hoped to dilute the influence of the Japanese bureaucracy in the negotiations by establishing a direct negotiating link with politicians in the prime minister's office. Bo Cutter was selected to lead the U.S. delegation to the framework talks, and he actively encouraged the Japanese to appoint the deputy chief cabinet secretary—a prominent LDP politician—as his counterpart. I regarded this element of the strategy as particularly problematic and expressed misgivings. The purpose of Washington's proposal—to work around or go over the heads of the bureaucracy—was transparent. Since power in Japan rested principally with the bureaucracy, such a proposal was destined to be rejected and would merely offend those who remained in charge of the negotiation. Despite my reservations, the proposal resurfaced in communications with the prime minister. Predictably, it was ignored, though I suspect its repetition rankled.

For their part, the Japanese approached the framework negotiations in an aggressively defensive mode. They would have preferred to avoid the negotiations altogether. Since that was impossible, they concentrated on attempting to neutralize U.S. proposals while limiting their scope. A prime objective was "minimum specificity"—i.e., the avoidance at all costs of any pledge that might be construed as a numerical target. In addition, the Japanese sought to limit negotiations to problems within the government's reach, thus absolving themselves of any responsibility for guaranteeing increased imports by the private sector. They also insisted on subjecting any concessions made to the United States to most-favored-nation treatment, in order to avert difficulties with other trading partners. Beyond this, they wanted a process that could be portrayed as balanced and reciprocal, thus averting any impression that the talks would address only Japanese market access and regulatory barriers in Japan. They pushed hard to include discussions of the development of cooperative activities in order to accentuate the positive and avert any inference that our economic ties were marked exclusively by strife and discord. Determined not to be outmaneuvered in the field of public diplomacy, moreover, they quickly seized the high ground, portraying themselves as champions of free trade, while putting the Clinton administration in the dock as proponents of managed trade.

Several rounds of discussions yielded little progress on the central issues, and with time running out before the G-7 summit, Washington appeared reconciled to reaching no agreement. The Japanese government, however, was not eager to host a major multilateral event clouded by an apparent impasse over trade with its major ally. With time running out before the summit, Prime Minister Miyazawa personally conveyed a suggestion to Washington for breaking the impasse. While he emphasized that numerical targets were still unacceptable, Tokyo, he said, could perhaps live with what he termed "an illustrative set of criteria"—whether quantitative or qualitative—as long as the language in the framework agreement indicated that such criteria could be used only to gauge progress, not to serve as targets or commitments for future trade outcomes. This gave Washington enough running room to send its delegation to Tokyo ahead of the summit, and the two teams struggled toward an agreement throughout the G-7 meetings. In the end, agreement was facilitated by direct talks between the national security adviser, Tony Lake, and Hisashi Owada, the vice minister of foreign affairs. Yet although excluding MITI and Ministry of Finance officials from the critical discussions may have eased agreement on the framework, it probably hardened their determination to resist offering concessions when substantive talks began. By that time, Prime Minister Miyazawa had been replaced, and Vice Minister Owada had assumed other responsibilities.

The language ultimately agreed on skirted major differences. "This assessment," the agreement read, "will be based upon sets of objective criteria, either qualitative or quantitative or both as appropriate, which will be established using relevant information, and/or data that both governments will evaluate. These criteria are to be used for the purpose of evaluating progress achieved in each sectoral and structural area." Agreement on this complicated formulation did not extend to what precisely it meant.

Other issues fueled the nonstop negotiations during the summit. Most were finessed. For example, Washington wanted the Japanese to commit to getting their current account surplus down to between 1 and 2 percent of their GDP within three to four years and to raise their imports of manufactured goods as a share of GDP by one-third within the same time frame (i.e., from roughly 3.1 percent to 4 percent, still well below the 7.4 percent level that was average for other G-7 members). What we obtained was a commitment to "a highly significant decrease" in the surplus and a "significant increase in global imports of goods and services" over the "medium term." The agreement also left unspecified the market obstacles to be removed, as well as the criteria to be employed for assessing progress.

The Japanese wanted any agreements concluded to fall outside the retaliatory reach of section 301 of our trade law. Washington rejected this, insisting that violations of agreements would be actionable under U.S. trade laws. No compromise being possible, we agreed to disagree: the United States reserved the right to enforce agreements that were reached; Tokyo signaled its intent to pull out of negotiations in any area in which Washington proceeded with what Japan considered an unfair trade practices investigation.

The agreement received good press, but this initial skirmish was a harbinger of what was to come. Both sides interpreted the understanding in divergent ways. The framework did not chart a clear path toward an agreement; it provided merely an agenda on which to struggle. Some weeks earlier, Walter Mondale had been nominated to replace me. I was relieved that he, rather than I, would have to try to keep this process on track. A week later I left Tokyo.

The Tokyo Summit

The framework agreement, however important to the administration, was not the president's only preoccupation during the Tokyo summit. Indeed from my standpoint, the G-7 summit provided a timely opportunity to increase President Clinton's awareness of other features of our relationship with Japan and to reinforce the administration's interest in Asia. In addition to the time the president was to spend in G-7 deliberations, the Japanese eagerly arranged for him to make an official bilateral visit to Tokyo just prior to the multilateral summit. Ultimately, we were able to claim only a little more than twenty-four hours for this bilateral visit, but it proved to be time well spent. It offered an opportunity for the president to engage in bilateral discussions with the prime minister, meet a wider range of Japanese leaders, publicly address key issues in our relations with Japan and the Asian region, and enjoy at least some more or less spontaneous interaction with the Japanese public.

The formal talks with the prime minister and his entourage took care of themselves. They were cordial and substantive. Arranging for the president to meet a cross section of the Japanese establishment was

trickier. The only time available was used for a brief reception immediately following the president's arrival from the United States. I
wished to keep the numbers sufficiently limited so that Mr. Clinton
would have some opportunity to speak with each of the invited guests.
Thus the invitees made up a genuine A-list of the Japanese political,
business, academic, and journalistic elite: the major LDP faction leaders;
leaders of the major opposition parties; and representatives from the
business, journalistic, and academic communities. The press highlighted almost exclusively President Clinton's informal exchanges
with reformist politicians like Morihiro Hosokawa and Tsutomu
Hata—contacts that proved to be highly useful, inasmuch as the former became prime minister within days, and the latter within months.
Some interpreted the reception as a subtle effort to align the United
States with the LDP's opponents. That was not my intent, though privately I hoped the voters would shake up the political system. Recognizing the uncertainties of the Japanese Lower House election that was
to take place in little more than a week, my main objective was to see
that the president met as many of Japan's potential future leaders as
possible.

I was personally surprised when Mrs. Clinton appeared at the
reception at the president's side. The White House advance team had
informed us that she would skip the first night's events. Bonny and I
were delighted that she chose to join the occasion, for she had stirred
tremendous interest among both the Japanese elite and the public. Her
presence, however, highlighted the fact that our guests included no
Japanese women. Some among the U.S. press feigned shock and out-
rage at this omission, and the White House spin masters suggested that
the oversight was the embassy's fault. I was bemused by the furor but
readily accepted responsibility for putting together the invitation list.
My embassy colleagues and I had prepared it with the aim of including the leaders of Japan's establishment. In fact, we had invited two
prominent women—Mayumi Moriyama, former chief cabinet secretary in the Kaifu cabinet, and Sadako Ogata, the UN High Commis-
sioner for Refugees—neither of whom was able to attend. But with a
few notable exceptions, women were not prominent in the leadership
of Japan's political, bureaucratic, business, and journalistic institutions,
and this perforce influenced our choices. It had never occurred to me
that we should arrange the guest list to meet the standards of Ameri-

can political correctness—as interpreted either by the press or the White House. In any case, the flap was quickly overtaken by events.

The embassy was eager to have the president visit Waseda University. Robert Kennedy had spoken there in the early 1960s and had earned widespread admiration for standing up to the heckling of leftist students. We were eager for another young U.S. leader to engage in open discourse with a new student generation in Japan. This suggestion encountered much initial opposition from some in Washington, but in the end the resistance eased, and the university provided an excellent showcase for the president's call for a Pacific Community. His informal exchanges with students proved to be a big hit with both those in attendance and those who watched on TV. The questions were blunt, and the president's responses good-natured, candid, and well informed. He seemed reluctant to leave.

I hoped the president would phone the parents of a young Japanese exchange student, Yoshio Hattori, who had been slain the previous October in Louisiana. The Hattoris had paid a call on Bonny and me following their son's death, in order to present petitions urging stricter gun control in the United States. I was touched by the grace with which they sought to find some larger meaning in their personal tragedy. I shared their sentiments about gun control and admired their decision to raise money to support expanded U.S.-Japanese student exchanges. I was gratified that the president telephoned them to express condolences, though technical difficulties in arranging the call prompted him to arrive nearly twenty minutes late for a meeting at my residence with Indonesian president Suharto.

The president, Mrs. Clinton, and the entire Washington entourage appeared delighted by the outcome of their brief bilateral visit. The G-7 summit likewise went well from the president's standpoint. And, whatever the eventual consequences, the last-minute signing of a framework agreement for trade negotiations was frosting on the cake. Needless to add, I was greatly relieved at the outcome. This was the third presidential visit for which I had borne some responsibility as ambassador. The first, a scheduled visit by President Reagan to the Philippines in 1983, had been canceled abruptly following "Ninoy" Aquino's assassination. The second—President Bush's visit to Tokyo in January 1992—had scarcely gone according to plan. At least on this third try, the president seemed satisfied with the result.

In Pursuit of a Trade Agreement

I followed the subsequent trade negotiations—which got off to a rather leisurely start in mid-September—essentially through the press, supplemented by occasional chats with former associates. The discussions initially focused on the contentious subject of numerical targets, a subject on which the delegations were unlikely to find much common ground. While the U.S. side sought to distinguish between managing outcomes and establishing benchmarks against which to measure progress, such fine distinctions got lost in an increasingly acrimonious debate between the delegations. Nor did the administration do an effective job of explaining these distinctions to the American press and public. This became obvious when a number of the nation's leading economists signed an open letter criticizing the administration's strategy.

Unfortunately, this approach played into the hands of the Japanese trade bureaucracy. They relished the opportunity to transform the negotiation into a public relations contest, for they held the high political ground. They had learned the crucial importance of public diplomacy during the SII talks, and this time they took the offensive. They treated any reference to objective criteria as if it were a demand for market share. They used Washington's alleged insistence on numerical targets to solidify support within their business community and political establishment against any concessions to Washington. They neutralized the United States' natural allies on trade issues in Asia and Europe by telling them that if Washington prevailed in this negotiation, it would seek similar market share arrangements with them. In any event, they hinted, concessions extended to Washington would come at others' expense.

Positioned so advantageously, the Japanese bureaucracy felt no apparent obligation to come up with serious counterproposals. And Washington's trade representatives, outmaneuvered tactically, took out their frustrations on their counterparts, following up the acerbic exchanges at the bargaining table with leaks of unflattering portraits of the Japanese negotiators to the press. Distrust mounted on both sides. Washington's negotiating approach also appeared to reflect a misreading of political developments in Japan. Hoping they could enlist the support of politicians to close a deal, at least some of the administration representatives made little effort to conceal their disregard for their bureaucratic counterparts. But the July 18, 1993, Lower House elections brought to power a coalition government whose unity was extremely fragile. Able to agree on little beyond the desire to oust the LDP and pass an electoral reform bill, it could fashion no detailed policy on trade issues and, like its predecessor, was inclined to defer to the bureaucracy on such matters. Thus the bureaucrats stonewalled, and no politicians had the strength to discipline them even had they possessed the disposition to try.

By the time Prime Minister Hosokawa visited President Clinton in Washington in early February 1994, both sides had concluded that no agreement was preferable to an attempt to paper over disagreements for cosmetic purposes. The result was ironic. In the mid-1980s, Washington began to insist on more verifiable results in trade agreements with Japan, among other reasons, in order to avoid losing control on trade issues to the Congress; now Japan's trade bureaucrats jumped on the opportunity ostensibly to champion free trade because it enhanced their prospects of deferring further market openings and delaying regulatory reform.

Both President Clinton and Prime Minister Hosokawa took a stab at portraying the results of the February summit as indicating a more mature relationship by noting that Tokyo and Washington could now agree to disagree. Some Japanese journalists reported that, exhilarated by the experience of standing up to the president, Prime Minister Hosokawa was "giddy" on the plane going home. If so, he was no doubt encouraged by some of the economic nationalists in his entourage. Others expressed a more sober view. Takakazu Kuriyama, Japan's ambassador in Washington, reportedly observed that it was scarcely a sign of maturity simply to put forward a position, stick to it, and otherwise refuse to search seriously for ways of resolving the problem. I am not sure whether he was speaking about Japan or America, but in some respects his words applied, it seemed to me, to both.

Following the summit, the administration appeared to contemplate several alternative policy options. One was to make Japan pay for its obduracy through the application of sanctions. Telecommunications appeared a logical target. The deadline for reviewing progress in implementing a 1989 telecommunications agreement was fast approaching, and Motorola had legitimate complaints about the way its access to the Japanese cellular telephone market had been curtailed. A second possibility involved talking up the yen. This tactic presumed that Japan's business community and government, alarmed by the deleterious effects of a strong yen on its most efficient export industries, would press for additional measures to stimulate domestic demand and/or deregulate the economy. A third possibility was to generate more pressure and a new deadline for negotiations through a reinstatement of the Super 301 provision of the 1988 Trade Act. Finally, the administration could avoid definitive policy announcements, making clear that the next move was up to Japan, thereby leaving its own options open.

In the end, the administration seemed to pursue each of these options in a limited way. Evidence of discord on bilateral trade issues exerted upward pressure on the yen; the prospect of sanctions spawned an early understanding on telecommunications (some in the Japanese press described this as the price Japan had paid for saying no at the summit); the administration revived Super 301, but it did so by administrative fiat and left itself plenty of time to negotiate by setting the deadline on September 30, 1994. Beyond this, Washington appeared quite content to let the Japanese government worry about further, perhaps more drastic, steps.

Initially, the Japanese government sought to squeeze whatever political benefits it could from having stood up to Washington. It warned against any attempt to manipulate the exchange rate and intervened heavily to calm currency markets. It attempted to neutralize threats of sanctions by hinting at countersanctions and a readiness to file a formal complaint with GATT authorities if any of the measures Washington pursued appeared to contravene GATT obligations. In a more conciliatory vein, it signaled its intent to pull together a series of trade-related measures to present to Washington in the course of the spring. The G-7 summit scheduled for July 1994 provided one possible deadline for this, but the meeting came and went with no major breakthrough.

In the end, the U.S. and Japanese delegations negotiated right up to and through the September 30 Super 301 deadline. By this time, however, both capitals appeared to recognize that a prolonged stalemate on trade could further destabilize the currency markets. For Japan, this meant diminishing the competitiveness of its blue-chip export companies; for the United States, it meant more pressure on interest rates at home and increases in the cost of doing business in Japan. Some key players in the administration seemed prepared tacitly to acknowledge that they had lost the public relations battle over numerical targets.

As the Americans downplayed objective criteria, the Japanese offered further procedural concessions to facilitate agreements. The negotiations were finally wrapped up on October 12, 1994, with agreements to improve market access in the insurance sector and to establish more transparent and reasonable guidelines for public procurement of medical devices and other products. Each side had worn the other down. The results were greeted with relief rather than any sense of triumph.

Spurred by the prospect of yet another summit—this time a meeting between Prime Minister Murayama and President Clinton in Washington on January 11, 1995—other unfinished business was removed from the table. Accords were signed concerning glass and financial services, and talks on autos and auto parts were scheduled to resume.

The auto/auto parts issue proved to be more intractable than many knowledgeable observers had anticipated. The bargaining provoked belligerent talk from both sides, and the press commentary was laced with predictions of an imminent trade war. A deal was finally struck only after a Super 301 deadline (May 28, 1995) had elapsed, just one day before punitive sanctions—100 percent duties on virtually all Japanese luxury car imports—were scheduled to go into effect thirty days later.

The agreement was not necessarily a bad deal, but neither was it a big deal. It was laced with sufficient ambiguity for both governments to declare victory. The accord promised significant deregulation of the Japanese after-sales market for auto parts, and the Japanese government promised to encourage an increase in the numbers of auto dealers handling U.S. car exports. In addition, Japan's major car manufacturers announced voluntary plans to expand their production of autos in the United States by roughly 25 percent from 1995 to 1998 and to increase substantially the local content in their American-made products.

President Clinton hailed the agreement's results as important, specific, and measurable. The Japanese claimed success in concluding an agreement without promising numerical targets or surrendering to U.S. threats. Yet, as in the past, the Japanese made their conciliatory gestures at the last minute to avert sanctions, and the administration packaged vague promises as if they amounted to ironclad commitments. For example, at the press conference called to announce the accord, Mickey Kantor, the U.S. negotiator, indicated that the number of Japanese auto dealers handling American products would increase by two hundred in 1996 and by a thousand by the year 2000, while sales of U.S. parts to Japanese transplant factories in the United States would rise by an additional $6.5 billion by 1998. His counterpart, Ryutaro Hashimoto, however, disclaimed any Japanese government involvement in such estimates and managed to have this specific caveat included in the communiqué: "The two Ministers recognize and understand that the plans newly announced by the U.S. and Japanese companies are not commitments and are not subject to the trade remedy laws of either country."[1]

While Japan's formal commitments were modest, market forces reinforced by this agreement will hasten the expansion of Japanese auto production in the United States and auto parts purchases from U.S. suppliers. Having published their plans, the Japanese manufacturers will have a hard time backing away from them, whatever they may say about them being forecasts rather than commitments. Some Japanese commentators are already lamenting the further hollowing-out of Japanese industry. But Japan's auto manufacturers will increase their profitability by moving more production to the United States, since for them this country is a cheap-currency, low-wage, high-skill production site. Needless to add, their new investments in the United States will mean more jobs for Americans—and, coincidentally, more competition for Detroit.

It remains to be seen whether the Big Three are prepared to make the investments that are essential to establish genuine access to Japan's distribution system. Chrysler disclosed an earnest of its intent in that regard shortly after the auto accord was signed. It announced that it would purchase the Seibu Motor Sales dealer network for more than $100 million and planned to establish two hundred sales outlets by the end of 1996 and five hundred by the turn of the century—a hopeful sign that it is getting serious about the Japanese market.

Thus the framework negotiations that had started with a bang ended with a whimper. Unquestionably, the agreements reached on telecommunications, public procurement, insurance, glass, financial services, autos, and auto parts will bring benefits to U.S. exporters of goods and services and to Japanese consumers. The result may be laudable; the process was not. Distrust between the negotiators grew. Polit-

---

1. Andrew Pollack, "Agreement on Which Both Sides Disagree," *New York Times*, June 30, 1995, p. C5.

ical leaders on both sides evidently concluded that tough and aggressive tactics played well with nationalistic constituencies. The terms of the new GATT agreement did little to diminish the intensity of these bilateral negotiations. And it is noteworthy that during the two years it took to achieve these agreements, the U.S. bilateral deficit with Japan increased to its highest level ever.

Other Concerns

Trade was not, of course, the only bilateral policy concern. I noted that the Clinton administration's policy instincts toward both the Chinese and Russians were at cross-purposes with Tokyo's. With respect to Russia, the difficulties began with an indiscreet remark by President Clinton to President Yeltsin during the Vancouver summit in April 1993. Notes concerning the president's conversation with Yeltsin were left at a restaurant and found their way into the hands of the press. The Japanese consequently learned that President Clinton had reportedly warned the Russian leader that when the Japanese said yes to the United States, they often meant no, and it was very important that Yeltsin not allow the Japanese to behave the same way with him.

I learned of the incident first through a phone call from Warren Christopher, who explained the context of the president's remarks and asked that I relay the explanation to Vice Minister of Foreign Affairs Hisashi Owada. My call to him proved somewhat redundant, since by the time I was able to reach Owada, Secretary Christopher had already spoken with him. Owada was gracious, but I doubted that the explanation had been thoroughly convincing, since what prompted anxiety among the Japanese was less the words themselves than the clubby atmosphere in which an American president appeared to be coaching a former adversary on how to deal with a major Pacific ally. This concern was visible a few weeks later when Foreign Minister Kabun Muto commented to an audience of his Foreign Ministry officials, "With the cold war over, the U.S. and the Soviet Union have become the best of friends, and it seems to me that Japan is made out to be like a common enemy of theirs."[2] Muto, a politician who often said openly what was on others' minds, overstated the problem, but his remark accu-

2. Quoted in Ayako Doi, "Washington's Asia Policy: Fallout in Beijing," *Japan Digest* 5, no. 12 (March 28, 1994): 23.

rately reflected the sensitivity of the Japanese to hints of change in Washington's diplomatic orientation.

Prodded by encouragement from former president Nixon, moreover, the Clinton administration proved more forthcoming than its predecessor in proffering support to President Yeltsin, for whom the Japanese felt little empathy. While the Japanese government played along with U.S. and European efforts to mobilize additional financial support for Russia in the spring of 1993, they did so, I suspected, more to avoid being odd man out at the G-7 summit than from any belief in the efficacy of such aid. Meanwhile, they began to devote more attention to developing relationships with several central Asian republics that had seceded from the Soviet Union.

With the December 1993 parliamentary elections and Yeltsin's subsequent shift to the right on foreign policy matters, differences between Washington and Tokyo gradually diminished. In the United States, criticisms of the Clinton administration's Russian policy came increasingly to parallel those circulating in Tokyo (specifically, that there was too much attention paid to Yeltsin and too little to the other former Soviet republics). Meanwhile, the willingness of Congress to provide aid to Russia atrophied. Moscow's clout in East Asian affairs declined further. And Russia faded as a bone of contention in relations between Japan and the United States.

It likewise appeared that China policy might create new tension in the relations between Tokyo and the Clinton administration. I thought such fears were overdrawn, since the politics of China policy had changed in Washington. While the president had committed himself to a tough human rights posture toward Beijing during the campaign, he had no desire to alienate the Chinese or to undermine U.S. commercial interests in China. Nor did the Democratic majority in Congress wish to embarrass their president during his first months in office. Consequently, the problem was kicked down the road though an executive order issued in late May 1993 that extended most-favored-nation status to China until May 1994 but identified a number of specific human rights conditions that would have to be met for it to continue thereafter.

Naturally, the problem reappeared as that latter deadline approached. Although political as well as economic conditions in China were arguably improving, there was little visible progress on the specific conditions outlined in the executive order. Secretary of State

Christopher's high-visibility trip to Beijing in March 1994 highlighted the problem. Overt public pressure on what the proud and nationalistic Chinese considered domestic matters provoked Beijing to dig in its heels. Thus by the spring of 1994 the stage appeared set for an open confrontation that served neither nation's interests.

Japan urged moderation on both sides but took steps to distance itself from the U.S. policy. When Prime Minister Hosokawa visited Beijing a few weeks after Secretary Christopher's mission, he reportedly intimated to the Chinese that it was not wise for one country to try to impose its democratic values on another. If the Japanese were not seeking to exploit Beijing's difficulties with Washington, they were at the very least attempting to avoid complicating their own bilateral relationship with China by appearing to be too closely associated with this element of Washington's China policy.

At the same time, however, Tokyo's own relations with Beijing entered a new phase. Its determination to develop a strong relationship with China was increasingly accompanied by a growing disposition to express clearly Japanese misgivings about certain aspects of Beijing's conduct. As China's military budget grew and its capacity to project its power increased, nervousness spread among the Japanese. These anxieties were accentuated, no doubt, by awareness that Russia no longer tied down so many Chinese forces on its northern borders and by suspicions that the United States' readiness to shoulder Asian security burdens was gradually declining. Beijing's nuclear modernization efforts, manifested in renewed nuclear tests, also provoked outspoken expressions of Japanese concern. So, too, did China's attempts to reinforce the limits on Japan's unofficial dealings with Taiwan, efforts that resurfaced when Japan invited Taiwanese officials to attend the opening ceremonies of the Asian Games in Hiroshima in the fall of 1994. In this case, Chinese threats prompted Japanese officials to refer publicly to their 1991 aid guidelines, according to which they were to take into account recipient countries' records on defense expenditures, arms exports, and human rights in their decisions to allocate economic assistance. These were subtle hints that Tokyo would not roll over in the face of Chinese pressure. And Beijing's growing power reminded the Japanese anew of the continuing value to them of its alliance with the United States.

Much to the relief of the American business community and Asian governments, the Clinton administration officially delinked trade with

China from specific human rights conditions in May 1994. While China's modest gestures on human rights fell well short of the administration's hopes, Washington extended most-favored-nation treatment and chose to pursue its human rights interests without the annual threat of sanctions. Though other difficulties surfaced and Washington's relations with Beijing remained more correct than cordial, the United States and Japan both recognized a growing need to play the triangular diplomatic game with Beijing in a prudent manner.

Another issue on which subtle differences emerged related to the president's call for a Pacific Community and his attempts to hasten the institutionalization of APEC. The Japanese supported APEC, to the point of putting on hold their reaction to the East Asian Economic Caucus proposed by Prime Minister Mahatir bin Mohamad of Malaysia. President Clinton's call for a Pacific Community was greeted politely, if without notable enthusiasm, and Prime Minister Hosokawa readily accepted President Clinton's invitation to attend the Seattle leaders meeting, although he appeared rather aloof throughout the gathering. Japanese ambivalence toward the president's APEC initiative was quite apparent. On the one hand, they welcomed any sign of the United States' enduring engagement in the Pacific; on the other, some feared that Washington's activism might diminish Japanese opportunities for leadership in this regional enterprise and force Tokyo to make unpalatable choices.

The Japanese government continued to resist any formal endorsement of Prime Minister Mahatir's proposal for a more exclusive East Asian economic grouping. But the signs of growing interest were unmistakable. Prominent business groups such as Keidanren and Keizai Doyukai publicly signaled their support for Japanese participation in the EAEC. A Pacific study group hosted by Ministry of Finance officials and containing some of the most powerful Japanese political and business figures appeared to be moving in the same direction. During the ASEAN Regional Forum meetings held in Bangkok in July 1994, Foreign Minister Hata attended a luncheon meeting to which only the proposed members of the EAEC were invited. And with increasing frequency Japanese leaders seemed to dwell publicly on the differences between Asian and American values—a focus some regarded as an attempt to lay a subtle basis for Japan's efforts to carve out a leadership role in the Pacific.

While postponing a definitive endorsement of the EAEC, the Japanese moved to upgrade their bilateral contacts with Asians in the fields of security, finance, and trade; to accord a higher priority to their trade and investment flows in the region; to defend more assertively Japan's model of development in international financial institutions; and to identify more closely with those affirming the uniqueness of Asian values.

On some issues, to be sure, collaboration with Washington assumed greater urgency—the North Korean nuclear issue, for one. Successful acquisition by Pyongyang of a nuclear capability posed a security danger for Japan and raised a highly controversial issue for its political establishment. Pyongyang's intransigent rejection of full-scale international inspections and its threat to withdraw from the NPT lent urgency to collaboration among those most directly affected: Korea, Japan, China, and the United States. Any effective strategy would demand Japan's cooperation, not least because coercive sanctions against the North required the termination of remittances from Korean nationals living in Japan to their relatives in North Korea.

Japanese officials regularly reaffirmed their readiness to implement sanctions against the North if the UN Security Council mandated such measures. Yet Tokyo displayed little desire to follow through on that resolve. Political factors complicated the calculations of even those Japanese who were prepared to tackle this tough issue. For example, Ichiro Ozawa sought to induce key defections from the LDP in the spring of 1994 in order to establish a coalition that did not rely on support from the Socialists. The transparent motivation was to enable the Japanese government to support UN sanctions against Korea. The effort failed. The reformists' minority government fell, and an LDP-Socialist-Sakigake coalition took power. Some Japanese regarded former president Jimmy Carter as the midwife of this curious coalition, and in some respects they may have been right: Carter's trip to Pyongyang in late June 1994 took the steam out of Washington's move toward sanctions. This in turn allowed the LDP to contemplate a coalition with the Socialists without placing relations with Washington at risk over the Korean issue.

The dominant elements in Japanese politics still prefer to avoid a confrontation in Korea. Like the South Koreans and Chinese, they appeared worried about backing Pyongyang into a corner and favored a gradualist strategy that would defer sanctions as long as possible. Understandably, then, the Japanese government publicly welcomed the U.S.-North Korean agreement when it was concluded in October

1994 and agreed to join South Korea in subsidizing the cost of light water reactors to be supplied to Pyongyang. They clearly hoped that this agreement would also open the door to progress in their own normalization talks with the North.

More generally, bilateral security relations with Japan remained relatively smooth. This was facilitated by several factors. For one thing, the late Secretary of Defense Les Aspin announced early on that the United States contemplated no major adjustments in either the U.S.-Japan Security Treaty or in U.S. force levels in the Pacific. The administration also agreed to hold the first "two plus two" ministerial meeting on security with Japan, and Washington was increasingly receptive to a regional forum for discussing security issues in Asia; both countries recognized that they faced major uncertainties in Northeast Asia, against which the Security Treaty remained a valuable hedge.

These considerations notwithstanding, security ties were not trouble-free. The Clinton administration's initial proposals for collaboration on theater ballistic missile defenses encountered strong resistance from the Japanese bureaucracy and business community, which perceived the proposals as an American effort to secure access to commercial technology in return for defense cooperation. When the Sharp Corporation refused to give the Pentagon an advance peek at its leading-edge flat panel display technology or to make such panels to military specifications, the Defense Department responded by creating and financing a consortium of U.S. companies to develop comparable technology at home. As the pressures on Japan's defense budget intensified in 1994, the Japanese Defense Agency threatened to apportion reduced defense outlays in a way that would leave host nation support payments to the United States short of those promised in the 1991 Cost-Sharing Agreement. The Clinton administration's handling of crises in Somalia, Bosnia, and Haiti left many Japanese wondering whether Americans were still prepared to shoulder military enterprises entailing risks and possible casualties. And trade frictions generated mistrust and resentment that threatened to contaminate our security relations.

Happily, both capitals recognized a need to surmount such problems and to keep security relations on track. A study group was created to examine possibilities for collaborating on theater ballistic missile defenses. Progress was made in achieving more balanced exchanges of defense technology. Despite acute political pressures, the Japanese government fully funded its host nation support pledges. The blue-ribbon commission established by the Hosokawa government to reconsider defense policy issued a ringing endorsement of the U.S.-Japan alliance. And Secretary of Defense William Perry and Joseph Nye, his assistant secretary for international security, highlighted the need for more attention to U.S.-Japan security links. By the time of the Clinton-Murayama summit meeting in January 1995, a conscious effort was visible on both sides of the Pacific to devote more attention to security cooperation.

Thus by mid-1995 the U.S.-Japan relationship, despite numerous difficulties, remained vital to both countries. A number of modest trade agreements had been signed. A substantial measure of parallelism had been preserved in U.S.-Japanese policies toward Asian issues. The administration had reaffirmed U.S. support for Japan's bid for a permanent seat on the Security Council, differences had narrowed over international environmental issues, and the alliance had survived.

Yet the psychological underpinnings of the relationship were shaky. Politicians on both sides of the Pacific appeared absorbed in other matters. The fiftieth anniversary of the end of World War II threatened to rekindle unhappy memories of that conflict. Japanese and Americans alike concentrated more on the competitive than on the collaborative aspects of the relationship. And despite the continuing convergence of many national interests, few thoughtful Americans and Japanese could take the future of the bilateral relationship for granted.

7 | Whither Japan?

Prospects for future U.S.-Japan collaboration depend heavily on the directions in which Japan's economy and politics evolve over the next few years. Japan is not destined to look "more like us."[1] But powerful forces of change are visible, and both domestic and international pressures are propelling Japan toward acceptance of a more permeable market, more competitive politics, a more transparent regulatory system, a more cosmopolitan society, and a less U.S.-centered foreign policy. These forces are consequently altering Japan's competitive position in the world economy, its foreign policy priorities, its strategic options, and its attitudes toward its Asian neighbors and the United States.

A host of uncertainties remain: To what extent will structural adjustments in Japan's economy slow its growth and accelerate its internationalization? Will more competitive politics in Japan lead to greater direction of the bureaucracy by elected representatives of the people and hasten administration reform and economic deregulation? What kind of military power will Japan seek to develop in pursuit of a more active and ambitious diplomacy? Will Japan's growing interest in Asia alienate it from the United States? These are the questions this chapter attempts to answer.

1. The title of an interesting book about Japan and America by James Fallows, published by Houghton Mifflin in 1989.

Is the Sun Setting on the Japanese Economy?

The prolonged recession from which Japan is now emerging has temporarily shaken Japanese self-confidence, provoking renewed debate about its economic priorities and concealing elements of its residual strength. The protracted sluggishness of Japan's domestic economy, juxtaposed against the revival of the United States' fortunes, has reminded Americans that Japanese industrialists are not ten feet tall. Since 1991 Japan's economy has expanded at less than one-third the rate of the United States'. Its drive for the lead in many key technologies has temporarily stalled. Many investments made in the United States in the flush of Japan's success in the eighties are being liquidated at a considerable loss. The Tokyo stock market has lost more than half its value since 1989. And the reputation of Japan's economic bureaucracy for long-term strategic thinking has been damaged by its misjudgments regarding the seriousness of the current slump and its failure to find a means of escaping it. Meanwhile, South Korea, Taiwan, and other newly industrializing Asian economies are mounting an ever sterner challenge to Japan's superior manufacturing. The Japanese consequently feel squeezed, pressured simultaneously by the resilience of the USA's high-technology sector and the growing competitiveness of its East Asian neighbors. This is not exactly what Japanese officials and industrialists expected of the 1990s.

The Japanese economy has experienced its share of cyclical downturns in the postwar period. Yet with few exceptions, they fell into the category of "growth recessions," in which the GNP growth rate merely dipped down to 3 percent. This time, however, the recession met the technical requirements of U.S. economists (that is, two consecutive quarters of negative growth); it revealed structural as well as cyclical features; and it has proven uncommonly difficult to shake. Indeed, it has raised questions about the future efficacy of several notable features of Japan's brand of capitalism.

First, central elements of Japan's postwar management paradigm—for example, lifetime employment, seniority pay, cross-shareholding arrangements, and single-minded preoccupation with market share rather than profitability—have become heavy burdens on the cost structure of many Japanese companies (mainly large manufacturing firms). Readily affordable when the economy was growing 4 to 5 percent per year, as it did from 1970 to 1990, now, with growth stuck below 1 percent since 1991, they are regarded by some observers as costly luxuries that many firms can ill afford. The Japanese press is laced with reports about efforts to downsize local firms, experiment with merit pay packages, liquidate shares in *keiretsu* firms, and augment companies' profitability even at the expense of market share. Such anecdotal evidence of change tends to overstate the scope of the adjustments to date. In fact, while costs have been cut in many resourceful ways, few employees have been fired, and few firms have undergone American-style restructuring. Of course, Japanese-style reengineering doesn't mean firing people; it entails searching for other ways of boosting productivity. But Japan now faces a vicious cycle. Massive trade surpluses have augmented the strength of the yen, diminishing the profitability of Japan's premier exporters. This increases pressure on jobs and lowers consumer spending at home while stimulating even greater efforts to find markets abroad, which in turn strengthens the yen still more. Hence the longer slow growth persists in Japan, the greater the pressure will be to modify structural features of the Japanese system—if not through deliberate industrial restructuring, then through the side effects of yen appreciation.

Second, there are growing doubts about the future viability of the catch-up capitalism that enabled Japan to enter the front ranks of the world's industrial powers. The strategy was simple and effective. The Japanese monitored promising technological and product developments around the world and then figured out how to commercialize them faster, better, and cheaper than anyone else. Now that Japan is the world's preeminent manufacturer, at the cutting edge of many technological developments, however, the strategy is obsolescent. Some of Japan's Asian neighbors have become skillful players in the catch-up game, licensing Japanese or U.S. technology and emulating their manufacturing techniques. The test for Japan is whether it can provide comparable leadership in scientific research and technological innovation—whether it can establish the architectural standards for key technologies of the future.

To date, the performance of Japanese industry has been disappointing. Its computer makers followed IBM down the mainframe track, missing in the process the higher–value-added opportunities in work stations, peer-to-peer computing, and software. Tokyo's efforts to stall Motorola's entry into Japan's cellular telephone market was a backhanded tribute to the U.S. firm's lead in developing cellular telephony.

The Japanese government recently acknowledged that its industrial policy efforts to blaze the trail in HDTV research had come up short; American digital technology surpassed the performance of Japan's analog system. And Japanese companies are scrambling to find a niche for themselves in the lucrative market for multimedia products. These dispiriting setbacks have prompted anxiety among thoughtful Japanese that their educational system stifles originality and creativity and that their regulatory arrangements inhibit their country's ability to spin off the kinds of innovative and entrepreneurial start-up firms that flourish in the United States.

Third, the current recession has thrown into bold relief the disparity in prices between Japan and its overseas competitors. For decades, Japanese authorities have utilized a variety of means to discourage consumption—not least, by limiting imports of manufactured goods. This enabled Japanese manufacturers to run the high margins at home that were used to subsidize aggressive pricing abroad. As the yen has grown stronger, however, exports have become less profitable, and many Japanese firms need those higher domestic margins to cover shrinking profits or even losses in their export trade. This tends to make many firms even more reluctant to welcome foreign competition, even as it tempts them to utilize more imported materials and parts to cut costs.

As the yen has grown stronger, moreover, Japan's long-suffering consumers—plagued now by low wage settlements, meager bonuses, less overtime, and new uncertainties about job security—have become more attentive to these price differentials. Changes in the purchasing habits of consumers and the procurement policies of some companies have been among the results. This is evident in the proliferation of discount stores, the growing volume of catalog sales, and price deconstruction—the trendy term for declining prices—in the Japanese market.

The high yen is also prompting changes in the relations between Japanese manufacturers and their suppliers. Rising costs associated with the strong yen have forced most large firms to raise export prices, import more components, raise productivity, or move production facilities offshore. This increases the opportunities for foreign manufacturers to gain wider access to Japanese supply networks. Until recently, no Japanese automobile manufacturer purchased steel from non-Japanese sources. But reduced profit margins have forced both Mitsubishi and Honda to procure steel from Korea and to contemplate purchases from other foreign suppliers. Even a few leading politicians have begun advocating measures to reduce the huge disparity between prices in Japan and overseas. During his stint as prime minister, Tsutomu Hata proposed that Japan pursue a "real income doubling plan" by cutting prices in half rather than by doubling the GNP. The bureaucracy threw cold water on the plan, which also evoked a tepid response from the business community.

Fourth, looming demographic changes herald new burdens on Japan's public finances. Twenty-five years ago, citizens sixty-five years or older accounted for only 7 percent of the total population. In 1993 that figure was 13.5 percent; demographers expect it to rise to more than 17 percent by the year 2000 and to exceed 25 percent by 2020. That means that twenty-five years from now roughly a quarter of the Japanese people will be senior citizens, with more than 13 percent over 75 years of age. Thus Japan is rapidly becoming one of the world's oldest societies. Its ratio of retirees to workers is growing ever more extreme. It seems likely that this will reduce the size of Japan's labor force, retard its savings rate, and draw resources away from the manufacturing sector in order to permit heavier investments in health care, infrastructure, and various service industries.

These are formidable problems. They will challenge the resourcefulness of Japan's political establishment, its bureaucratic elite, its business community, and its citizenry. Yet these difficulties, however daunting, are scarcely harbingers of Japan's decline. The Japanese are never more purposeful than when coping with adversity. And in tackling such challenges, they possess many hidden strengths. Some of the problems, moreover, are exaggerated by both the Japanese and the U.S. press. A nation of worriers, the Japanese dwell on their shortcomings and play down their capabilities. Only an economy of unusual strength could amass a current account surplus of $127 billion in 1994. Japan's savings pool remains immense. According to a recent OECD report, Japan accounted for $819 billion in net national savings in 1993, or 56 percent of all new savings among OECD countries. The comparable figure for the USA was $75 billion, or 5 percent. In this context, it is not surprising that Japanese investments per worker exceeded those of U.S. companies by a factor of two or three.[2] Japan's currency is among the world's strongest. And it has a virtual

2. See Eamonn Fingleton, *Blindside* (New York: Houghton Mifflin, 1995), pp. 5–6.

monopoly on the production of a number of materials and components used widely in the manufacture of both consumer products and
industrial machinery.

The sun is not about to set on Japan's manufacturing sector; indeed,
in 1993 it surpassed the United States in total manufacturing output
for the first time. Japan's major exporters—Toyota, Hitachi, Canon,
NEC, etc.—have found ingenious ways of cutting costs and sustaining
competitiveness. Toyota, for example, reduced the number of models,
standardized the production of parts, and further increased the efficiency of the production process—without relinquishing its commitment to the central features of Japan's management system. The central
features of that system will survive, at least for now in the biggest manufacturing firms, because Japanese managers are still willing to pay a
high premium for social harmony, nonadversarial labor relations, and
cozy arrangements with *keiretsu* partners; moreover, most still believe
that their system provides them with substantial advantages over their
competition. Impressive arguments can certainly be mounted in
defense of that conviction.[3]

It is true that Japan's computer industry has not achieved the
global dominance its U.S. competitors feared only a few years ago.
And in some key technologies—such as microprocessors, software,
and the like—they are well behind leading U.S. firms. Yet Japan's
computer industry continues to run a sizable surplus in its balance of
trade with the world and with the United States. In the multimedia
field, Japan may still be scrambling for a strategy, but its catch-up
instincts are much in evidence, and in some niches—e.g., memory
and display technologies—it has established a commanding lead over
foreign rivals. If Japan's distribution system remains inefficient, it is,
nonetheless, Daiei and Yaohan rather than Walmart or Nordstroms
that are making impressive inroads into the Asian regional retailing
market. Japanese banks are struggling under a mountain of nonperforming loans, but their asset base remains huge, and the full faith
and credit of the Japanese government still stands behind them.
Japan's population may be aging, but that is not reflected in the
country's savings rate, which has begun to increase again, in response
to hard times and economic uncertainties. Japan can adapt to an
aging workforce by improving the status of women in the work-

3. See Fingleton, *Blindside*, particularly pp. 204–56.

place. Some sectors of Japan's economy are struggling, but both government and industry remain devoted to developing new industries for the future. A report published by MITI's Industrial Structure Council in mid-1994 identified twelve growth sectors for the twenty-first century: housing, health care, energy, information services, distribution, business consulting, new manufacturing technology, human resources, urban facilities, environment, leisure activities, and international travel and conferences. Coincidentally, if this MITI vision were effectively implemented, it could shift Japan's economy away from its current dependence on exports to a trading posture fueled more by domestic demand and more capable of absorbing a much larger share of imports from Asia, the U.S., and Europe than it currently does.

Beyond this, the Japanese continue to manage economic fundamentals extremely well. They save assiduously; their work ethic remains strong; they spend more for civilian research and development than any other country does; and they have weathered a prolonged downturn with modest unemployment and low inflation. Although younger Japanese may not share the single-minded devotion to their companies that was emblematic of the postwar generation, they remain highly educated, well motivated, and extremely competitive by any international standard.

Japan, moreover, has positioned itself better than anyone else in the East Asian regional economy. It consequently can expect a strong bounce out of the high growth in its neighborhood. The accelerated relocation of Japan's production facilities overseas is further hastening its integration into Asian markets. While reducing the export of many of Japan's consumer products, this is bolstering demand in Asia for Japanese capital goods, specialized components, and services. No wonder Japan's exports and investments in Asia are rising simultaneously. And many of the imports now finding their way into the Japanese market come from overseas affiliates of Japanese companies.

Finally, despite current problems caused by the recession and the Kobe earthquake, Japan's past fiscal prudence assures it a wider range of future policy options than virtually any other advanced country in the world can claim. We could not spend our way out of our recession in the early 1990s; the U.S. fiscal deficit deprived us of that alternative. Japan, however, is one of the few governments in the world that until recently regularly amassed sizable surpluses in its consolidated budget.

If it has been reluctant to stimulate domestic demand through tax cuts or massive public works spending, this reflects the policy convictions of Ministry of Finance officials rather than objective constraints on their policy options.

For these reasons, despite the daunting challenges it faces, Japan remains a formidably competitive economy, many of whose manufacturing industries will emerge from the current slump leaner and more efficient than ever. The key question for us is how rapidly the internationalization of Japan's economy will unfold. The process has been under way for decades, but its contours are changing. During much of the postwar period, trade was the engine of Japan's growth, and foreign direct investment was relatively modest: less than $4 billion in 1970. Japan imported raw materials, energy, and food while exporting finished products. And the United States was its dominant overseas market, accounting for nearly 40 percent of its exports as recently as 1989.

Today production facilities are being relocated abroad more rapidly, and Japan's direct foreign investments have increased dramatically—from $36.5 billion in 1980 to perhaps a cumulative total of $500 billion in 1995—as a result of a strong yen and the need to take advantage of cheap foreign labor and strengthen access to foreign markets. Manufactured goods like autos remain a staple export, but Japan's surpluses are now buoyed by overseas sales of office equipment, semiconductors, communications equipment, advanced materials, production machinery, and high-tech products of all kinds. Manufactured goods accounted for 56 percent of all imports in 1994—a sizable increase in the past five years. Moreover, while the percentage of Japan's exports to the United States has dropped to 30 percent, 40 percent are now directed to Asia.

Although the Japanese market has undeniably become more open to imports of industrial products, however, it continues to lag behind other major industrialized countries in its levels of intra-industry trade, openness to manufactured imports, and receptivity to foreign direct investment. Progress toward internationalization, moreover, has been slow in key service sectors, which remain highly insulated from international competition. Japan's administrative elite will continue to manage the public sectors and defend the underlying framework of the Japanese economic system, often at the expense of long-suffering consumers. This will continue to generate frictions with trading partners.

Two examples, supplied by Kenichi Ohmae, illustrate the persistence of these problems. The postal service—owned and operated by the government—charges roughly twice as much for postage as does its U.S. counterpart. Logically, the direct mail industry should seek low-cost alternatives to mailing from Japan; after all, Japanese marketing people could send direct mail advertising pieces to Japanese households far less expensively from the United States or Hong Kong than from anywhere in their own country. But the government has made it illegal for Japanese companies to mail such materials into Japan from abroad. The penchant for excessive regulation also results in a cost structure for Japan's airlines that is roughly twice as high as that of their major competitors—a principal reason they have been losing market share on international flights. To assuage the pain of high losses on its international routes, the government subsidizes JAL and ANA by allowing them to charge such extraordinarily high prices for domestic flights that it is now cheaper to fly round-trip from Tokyo to Chicago than between Tokyo and Okinawa.[4] Such examples are legion. They help explain both why public support for deregulation is growing and why it will not come overnight.

Some developments should have a positive effect on U.S.-Japan trade relations. With the volume of Japanese imports expanding, U.S. producers of products ranging from personal computers to apples, from semiconductors to cellular telephones, and from pharmaceuticals to financial services should be able to increase their sales and in some cases their market share in Japan. As Japan's economy revives and the United States' recovery slows down, the bilateral trade imbalance should again begin to recede. The continuing growth of service trade as a percentage of international trade should reinforce this tendency: U.S. firms are currently the world's most efficient producers of many services; Japan's are still at a comparative disadvantage in many service sectors—not least because, as noted, they have long been shielded from tough international competition. Trade tensions should also be tempered by the continuing proliferation of strategic alliances among American and Japanese companies.

Some of the informal barriers to foreign investment in Japan are likewise coming down. Property prices continue to decline. In a soft

4. See Kenichi Ohmae, "Letter from Japan," *Harvard Business Review* (May / June 1995): 154.

labor market, the difficulties of recruiting local staffs have eased. And with many small and medium-sized firms struggling for survival, opportunities for acquisitions and mergers should increase. A weak dollar, of course, raises the cost of doing business in Japan, and this is perhaps the reason why U.S. direct investment there, while up, has not kept pace with the opportunities currently available.

Yet one cannot count on a durable lull in trade tensions. The trade imbalance remains too large, and the limits on market access in Japan are still too great to warrant complacency. In Japan's brand of highly regulated capitalism, moreover, the government continues to control the terms of competition against new entrants to the market. And while the politicians perform what Bagehot termed the "ceremonial functions" of government, the bureaucracy continues to dominate the "efficient functions"—that is, they manage the economy, run the government, and generally call the tune. The question is, therefore, whether more competitive politics are in prospect, and, if so, whether this will help open the door to genuine administrative reform and a significant deregulation of the economy.

The Prospects for Political and Administrative Reform

On July 18, 1993, the Japanese voters turned the Liberal Democratic Party out of power for the first time since the party was established in 1955. It was ousted because repeated scandals had marred its image, a prolonged economic downturn had reduced public tolerance for LDP corruption, its leaders' complacency in the face of public demands for political reform fueled the rise of reformist parties, defections from within the LDP's ranks gave a reform coalition a majority of votes in the Lower House, and the end of the cold war made the Socialists a plausible coalition partner.

While the appearance in power of Morihiro Hosokawa's reform coalition was a pleasant surprise, it scarcely represented a radical break with the past. After all, the LDP had not exactly been repudiated. None of its incumbent leaders had been defeated, though a number had migrated to other parties. When the new reform coalition's cabinet was invested, the prime minister, foreign minister, finance minister, and MITI minister all turned out to be former LDP members with roots in the old Tanaka/Takeshita/Kanemaru machine.

Still, public and press enthusiasm for change was palpable. And the agenda the coalition proclaimed—reform of the electoral system, deregulation of the economy, greater priority to consumer interests, enhanced political discipline over the bureaucracy, and greater Japanese responsibility for international peacekeeping and the promotion of free trade—was genuinely progressive. It earned high approval ratings from the Japanese public and converged nicely with the United States' interests.

Despite strong public support, however, the coalition's rule was short-lived. Its only major legislative accomplishment—a potentially significant one, to be sure—was electoral reform. Japan's old multi-constituency election system, dating back to the 1920s, was altered to reduce the number of seats in the Lower House from 511 to 500 and to transform 60 percent of those seats into single-member district elections of a winner-take-all variety. The other 40 percent of the seats were to be determined by proportional representation based on lists of party representatives in eleven regional districts. Each voter now gets two votes: one for a candidate in his or her electoral district and another for the party of his or her choice.

By mid-summer 1994, Prime Minister Hosokawa had fallen victim to allegations of financial improprieties that had taken place before he became prime minister, and his successor, Tsutomu Hata, had succumbed to a parliamentary vote of no confidence. The Socialists and LDP—determined adversaries for a generation and the two principal losers in the 1993 election—forged a marriage of convenience to reclaim control of the government. They were joined in this coalition by the Sakigake Party, a reformist group that had defected from the LDP in 1993 under the leadership of Hiroshi Takemura. Although the LDP and the Socialists had been bitter political adversaries for decades, their views differed little on many of the trade and regulatory issues that were salient for the United States. And personal relations among some key leaders were surprisingly cordial.

A major political realignment is under way in Japan. But its future shape is far from clear. Some of the proponents of electoral reform hope that the new election rules will usher in competitive politics between two or three large, programmatic parties. At present, the competition is between two fragile coalitions composed of strange bedfellows. They are destined to undergo further transformation. Inherently unstable, the alliance between the Liberal Democrats and Socialists is unlikely to be a durable feature of the landscape, if only

because the Socialist Party, already weakened, appears destined to suffer further debilitating losses. The Socialists paid a high price for their
entry into a coalition with the LDP. They were obliged to cast aside
virtually all the cherished beliefs they had embraced throughout the
cold war—i.e., opposition to the U.S.-Japan alliance, rejection of the
constitutionality of the Self-Defense Forces, resistance to the development of civilian nuclear power, and antagonism toward the Re-
public of Korea. Thus, in return for the premiership, the Socialists
finally joined Japan's cold war political consensus, albeit long after the
cold war had ended. In the process, they alienated many of their loyal
supporters, virtually assuring additional splits in the party and a further erosion of voter support. This was apparent in the July 1995
Upper House elections, in which the Socialists retained less than half
of the forty-one seats they had previously controlled. Visible rifts have
also appeared within the reformists' ranks. These are inspired vari-
ously by antipathy toward Ichiro Ozawa, the architect of the 1993
reform coalition and the New Frontier Party (NFP); reservations about
the NFP's growing dependence on the political support of the Komeito Party and the financial backing of its religious arm, the Soka
Gakkai; and the temptation some anti-Ozawa members feel to rejoin
the LDP in order to regain the perquisites of power and forge a stable
governing majority.

The Murayama government, initially expected to survive only
briefly, has already been in power longer than the Hosokawa and Hata
cabinets that it replaced. Political reform efforts have stalled, at least
temporarily, and some commentators question whether the New
Frontier Party can legitimately claim the mantle of reform. The effort
to promote deregulation of the economy has lost momentum. Cyni-
cism about the prospects for change is again widespread. Some pundits even predict that the LDP will reestablish its majority in the Lower
House when the next elections are held.

Such an outcome is certainly possible but not in my judgment very
likely. When given the chance, Japanese voters have expressed growing
dissatisfaction with the political status quo, and a large floating vote
lends uncertainty and volatility to future elections. The LDP lost its
majority in the Upper House in 1989 and in the Lower House in 1993.
In recent Upper House elections, the opposition New Frontier Party
gained more new seats than did the LDP. And in April 1995 local elections, LDP-endorsed gubernatorial candidates in Tokyo and Osaka were

defeated by ex-comedians. As Nihon Keizai reported, "The voters said 'No' to the *dango* (collusive bidding) of politicians and bureaucrats. . . . It's clear that their judgment was based on disappointment with political parties that align themselves without regard to policy, and with a bureaucracy that stands accused of colluding with businessmen."[5]

It is also important to remember that the rules for Lower House elections have been changed, and until a few elections have been conducted, one can only speculate about the possible effects of that revision. Surely there will be some. At a minimum, representation of urban and suburban voters will increase, and those segments of the electorate have consistently exhibited greater sympathy for consumer interests and political and administrative reforms. Finally, the decline of the Socialist Party and the deep divisions among leaders of the formerly dominant Tanaka/Takeshita/Kanemaru faction in the LDP leave a potential political vacuum that will invite intensified political competition, the results of which are as yet unpredictable.

Greater competition can increase the quality of Japanese political leaders and improve their public standing. This is important because Japan's political system currently accords only limited influence to politicians. It is dominated by an iron triangle of senior officials, conservative politicians, and prominent industrialists. To oversimplify the dynamics of this arrangement, the politicians pass the laws that bureaucrats draft, the business community bankrolls politicians in return for their help in securing favors from the bureaucracy, and the administrative class manages the important business of governing the country. Reform movements have periodically surfaced with the ostensible aim of altering these arrangements and enhancing the power of the political class and those who vote them in or out of office. Few of these efforts have exerted a durable influence. Perhaps this reflects the preference of the Japanese people for strong central authority capable of managing controversy and ameliorating conflicts within the society. More likely, it is a tribute to the ascendancy of a bureaucratic leadership as determined to avoid direction from politicians as it is to prevent "confusion" in the marketplace. In this context, political reform must be regarded as a difficult uphill struggle against significant odds.

5. Quoted in Ayako Doi, "Big City Elections: A Vote Against the Mandarins," *Japan Digest* 6, no. 15 (April 17, 1995): 24.

Until Japan's political realignment takes clearer shape, however, the resulting confusion leaves control over public policy where it has traditionally rested—in the hands of the bureaucracy. The dominance of the bureaucracy is reinforced by a number of factors: the large number of ex-bureaucrats in the Diet; the *amakudari* system, through which retired officials run many of the country's private firms and public corporations; the politicians' dependence on the bureaucracy to draft laws that typically concede officials exceptional latitude in their interpretation; and—at least heretofore—an electoral system that breeds factionalism in the political parties, leaving them weakened in their struggle to hold the bureaucracy accountable.

Not that the bureaucracy is a monolith. On the contrary, sectionalism among and within ministries is as strong as ever. But without strong political leadership, disputes go unresolved, policy is marked by drift, and it is difficult to shake the status quo. Opening markets, deregulating the economy, devoting more attention to consumer interests, and shouldering larger international responsibilities are regularly affirmed as future aims by Japanese politicians, blue-ribbon commissions, and academic and journalistic commentators. But they are not the highest priorities of those elements of the Japanese bureaucracy that count the most. The Finance Ministry, secure in its position as primus inter pares among the ministries, drives policy through its control of budgetary and tax issues. And it has demonstrated scant interest in deviating from its well-established preference for economic nationalism, an austere budget, the suppression of domestic consumption, blank-check grants of rule-making authority, and a continuing drive to expand the nation's productivity. The administrative and institutional arrangements in Japan were designed to facilitate a disciplined national effort to catch up with and, if possible, surpass the West while minimizing foreign influence over Japan's economic and political system. Senior officials have not seen fit to modify that strategy fundamentally, and they appear reluctant to undertake any wholesale overhaul of Japan's political and administrative arrangements at a moment when international strategic, political, and economic uncertainties are multiplying.

Japan thus stands at an important turning point. Its government functions most efficiently when there is a consensus on objectives and their implementation can be left to a lean and effective bureaucracy. When new challenges arise, the government appears to temporize. Yet

Japan now faces a host of novel challenges. How should it reshape its economy to preserve its competitiveness while improving the welfare of its citizens? How should it define its new international responsibilities? How can it maintain its security in a post–cold war setting? Should it identify its international priorities essentially with the West or with its Asian neighbors? Must it choose? These are issues of identity and national purpose. They are quintessentially political in character. In a democratic society, they demand public debate. And for the debate to be meaningful, elected representatives of the society must be prepared to insist on bureaucratic compliance with authoritative expressions of the public's will. Political reform is incomplete without administrative reform; political accountability impossible without bureaucratic responsiveness. Hence, Japan faces a dual challenge: to define new purposes through a more competitive political process, and to subject its bureaucratic establishment to greater political direction.[6]

If the new election system does yield more competitive politics between more programmatic parties—and this remains a big if—issues that in the past were resolved in backroom negotiations among LDP faction leaders and senior bureaucrats should be pushed out into the open where they can be publicly debated. While neither the LDP nor the New Frontier Party possesses strong ideological and programmatic tendencies, they do appear, broadly speaking, to represent differing inclinations on the issues of greatest moment to Japan. The LDP is more committed to the status quo at home and possesses more nationalistic reflexes on foreign policy; the New Frontier Party appears more favorably disposed to deregulation of the domestic economy and an expansion of Japan's international responsibilities. If parties with differing platforms alternate in power, over time pressure to enhance bureaucratic responsiveness to political direction should increase. Hints of this were visible in 1993, when the Hosokawa government purged a senior MITI official who was perceived as being too closely affiliated with the LDP. But a genuine realignment of Japanese politics will take time, and the emergence of a simpler and more competitive party system is by no means foreordained. Nor, certainly, is the politicians' ability to subject proud bureaucracies to political direction.

Failure to achieve more competitive politics certainly will delay pos-

---

6. These are the leitmotifs in Ichiro Ozawa's book, *A New Blueprint for Japan's Future* (Tokyo: Kodansha International, 1994).

sibilities for genuine administrative reform, in which Japan's trading partners have a huge stake. To be sure, important interests call with growing frequency for administrative reform. The business federations regularly advise it; political leaders routinely acknowledge its necessity; the Murayama cabinet promised a comprehensive five-year program of regulatory reform; and the press has appointed itself cheerleader and watchdog. To date, however, the results have been meager. The reasons are clear. The business community's support for deregulation is soft— long on generalities, equivocal on specifics. Few political leaders have offered more than ritualistic support, since it is within the interstices of an extensive and opaque regulatory system that Japanese politicians are able to extract rents in return for favors to constituents. A few individuals who have publicized the stultifying effects of the current administrative arrangements have achieved notoriety, but their complaints have as yet brought little tangible change.[7] The most consequential resistance comes predictably from the bureaucracy, and that resistance is intense. Administrative reform is a direct assault on the source of the bureaucracy's power. Heretofore, senior officials have successfully eviscerated every reform effort, reducing ambitious proposals to meaningless gestures. And they appear determined to continue doing so.

Some deregulation, to be sure, is inevitable; indeed, modest steps have already been taken. But efforts are unlikely to attain significant momentum until those who manage the economy are persuaded that the current regulatory system—which tends to prohibit anything not expressly authorized—is eroding Japan's competitiveness. It is noteworthy that the Maekawa Report, issued in 1986, urged deregulation principally in order to mollify foreign trading partners and to harmonize Japan's practices with the international community. The bureaucracy ignored most of its central recomendations. Today deregulation is being suggested in order to lower prices, stimulate investment, eliminate restrictions on business activities, boost productivity, and relieve relentless upward pressure on the yen—all more politically compelling justifications. But pending either political reform or unexpected displays of bureaucratic self-abnegation, progress toward significant administrative reform appears likely to remain slow. Under these cir-

7. Masao Miyamoto's book *The Straitjacket Society* (Tokyo: Kodansha International, 1994) provides much anecdotal evidence of the perverse consequences of excessive regulation. Miyamoto has received impressive publicity and lucrative book contracts but was recently fired by the Health and Welfare Ministry.

cumstances, dramatic initiatives in the field of defense and foreign policy are also unlikely. Heightened nationalism provides a defense against foreign pressure for trade concessions. And weak political leadership and bureaucratic sectionalism reinforce minimalism as the watchword of foreign and security policy.

Will Japan Become a Major Military Power?

Since the Meiji Restoration, Japan has viewed its neighbors as rivals—militarily powerful and potentially antagonistic. Today Tokyo again has reason to regard its neighbors warily. North Korea has recently advertised its nuclear ambitions; nationalism is again on the rise in Russia; China's assertiveness on certain territorial issues (e.g., the Spratly Islands) has increased, against the backdrop of an ambitious program of military modernization. Meanwhile, some Japanese question the reliability and durability of the U.S. strategic guarantee under post–cold war conditions. It is scarcely surprising, therefore, that many wonder whether Japan will make a bid for major military power status in the years to come.

In fact, Japan's military power is already significant, and its military potential has reached a level that no Asian nation can ignore. Its defense budget is the third largest in the world. It has acquired frontline equipment of impressive technical sophistication The strength of Japan's economy and its impressive technical and human resources assure it a formidable military mobilization base. Few doubt Tokyo's ability swiftly to acquire nuclear capabilities, if provoked. And its advanced space program would enable it to field ballistic missile delivery systems of intercontinental range in short order.

Japan's military capabilities and its readiness to utilize them have gradually expanded in recent years. Since the mid-1980s Tokyo has extended its naval defense perimeter a thousand miles to the south of Tokyo. On three occasions since 1992 it has dispatched Self-Defense Force units abroad in support of UN peacekeeping or disaster relief operations. In 1994 an advisory group on security policy commissioned by Prime Minister Hosokawa recommended that Japan augment its intelligence gathering through the deployment of satellites and develop stronger logistic support for its UN peacekeeping activities. Press reports in mid-1995 suggest that the Japanese navy plans to acquire within the next three or four years four flat-deck 8,900-ton amphibious landing ships that could be converted into mini–flat tops capable of carrying Harrier jump jets.[8]

Postwar constraints on defense activities have gradually weakened in Japan. Politicians now speak more openly about Japan's national interests. Proposals to revise the constitution enjoy resonance among some prominent politicians within the government and the opposition; the *Yomiuri Shinbun*, Japan's most widely read daily newspaper, even published a proposed draft. Socialist opposition to Japan's defense programs has softened. Press reports openly acknowledge that the Japanese government explored the efficacy of a nuclear option at the time of Eisaku Sato's government in the late 1960s. (The report resulting from this analysis apparently concluded that Japan possessed the technical capacity to acquire nuclear weapons but that any effort to develop them would be strategically and politically counterproductive.) And some conservatives who express a desire to see Japan become once again what they term an ordinary country presumably wish to see a fuller development of Japan's defense capabilities. (There are exceptions, notably Ichiro Ozawa, whose book, *A New Blueprint for Japan's Future*, argues that extension of Japan's defense capabilities should be limited to supporting peacekeeping operations authorized by the United Nations.)

Interpreting this gradual expansion of Japan's defense capabilities and guidelines in the light of its mercantilist tradition, its past quest for regional preeminence, the highly competitive nature of its society, its acute consciousness of rank and status, and the bias of Japanese institutions in favor of state interests rather than individual welfare, some observers argue that the disparity between Japan's economic power and its military status will inevitably narrow. Yet powerful constraints on Japan's defense efforts remain in place, and its leading politicians certainly understand the high costs and adverse consequences any major Japanese military buildup would stimulate in the absence of a clear, palpable, and unprovoked threat to Japan's security. There is still substantial support in Japan for an international role as a "global civilian power"— an extension in a slightly different form of its long-established Yoshida line. Pacifism continues to run deep in Japan's mass culture.

As a trading nation, Japan has made use of export-led growth. It has supplemented its export capabilities by recycling its immense trade

8. See *Japan Digest* 6, no. 23 (June 19, 1995): 12.

surpluses through heavy investments throughout the world. Protection of its commercial interests requires peace and the confidence of its trading partners. Both could be jeopardized by a major military buildup. In addition, at a time when Japan faces stern economic competition from both advanced and developing countries, diverting financial resources and engineering and scientific talent from the civilian into the defense sector would impose unwelcome burdens on the competitiveness of Japanese firms. And while Japan's overseas investments are a considerable asset in times of peace, when conflicts threaten they provide potential hostages to foreign interests.

Constitutional and political inhibitions against a Japanese quest for major military power remain strong. Indeed Prime Minister Murayama was reluctant to utilize Self-Defense Forces even for disaster relief during the Kobe earthquake. In the political realignment currently under way in Japan, dovish elements are distributed broadly within both the governing and opposition coalitions. The Japanese public displays little interest in revising or eliminating constitutional impediments to an expanded security role in the world. And budgetary constraints on the Defense Agency budget remain tight.

The Japanese fully understand the high costs a military buildup would impose on their relations with Asian neighbors. Japan has just begun to overcome the legacy of its colonial and wartime conduct in Korea, China, and Southeast Asia. A significant enlargement of its defense capabilities—particularly if accompanied by friction in its relationship with the United States—would reawaken fears among its neighbors and complicate Japanese efforts to carve out a stronger leadership position in Asia. Japan's geographic limitations and its resource deficiencies make it unlikely that it could become a strategic superpower—a nation able and willing to extend protection to others.[9] Hence any rapid expansion of Japan's military power would be more likely to be perceived by neighbors as a threat than as a source of reassurance.

None of these considerations guarantees that Japan will indefinitely forgo the acquisition of power projection capabilities, a nuclear deterrent, arms exports, or the assumption of overseas military responsibil-

9. For elaboration of this point, see Michael M. May, "Japan as a Superpower?" *International Security* 18, no. 3 (winter 1993/94): 82–187.

ities outside the framework of UN peacekeeping. But they do make any of these developments unlikely in the absence of a decisive rupture of the U.S.-Japan alliance. Just as the termination of Japan's alliance with the United Kingdom set Japan adrift after World War I, an end to the U.S.-Japan Treaty of Mutual Cooperation and Security would unhinge the moorings of Japan's contemporary diplomatic and security policy. Thus the United States' reputation as a reliable ally remains perhaps the most significant inhibition to Japan's incentive to seek strategic autonomy.

Coincidentally, it appears unlikely that Japan would throw its technological weight around by withholding components of U.S. defense systems. It did not do so during the Gulf war, and I doubt that it will. While the Sharp Corporation recently refused to manufacture leading-edge liquid crystal display technology to U.S. military specifications, its motivations were principally commercial, and the Defense Department responded by extending subsidies to potential domestic suppliers. If the Japanese government encouraged its companies to withhold technical support or critical supplies from the United States, its reputation as a reliable commercial partner and security ally would be irreparably damaged. And it would quickly discover that it suffers substantial disadvantages in such a game. The long–lead-time items in defense production are systems integration capabilities and an R-and-D base. In both fields, U.S. superiority is clear, and the lead times would give us ample opportunities to overcome deficiencies in other aspects of our defense industrial base.

The force of inertia, as well as a clear-eyed appraisal of its interests, will likely impel Japan to continue to rely on the alliance, and Tokyo clearly has welcomed recent signs that the Clinton administration seeks to reinforce the bilateral security relationship. Yet the juxtaposition of a huge economic base and immense technological power with extraordinary dependence on the United States remains something of an anomaly. Moreover, the brutal rape of a Japanese teenager by U.S. servicemen in Okinawa in October 1995 provoked an emotional nationalist reaction. Several members of the Diet called for the reduction or elimination of the American military presence, and the incident exposed the reluctance of a weak coalition government to publicly defend the alliance. This may further reinforce a visible tendency among the Japanese to question the future efficacy of the alliance at a time when the USA appears to be turning inward and defining its security interests with greater circumspection and less generosity. They have observed the sharper edge to our trade negotiations and the growing intensity of bilateral commercial competition. In Somalia and Bosnia, they witnessed the speed with which the United States appeared to retreat from security duties in the face of high risks and a few casualties. As Japan's obligations to provide financial support to our forward-deployed units grows, moreover, it may judge that the costs of our guarantee are going up as its value recedes. And as the Japanese continue to place the building blocks for strategic independence in place—through, for example, the growth of their space program, their civil nuclear effort, and their aviation and aeronautics industry—the marginal costs of a strategic breakout will gradually decline.

In strategic terms, the Japanese have three broad alternatives. First, they can stick with established policy—reliance on the U.S. alliance—while continuing to improve the quality and capabilities of the Self-Defense Forces, with particular emphasis on guided missiles, telecommunications, aeronautics, and remote-controlled observation systems; extending their participation in UN peacekeeping activities; and taking an active part in developing the ASEAN regional forum and its security dialogue.

Second, they could seek to align themselves with another major power. At present this scarcely appears realistic. An alignment with Russia could theoretically offer Japan relief from its dependence on the United States, access to resources in Siberia, and a possible means of recovering the Northern Territories. For Russia, close links with Japan could bring desperately needed financial help. But apart from the fact that Russians and Japanese have scant empathy for one another, the risks for both far exceed any potential benefits. The U.S. and Chinese markets are worth much more to Japan than Russia's; Tokyo can achieve access to Siberian resources without a security connection to Moscow; and a Japanese alignment with Russia could provoke a counteralignment between Japan's main potential rival at sea (the United States) and Russia's principal potential rival on land (China). A Sino-Japanese alignment is more plausible, though still remote. For China, Japan offers an attractive source of aid, investment, and technology; it provides China with a possible source of leverage on U.S. policy; and its market is a genuine magnet. For Japan, close ties with Beijing are useful in Tokyo's relations both with Russia and the United States and central to its efforts to carve out a larger regional role. Nonetheless, a security connection between these two Asian giants is counterintuitive, except in the context of a threat that Russia no longer poses and the United States will not provide. Without such a pretext, a Sino-Japanese alliance would serve no obvious purpose; it would alarm Japan's neighbors while inviting U.S. enmity.

Third, they can embark on an independent strategic course that would imply a readiness to give up the alliance with the United States and perhaps acquire nuclear weapons. This would relieve Japan of its dependence on the United States and provide it with the muscle to support an autonomous diplomacy, satisfy some Japanese ultranationalists, and supply new business to Japan's defense industry.

Pursuit of the first option appears the most likely course of action for the Japanese. It allows Japan to temporize, avoiding—or, at a minimum, deferring—a more drastic alternative. It avoids the costs associated with a strategic breakout while reminding others of Japan's capacity for greater military independence, should its interests be ignored. As Japan's capabilities gradually increase, of course, uncertainties about its future intentions may grow. And in a climate of uncertainty, the possibilities for miscalculation would increase on all sides. Singapore's former prime minister, Lee Kwan Yew, recently reminded the Japanese of the risks of its own miscalculations, noting that it "risks serious deterioration in [its] bilateral relations with the U.S. if it persists with its current [mercantilist] practices. . . . So Japan must weigh its trading interests against its need for an indispensable U.S. counterweight to a China growing in weight and influence, and a Russia which is still well-armed but unstable."[10] For the foreseeable future, expectations of strategic rivalry, let alone renewed military conflict, between Washington and Tokyo, are more the grist of fanciful novels[11] than compelling analysis.

Japan Between East and West

For more than a century, Japan has been poised uneasily between its Asian roots and the aspiration to transcend its Asian identity. At the G-7 summit in Williamsburg, Virginia, in 1983, Prime Minister

10. "Japan Must Open Market Before Taking Leadership," *Nikkei Weekly*, July 3, 1995, p. 15.
11. See, for example, Tom Clancy, *Debt of Honor* (New York: Doubleday, 1994).

Yasuhiro Nakasone proclaimed Japan a member of the West. Yet many Japanese feel they do not fit comfortably within the Western camp. And Washington's occasional talk about a constellation of countries "from Vancouver to Vladivostok" prompts questions as to whether they are welcome. Among Asians, Japan is widely respected for its remarkable postwar economic record. Its aid, its investments, its exports, and its technology are welcomed by all. Its model of catch-up capitalism is widely emulated. Its popular culture has begun to elicit growing interest among its neighbors. And many prominent Japanese are currently calling for the "re-Asianization" of Japan's foreign policy.

Many Asians, however, remain ambivalent about Japan. Its economy accounts for nearly two-thirds of Asia's gross product; hence its strength inevitably provokes some fears of domination and exploitation. Many are uncomfortable with Japan's preferred "flying geese" model of regional development, for it seems to assign them a position of permanent subordination to Tokyo's lead. There are contradictions, moreover, in Japan's active promotion of export-led growth and its reluctance to absorb a much larger share of Asia's manufactured products. Uncertainties persist as to how a more powerful Japan might define its regional objectives. And the past casts a lingering shadow over Tokyo's relations with its neighbors—particularly Korea and China.

Japan's Nobel prize–winning author, Kenzaburo Oe, has underlined the continuing salience of Japan's need to come to terms with its past. "For the Japanese to be able to regard twenty-first century Asia not as a new economic power rivaling the West but as a region in which Japan can be a true partner, they must first establish a basis that would enable them to criticize their neighbors and be criticized in turn. For this, Japan must apologize for its aggression and offer compensation. This is the basic condition, and most Japanese with a good conscience have been for it. But a coalition of conservative parties, bureaucrats and business leaders opposes it."[12] Failure to face these issues squarely leaves Japan's postwar reconciliation with its neighbors incomplete and younger Japanese ill-informed.

In fact, younger Japanese should increasingly be able to address these issues with greater detachment and less anguish. And however

12. Kenzaburo Oe, "Denying History," *New York Times Magazine*, July 2, 1995, pp. 28–29.

reticent conservative bureaucrats and politicians may be about coming to terms with Japan's historical responsibility in these matters, they no longer monopolize the information available to the Japanese public. The international media sees to that. Several years ago, for example, a teacher in a Japanese school in Singapore made a documentary about Japan's 1941 invasion of Singapore in order that his students might better understand local attitudes toward Japan. The documentary was straightforward and evidently graphic. Its effect on the students was reportedly profound. Once this story broke in the Singapore press, it created a media stir back in Japan, sparking press commentary for weeks. When accusations that Japan had officially recruited Koreans and other Asians to serve as "comfort women" for Japanese soldiers, the designated government spokesperson denied official complicity. The denial did not stand up to careful scrutiny, and the ensuing media coverage exposed many activities that had long been ignored in Japan's public discussion of wartime events. The fiftieth anniversary of Pearl Harbor likewise brought documentaries produced at home and abroad that received wide exposure and further illuminated dark corners of the past. Japanese textbooks are beginning to acknowledge colonial and wartime misdeeds more candidly, and the fiftieth anniversary of the war's end has added further detail. So will the widespread availability of CD-ROMs providing data on this period from a rich diversity of international sources. Thus in Japan as in other countries the information revolution is eroding the capacity of officials to control public perceptions of historical events.

Prime ministers Hosokawa, Hata, and Murayama have expressed more forthrightly, more sincerely, and more spontaneously than any of their predecessors official regrets for Japanese conduct in the 1930s and 1940s. But when Prime Minister Murayama recently staked much political capital on securing a Diet resolution expressing Japan's remorse for its prewar and wartime conduct, determined opposition from conservative politicians and veterans' groups resulted in watered-down language that forfeited any goodwill the resolution might have engendered abroad. Even then, the resolution had to be rammed through the Diet in the face of a boycott of seventy LDP members and all the main opposition delegates. And this sorry episode came on the heels of the late former foreign minister Michio Watanabe's public assertion that Japan had "amicably" taken over control of the Korean peninsula in 1910—a statement that South Korea's Prime Minister Lee

Hong Koo denounced as absurd and for which Watanabe was compelled to apologize.

Needless to add, time heals old wounds. And these memories are more vivid in the minds of Koreans and Chinese than those of Malaysians, Indonesians, and Thai. Indeed, during a recent visit by Prime Minister Murayama to Kuala Lumpur, the Malaysian prime minister chided him for worrying so much about the past and urged him to assert stronger leadership in Asia.

In some respects, Japan is well positioned to do so. Its consumer products are universally admired and widely imitated. Its capital goods now fill Asia's booming factories. Its official development assistance dwarfs that of the United States and all other donors, and its support for infrastructure projects has been shrewdly designed to generate commercial opportunities that are eagerly exploited by Japanese companies. Its commercial loans and technology transfers represent significant sources of leverage. Its communitarian values are compatible with Asian inclinations. So are its pragmatic approach to government–private sector cooperation and its industrial policy tradition. And the strong yen, by accelerating the relocation of many Japanese production facilities into neighboring Asian markets, is hastening Japan's integration into the regional economy. Already it has outpaced our own. And pressure is growing to denominate more of Asia's trade in yen and to utilize it as an international reserve currency.

Nor has Japan neglected to solidify its position within the Asian community. For some years it has spoken for Asian interests within the G-7 and other international fora. It has carved out a substantial role in regional institutions. It has encouraged industrial policies for the ASEAN countries that harmonize with its own industrial plans. It is cultivating closer bilateral links with its neighbors in every field. It has opened its universities to large numbers of Asian students. And its officials have invited innumerable Asian counterparts to Japan to participate in courses on development challenges, industrial policies, and financial issues.

Foreign direct investment constitutes a principal instrument of Japan's strategy in Asia. Through 1994 Japan's cumulative direct investment in Asia came to $64 billion—two-and-a-half times the estimated American total. Its need to recycle a massive trade surplus and the effects of a high yen on the cost structure of many Japanese industries have fueled the outflow of funds, not only from Japanese multinationals but also from small and medium-sized enterprises that throughout the region provide components and parts for Japanese multinationals as well as for local manufacturers. This investment affords broad segments of Japan's industry access to growing overseas markets while keeping their cost structures competitive internationally.

Some see in this external migration of Japanese capital a sinister plot to integrate the Asian economy under Japan's leadership. Undoubtedly one could find senior Japanese officials, prominent politicians, and business leaders in Tokyo who harbor such ambitions. But corporate investment decisions are driven principally by commercial considerations. Of course, as Japanese investments in the region grow, so in general will the influence of the Japanese government. When it talks, Asians certainly listen. But they will not blindly follow Tokyo's lead. Like developing nations everywhere, the industrializing countries of Asia are sensitive about their sovereign prerogatives. They are determined to increase the local content of foreign subsidiaries operating within their borders. They drive increasingly tough bargains over the transfer of technology and the inclusion of local nationals in the management structures of foreign firms. Japan's overseas investments also constitute hostages to Asian demands for wider access to Japan's market.

Fears of Japan's domination of the Asian regional economy are likely to prove no more prophetic than Jean-Jacques Servan-Schreiber's apprehensions in the mid-1960s about Europe's domination by U.S. multinationals.[13] While Japan is creating a formidable production network in Asia, it is not alone. The nexus between China and the overseas Chinese community in Southeast Asia provides one counterweight; U.S. and European multinationals supply another. Most important, however, is the fact that most Asian countries are financing their growth principally through high rates of internal savings. As their economies prosper, they are becoming major foreign investors in their own right. As always, competition—among investors and exporters—provides the principal check against any nation's ability to establish dominion. This unquestionably accounts for the evident desire of Southeast Asian countries to see U.S. investment levels and commercial activity in the area increase. And we have a comparable interest in ensuring that our companies participate fully in the burgeoning prosperity of Asia.

Ironically, if some Asians worry about the weight of Japan's economic influence, many Japanese now betray apprehensions that they have missed their moment in the sun. While they have been mired in recession, the world's attention has been seized by China's relentless industrial advance, even as Korea, Taiwan, Singapore, Hong Kong, and others have been chipping away at Japan's competitive edge in fields ranging from semiconductor manufacturing to high finance. Other Japanese worry that the United States will bypass them in Asia. Recalling that the USA's relations have rarely been simultaneously good with both Japan and China, some fear current trade frictions between Washington and Tokyo may tip the balance of U.S. interest toward Beijing, whose large and rapidly growing market exerts a magnetic attraction on many American multinationals. Worries that Japan's market is losing its allure are reinforced by the exodus of many U.S. firms from the Tokyo Stock Exchange in favor of cheaper and less heavily regulated financial centers in Hong Kong and Singapore. And many other U.S. companies are seeking to develop corporate strategies for Asia that work around Japan's high-cost, high-regulation market in favor of lower risks and higher returns elsewhere. At a time when transportation routes all over Asia are expanding rapidly, domestic constraints on Japan's ability to extend its airport runways and reduce costly fares and handling services have diminished Tokyo's chances of becoming the major regional transportation hub. And regulatory excesses pose obstacles to Nippon Telegraph and Telephone and private Japanese telecommunications companies in their quest for a decisive role in this key industry in Asia's future.

Despite these concerns, or perhaps because of them, Japan is devoting more and more attention to its interests in Asia. This is understandable. Security concerns about other major powers have temporarily diminished. The center of gravity in the global economy continues to shift toward the Pacific. Asia provides an arena in which Tokyo can exert more visible leadership and a natural constituency for its efforts to play a wider global role. Interest among Asians in Japan's experience is high. And trade frictions with Washington have stimulated nationalist reactions in Japan that encourage its government to stake out more independent policies in its own backyard.

Yet the Japanese will seek, if at all possible, to avoid a choice between its Asian neighbors and its American ally. Tokyo's stake in the North American market remains immense; more than a quarter of its exports still wind up in the United States, and the percentage is larger if one adds the sales of its foreign affiliates. More and more of its companies are tied through strategic alliances to U.S. firms. Japan's hopes for a permanent seat on the Security Council require the USA's assent. In addition, Tokyo's relations with its neighbors would be complicated by a withering of its defense cooperation with Washington. And the alliance with the United States represents a valuable form of insurance at a time when the regional security environment remains fraught with uncertainties. It is therefore not surprising that many Japanese remain attached to the image of Japan as a bridge between East and West. It is a comforting metaphor. Certainly, it is easier to be a bridge than a broker.

But asserting leadership requires balancing interests, imposing priorities, and shouldering risks. It demands the use of political capital rather than merely its accumulation. And it will require a further opening of Japan—to foreign products, to foreign capital, to foreign students, to foreign ideas, and even perhaps to foreign immigrants. Ironically, then, Japan's hopes of retaining its alliance with the United States and exerting greater leadership in Asia may compel it to accelerate the reform of its political system and the opening of its market. In the post–cold war era Japan cannot expect Asians fully to exploit the potential of Japanese-style export-led growth unless Tokyo provides a more substantial market for Asia's exports. Nor can it expect Washington's support for its security if it exhibits insensitivity to U.S. interests in Asia.

8

The Challenge for America

The United States and Japan remain mutually dependent on each other. Yet neither government expects as much from the bilateral relationship as it once did. This chapter explores the adjustments in the terms of interdependence that have resulted from changes in the global strategic balance, the world economy, and domestic politics in both countries. It concludes by suggesting a variety of actions the United States should take in order to assure that the relationship with Japan continues to serve our interests in the future.

The Changing Terms of Interdependence

The end of the cold war undermined the central trade-off that marked the relationship between Tokyo and Washington from the early 1950s to the late 1980s—i.e., U.S. indulgence of Japan's mercantilist trade policy in return for Japan's acquiescence in the United States' cold war strategic leadership. With the easing of East-West tensions, Washington has concentrated on reestablishing the industrial and financial underpinnings needed for a global leadership role, while Japan has focused on increasing its diplomatic autonomy. Each acknowledges the continuing utility of the alliance, but neither is willing to sacrifice as much as it once did to preserve it.

The terms of our mutual dependence have altered in complex

ways. In the security field both the United States and Japan enjoy wider diplomatic flexibility in the absence of an immediate Soviet or Russian threat. Objectively, however, Washington has regained greater maneuverability. The United States is the world's sole remaining military superpower. It continues to value its defense cooperation with Tokyo, but it can defend itself with or without the alliance with Japan against all plausible military contingencies that directly threaten it. Japan, on the other hand, has developed key building blocks for strategic independence but remains reluctant to pursue that path. Its alliance with the United States continues to be a valuable means of bolstering its security, reassuring its Asian neighbors, hedging against an ascendant China, and avoiding a divisive domestic debate about its strategic alternatives.

In the economic sphere, the picture is more complicated. Both Washington and Tokyo have attempted to fortify their economic self-reliance, yet each remains extremely dependent on the other. The United States belatedly has taken some serious steps to reduce its fiscal deficit; its manufacturing firms have undergone painful but beneficial restructuring; it has forged a stronger North American economic base through the ratification of NAFTA; a more proactive governmental export promotion effort has been targeted at the so-called big emerging markets in Latin America and Asia; and it depends less than it did five years ago on Japan's purchases of U.S. government securities to finance its debt. Though we continue to run a large deficit, its size as a percentage of GDP is now considerably smaller than it was in 1989.

Nor are we as reliant as we were on Japanese foreign direct investment to create jobs and spur growth. A significant portion of the funds Japanese financial institutions invested in U.S. real estate and equities in the late 1980s and early 1990s are being repatriated to fortify the balance sheets of troubled banks, securities houses, and insurance companies at home. (Of course, in a period of slower growth, the United States would miss the large Japanese portfolio and direct investment that offset our low savings rate in the 1980s.) And while we continue to purchase more than a quarter of Japan's exports, Japan's imports of U.S. goods and services stagnated during its recession and now represent little more than 10 percent of our global export trade.

Japan is not the economic juggernaut it appeared to be five years ago. Its banking system is particularly fragile, having suffered enormous losses on domestic stocks and real estate, not to mention a number of imprudent investments abroad. Still, its manufacturing sector is the largest in the world, and the yen is, arguably, the world's strongest currency. Japan is piling up trade surpluses at record levels, and its pool of national savings is without equal. Through its investment, aid, and technology transfers in Asia, it has established an unrivaled position in the world's most dynamic market. It now exports more to Asia than to the United States. And despite the United States' prowess in developing information-age technologies, Japan is still running huge trade surpluses with us in semiconductors and transistors, computers and peripherals, and even telecommunications. Eamonn Fingleton contends that "the combination of a huge manufacturing work force and high productivity enable the Japanese economic system to aim for almost complete self-sufficiency in advanced manufacturing."[1] This seems improbable. But Japan certainly has developed extraordinary strength in the manufacture of key consumer items, basic materials, and production machinery.

Politically, our mutual dependence appears likewise to have been attenuated somewhat. Preoccupied with domestic issues, the Clinton administration has generated fewer international initiatives for which Japan's financial or political support was critical. (Supplying light water reactors to replace North Korea's old graphite reactors is an important exception.) And as Washington has focused on tough trade talks with the Japanese, it has played down its common agenda with Tokyo. The Japanese government, meanwhile, has sought to bolster its standing among its Asian neighbors by distancing itself somewhat from various U.S. initiatives on human rights, APEC, and China's entry into the World Trade Organization. Cooperation in international organizations appears less visible, in part because Japan is not currently a member of the Security Council, and Tokyo has become more assertive in promoting its own model of economic development in international institutions.

Meanwhile, each country has been devoting more time, effort, and resources to other relationships: the United States with Russia, Eastern Europe, Latin America, and the Middle East; Japan with the rest of Asia. As mentioned in the previous chapter, this has prompted Japanese anxieties about "Japan passing" by Americans eagerly shopping for market openings and influence elsewhere in Asia, while U.S. officials worry

1. See Eamonn Fingleton, *Blindside* (New York: Houghton Mifflin, 1995), p. 76.

conversely about a possible Japanese bid to lock up the Asian market or back Malaysian prime minister Mahatir bin Mohamad's East Asia Economic Caucus and its more exclusive brand of Asian regionalism.

In some respects, the combined weight of the United States and Japan in the world economy has declined. Europe's integration, the revival of Latin America, the dynamism of China, the rapid growth of Asia's new industrializing economies and ASEAN all reduce the relative economic influence of both countries. And neither of us can dominate new institutions, such as the World Trade Organization and the Asia Pacific Economic Cooperation initiative, that have emerged on the trade front. Whether an awareness of this relative decline of our clout will inspire greater efforts to collaborate or a more spirited competition for influence in Asia and elsewhere remains unclear.

The attempts of both Washington and Tokyo to alter the terms of interdependence to their own advantage have not produced a more comfortable relationship. Elements of rivalry are more visible; cooperative endeavors require more self-conscious effort. Macroeconomic coordination has been sporadic at best. Trade talks, despite the conclusion of several agreements in 1994 and 1995, are marked by bitter acrimony, threats, and counterthreats. And the trade imbalance remains huge.

These difficulties notwithstanding, it is unlikely that the U.S.-Japan relationship will break down. Each country possesses too large a stake in the other's prosperity. Japan may have diversified its trade, but it still exports far more to us than we do to them. While the U.S. manufacturing sector has surely revived, the quality of its industrial production depends heavily on materials, components, and production equipment supplied by Japanese firms. As the world's largest debtor, we will need to tap Japan's savings pool, and in deploying their savings abroad the Japanese will find the help of innovative and efficient U.S. banks and security firms invaluable.

Thus our mutual dependence persists. Threats of economic sanctions, whatever their motive and rationale, carry with them the implicit danger that we may shoot ourselves in the foot. This reality, evident yet again in the recent fracas over autos and auto parts, will continue to exert a restraining influence on our negotiators and impel them to search for solutions that offer benefits to both sides. And the most obvious and logical way to reduce our respective external imbalances—by reducing our domestic savings/investment imbalances—

would improve the health of each of our economies while doing no harm to trading partners.

Ironically, managing our economic ties may prove less treacherous than maintaining the overall alliance. The cohesion of all of the United States' alliances has suffered since the cold war ended—a natural consequence of the removal of an obvious and immediate threat. Yet the U.S.-Japan alliance remains unique in certain respects. Two in particular stand out. First, the asymmetries in the U.S.-Japan alliance create a more acute "free rider" problem than we have experienced in Europe or with other Asian allies. Since the United States extends a security guarantee that Japan does not reciprocate, Washington has naturally expected Tokyo to compensate for this uneven bargain in other ways. Tokyo's substantial financial contributions to the maintenance of our forward-deployed forces in Japan represents one form of compensation. These payments have been ample, and their political effects real. But the continuing imbalance in our respective contributions to a variety of other common goods whose benefits we share—security, open markets, basic scientific research, the protection of the environment, the development of the institutions that foster regional cooperation, and so on—leaves political support for the U.S.-Japan alliance in greater jeopardy than is the case, for example, with NATO.

On the other hand, while the disintegration of the Warsaw Pact left NATO, despite fighting in the Balkans, without a major security threat, North Korea's pursuit of nuclear weapons poses immediate dangers that underscore the continuing relevance of the U.S.-Japan alliance. Yet the framework for operational cooperation between U.S. and Japanese forces in relation to Northeast Asian military contingencies remains ill defined. A crisis in Korea would expose those limits in a way that could revive many of the anguishing problems that plagued our relationship with Japan during the Gulf war.

Difficulties over trade and security echo in the diplomatic and political spheres. Japanese doubts about our reliability as an ally or resentment over what they perceive as U.S. high-handedness in trade talks could fuel efforts to stake out a larger role for themselves in Asia at our expense. Conversely, U.S. irritation at Japan's reluctance to open its market or step up to tough international issues could encourage Washington to downgrade the priority it has accorded this relationship in favor of building stronger links with other Asian nations.

Domestic political developments in both countries, moreover, complicate efforts in both Washington and Tokyo to undertake the steps necessary to put the relationship back on track. In Japan, weak coalition governments have exhibited neither the strength nor the will to deregulate the economy or open the market wider to foreign competition over the objections of a determined and powerful bureaucracy. And the halting steps toward a political realignment raise doubts about prospects for administrative reform in the absence of further external shocks to the system. In the United States the Clinton administration has turned its attention decisively to domestic matters. And while the 1994 mid-term elections brought Republican control of Congress for the first time in forty years, the new majority has likewise focused its attention on domestic reform, though with a decidedly different agenda. To the extent it concentrates on achieving greater fiscal prudence and providing incentives to increase savings and investment, its efforts could in time ease U.S.-Japan trade tensions. But achieving such results generally requires bipartisan support, and with presidential elections again looming, the prospects for that are, at best, uncertain. The politics of trade policy, meanwhile, has changed. In the 1980s U.S. companies sought the government's help in protecting the home market from Japanese competitors. Now, more confident of their competitiveness, they seek Washington's help in opening foreign markets.

Returning U.S.-Japan relations to a sounder footing will not be an easy task. But it remains critical to the defense of U.S. interests in a region that contains a large percentage of the world's people and much of its most efficient manufacturing. The balance of power in Asia remains critical to our security. In the search for an equilibrium, Japan is a natural ally. It is a maritime trading nation with no territorial ambitions and a huge stake in the freedom of the seas. Its economic power is so great that significant decisions regarding the multilateral trading and financial system require its assent. And as a democracy with a modest nonnuclear military establishment, it values our security commitment. Whatever our bilateral trade difficulties, Japan remains our largest overseas commercial partner. Efforts to cope with regional problems in Asia—whether in Korea, the Taiwan Straits, or the South China Sea—have little chance of success without parallel U.S. and Japanese diplomatic efforts. And the quest for a Pacific Community will stand or fall on our ability to work out an acceptable accommodation among the basic interests of the major Asian powers—first and foremost, the United States and Japan—just as the success of the European Common Market depended on an accommodation between the interests of French farmers and German industrialists.

These shared interests are often forgotten as we struggle over one or another trade issue. But several trends should improve prospects for easing U.S.-Japan tensions over trade in the future. First, the globalization of finance and production is prompting U.S. and Japanese companies to strike up more and more of the strategic alliances that Peter Drucker has described as the principal force driving the integration of the world economy.[2] Intensified collaboration among our companies may not produce a borderless economy, but it is smoothing off some of the rough edges of technonationalism on both sides of the Pacific. Intel may dominate the design of the world's most sophisticated microprocessors, but it relies on Sharp for the manufacture of the memory devices it designs. Mazda remains a formidable auto manufacturer, but its future depends on its relationship with Ford. Ito-Yokado bought out the Southland Corporation's stake in the 7-Eleven retail store chain, but its bid to reduce the prices of consumer items to Japanese customers depends importantly on outsourcing arrangements with U.S. and other foreign suppliers. Examples of such cooperative relationships multiply daily.

Second, there has been a perceptible convergence in the U.S. and Japanese brands of "corporate" and "cowboy" capitalism. This is a tribute to the power of competition. As each nation's firms struggle for market share and profits in a global economy, they tend to emulate those of their competitors' practices that produce favorable results. In the late 1980s U.S. firms seemed more often the pupils; Japan's the mentors. Many of our most successful companies augmented their competitiveness by adapting certain Japanese practices—e.g., lean production methods, just-in-time delivery systems, total quality management, less adversarial patterns of labor-management relations, and more durable links between manufacturers and suppliers—to their own requirements. The benefits were enormous, as the enhanced productivity of the U.S. manufacturing sector attests.

The tables have turned in the 1990s, when Japanese managers are examining our experience in restructuring to find new ways of cut-

2. See Peter Drucker, "Trade Lessons from the World Economy" in *Foreign Affairs* 73, no. 1 (January/February 1994): 102–4.

ting costs while increasing efficiency. They are studying our educational system and corporate culture for clues as to how the USA continues to spawn successful start-up companies marked by technological virtuosity and entrepreneurial spirit. They are adapting features of
our distribution system to provide greater convenience and lower
prices to consumers. And they are finding in our service sector many
innovative ways of using information technology to improve the productivity of their own firms.

Thus the globalization of the marketplace is driving us to harmonize to a greater degree our industrial structures and our business practices. Nor have governments been immune from this process of mutual
emulation. Over the last decade U.S. officials and politicians have
rediscovered the virtues of fiscal prudence and the benefits of export
promotion. Washington has provided new incentives to commercialize technology for civilian use and relaxed antitrust guidelines to facilitate international competitiveness. Conversely, Japanese officials are
acquiring a growing awareness of the need for deregulation and more
rigorous enforcement of the antimonopoly law. Indeed, MITI's annual
trade white paper warned in early 1995 that Japan risks being left
behind in the global economy unless it hastens to deregulate, cut
prices, and make itself more attractive to foreign investors.[3]

The homogenization of our economic systems is neither possible
nor desirable. It would eliminate the diversity that makes life interesting and trade necessary. But the convergence under way has, I believe,
undermined a hypothesis advanced by geoeconomists a few years
ago:[4] namely, that acute conflict between differing forms of capitalism
would displace the cold war struggle between capitalism and communism. Certainly, economic competition with our allies has intensified,
but it is no life or death struggle.

In an age of mobile capital and rapidly expanding foreign direct
investment, the nature of national competitiveness is also changing.
With its mercantilist tradition, Japan has tended to measure its competitiveness by the size of its trade surplus, and it puts much effort
into promoting exports and discouraging imports. But as Vincent
Cable has recently observed, "competitiveness is no longer predom-
inantly a trade issue. Rather, it is about creating the right business

3. See *Japan Digest* 6, no. 20 (May 29, 1995): 21.
4. See, for example, Edward Luttwak, *The Endangered American Dream* (New York:
Simon and Schuster, 1993).

conditions—infrastructure, deregulation of markets, skilled and educated labor, financial stability—to attract or retain mobile capital."[5] In some respects the United States, arguably, is faring better than Japan. For example, despite its strong domestic savings rate, at least some Japanese economists and commentators have acknowledged that a low level of foreign direct investment in Japan is an indicator of weakness rather than strength. A serious effort to facilitate foreign direct investment in Japan obviously would have a salutary effect on our relationship.

Third, the evolution of our economies is creating additional shared interests. As Japan's foreign direct investment grows, so does our mutual interest in fashioning clearer multilateral rules for protecting such investments. As Japan's preeminence in manufacturing is increasingly challenged by Asian neighbors, its interest in rules against dumping and countervailing duties will more closely resemble our own. As its manufacturing sector moves to higher and higher technological levels, its stake in effective multilateral rules to protect intellectual property should increase. And as Japan locates more of its production facilities overseas, its market is becoming more open to imports of manufactured goods. Of course, many of these imports are sourced from Japanese subsidiaries abroad, but the firms of other countries will benefit as well, since the links between Japan's overseas manufacturers and their suppliers will be less ethnocentric and exclusive than the *keiretsu* ties at home. Insistent demands for higher local content will see to that.

Fourth, our societies also face a growing array of common problems: how to care for an aging population; how to sustain jobs for our blue-collar workers as we compete in a global market; how to protect the environment from the ravages of industrial pollution; how to preserve growth without succumbing to those social pathologies that appear to accompany mature industrial status (drugs, crime, the erosion of family values, etc.); how to contain global public health problems such as AIDS; how to draw former socialist countries into the international economy; and how to cope with a wide range of natural disasters. Our approaches to these various issues will undoubtedly differ from case to case. But they will also invite—and occasionally

5. See Vincent Cable, "The Diminished Nation-State: What Future for the State?" in *Daedalus* 124, no. 2 (spring 1995): 32.

demand—increasing collaboration among groups within our countries, and, indeed, within our governments as well.

Finally, our shared strategic concerns did not disappear when the cold war ended. The United States' stake in Asia is growing. It is the region in which we have our largest and most rapidly growing trade. It is an area in which the interests of all the major powers intersect. It is the only region in which we might conceivably face superpower-sized security threats in the early twenty-first century. As trading nations, we and Japan share a vital interest in preserving the security of sea lanes and stability in the world's most dynamic economic region. As peaceful nations and status quo powers, we also share an interest in arresting the spread of weapons of mass destruction and preserving an alliance that produces an indispensable hedge against the strategic uncertainties that loom on the Pacific horizon.

What Is to Be Done?

All that said, the fact remains that U.S. relations with Japan are drifting. No immediate crisis looms, yet an undeniable awkwardness surrounds the relationship. The alliance between Tokyo and Washington has seen its ups and downs before, and ways have always been found to muddle through. We can probably do so again. Yet failure to overcome the current malaise will diminish U.S. opportunities to expand exports and investment flows to Japan, forfeit Tokyo's help in tackling a variety of regional and global problems, undermine the confidence that is essential for our alliance, and invite a more intense and open struggle between Japan and the United States over the future shape of Asian regionalism.

What then can be done to put our relationship with Japan on a more solid footing? The most immediately pressing problems, as usual, lie in the field of trade. And that is a good place to start. Both countries bear their fair share of responsibility for the sizable external imbalances that we run with each other and the world. It is time we each put our own house in order. Since the U.S. current account deficit reflects the disparity between our savings and domestic investment, only we can take the steps necessary to reduce or eliminate it. If we succeed, it will strengthen our position not only with Japan but with all our trading partners.

Thus the starting point for achieving a more balanced economic relationship with Japan must be a renewed emphasis on economic fundamentals at home. Our most urgent national requirement is to raise our abysmally low rate of savings. The future of our economic well-being depends on this. Yet the problem has not yet been accorded the attention and priority it deserves. President Clinton put deficit reduction on the national agenda in a serious way with his 1993 deficit reduction package, which promises some reduction in government dissaving. Little has been done, however, to provide stronger incentives to encourage personal and corporate savings and investment. Having evidently concluded from the Democratic Party's stunning defeat in the 1994 mid-term elections that there was no political payoff in deficit reductions, moreover, President Clinton left responsibility for the problem largely to the Republican-controlled Congress. Ironically, failure in the Senate of the proposed constitutional amendment requiring a balanced budget may have had the fortuitous result of denying politicians an easy way out—i.e., a chance to appear interested in reducing the fiscal deficit without having to make hard budgetary choices for several years. Since then, Republican leaders in both the House and Senate have put on the table detailed plans designed to balance the budget within seven years. And this has prompted the president—in a reversal of the customary executive and legislative branch roles in budgetary politics—to put forth a comparable plan of his own. For the first time in many years, leading members of both the House and Senate are likewise promoting reforms of the tax system designed to discourage consumption and raise personal savings and corporate investment. This is encouraging. But it will require a broad public consensus and/or political courage on both sides of the political spectrum to achieve the passage of such budget and tax reforms.

Second, we cannot afford to rely principally on exchange rate adjustments to cure our current account deficit. In an era of floating currencies, each day brings new evidence of the difficulty governments face in managing exchange rate fluctuations. When roughly a trillion dollars changes hands in the exchange markets each day, government intervention to bolster the value of a nation's currency rarely has more than a brief and superficial effect. Yet the periodic temptation to attack our trade deficit with Japan by talking up the yen occasionally appears irresistible to some in Washington. There are several possible reasons for this. A weak dollar increases the competitiveness of U.S. exports and should diminish our propensity to import. Conversely, a strong yen erodes the profitability of many Japanese exporters, and Treasury officials have assumed, perhaps, that a rising yen would force the Japanese government to take bolder steps to reduce its trade surplus by stimulating additional domestic demand or removing regulatory barriers to imports. The increased value of Japan's exports, however, offsets for lengthy periods the effect of their reduced volume in Japan, not least because the benefits of a strong yen are not generally passed on quickly or fully to Japanese consumers.

Whatever the logic, the results of such efforts can be perverse. A weak dollar encourages inflation at home while sharply increasing the cost of doing business abroad. This in turn discourages U.S. firms from investing in the Japanese market at a time when an increased corporate presence there is critical to the ability of our firms to achieve greater exports to Japan in the future. As the yen has grown stronger, the profitability of Japan's leading exporters has indeed suffered, but a strong currency also permits Japanese companies to acquire production facilities in Asia at fire-sale prices, thereby strengthening their regional position and reducing their future vulnerability to currency fluctuations. In late summer 1995 the Federal Reserve Bank and the Bank of Japan engineered a successful joint intervention in currency markets, which encouraged a substantial depreciation of the yen against the dollar. Whether the effects will prove more than evanescent depends on whether other fundamentals underlying each country's external imbalance are addressed.

Third, despite the Clinton administration's determination to include targets in trade agreements with the Japanese, it has generally ignored the objective criterion that perhaps has the most salience with Japanese consumers and companies: namely, the wide price disparity in Japan and abroad for a variety of tradable goods and services. This feature deserves much greater attention in our bilateral trade strategy. The readily verifiable price gap points one directly to those sectors of the Japanese economy in which limits on competition are most stringent. The restrictions—whether accomplished through tariffs, quotas, oligopolistic practices, arbitrary and opaque regulations, or a complex distribution system—drive up prices both for Japanese households (which pay much more than they should for life's necessities) and for Japanese companies (whose costs have been skyrocketing in the face of a rising yen). By focusing negotiations on these sectors—for example, agriculture, financial services, transportation, construction, telecommunications—and emphasizing the need for accelerated deregulation and dismantling of other limits on competition, we stand a better chance of gaining support for our negotiating objectives from significant Japanese constituencies, such as the press, consumer groups, the business community, and even some elements of the political establishment.

Fourth, we should resist generalized efforts to imitate Japan's industrial policy. MITI can claim some important postwar industrial policy successes, but it has also experienced its share of failures. We do not need our own Ministry of International Trade and Industry. The most helpful industrial policy Washington could pursue would be to adopt prudent fiscal policies that keep inflation low and provide incentives for savings and investment while improving the quality of our primary and secondary education and sustaining support for a high level of basic scientific research. This last deserves special attention at a time when traditional sources of support for such research—e.g., federal R-and-D budgets for NASA, the NIH, and the departments of Defense, Energy, and Agriculture—are all under intense pressure. To be sure, there may on occasion be justification for encouraging precompetitive collaboration among our companies to promote the rapid development of certain technologies critical to our national defense and industrial future. The Sematech consortium, for example, supported by both federal and corporate resources, has had a salutary impact on U.S. semiconductor manufacturing capabilities. Federal support to encourage work on advanced flat panel display systems has also been authorized and may perhaps be warranted in the light of the importance this technology will have on a variety of industries and defense systems. But on balance I believe such support should be reserved for exceptional cases rather than provided as a general rule.

We do need, however, to weed out many of our domestic laws and regulations that undermine the international competitiveness of industries in which we enjoy a significant comparative advantage. Too often we have pursued domestic policies with scant regard to their effect on our ability to compete abroad. We no longer have that luxury. Some of the items on the GOP's Contract with America address such concerns: for example, tort reform and proposed changes in product liability laws. The Clinton administration has focused on other ways of enhancing U.S. competitiveness (for example, by augmenting export promotion activities). A major test will be our readiness to take the steps necessary to preserve and bolster the competitiveness of our aircraft and aeronautics industry—which remains a crucial source of exports and a central pillar of our defense capabilities.

Fifth, in encouraging the opening of Japan's market and a resolution of bilateral trade disputes, we should rely more heavily on multilateral pressure. With the conclusion of the Uruguay round, multilateral trading rules have been tightened up and extended to new fields. Meanwhile, APEC is gathering momentum as a potentially valuable forum for fostering trade liberalization. In the post–cold war era we must increasingly define our trade negotiating objectives vis-à-vis Japan in terms that are defensible outside U.S. policy-making circles and capable of mobilizing the support of Japan's other trading partners. If we assert that Japan is an outlier, we must be prepared to defend that contention convincingly in multilateral bodies. If such claims evoke support, they will carry greater weight with the Japanese public, press, and government. If we cannot make the case persuasively beyond our borders, we are unlikely to achieve success in bilateral negotiations with Tokyo.

Pressure should be focused particularly on the excesses and lack of transparency in Japan's regulatory system. All of Japan's trading partners suffer from the arbitrariness of its administrative practices. It remains the only major democratic country without a code of administrative procedure. The preferential features of its administrative guidance system impose burdens on all foreign firms and undermine governmental claims of fidelity to the principle of national treatment. Emphasis on deregulation, moreover, would enable foreign negotiators to enlist support from Japanese constituencies that suffer from excessive bureaucratic direction.

While we must pay more attention to the overall health of the global trading system, we cannot, to be sure, forswear bilateral trade negotiations with Japan. Regrettably, the World Trade Organization's rules still do not cover many of Japan's most effective informal trade barriers. Bilateral sectoral negotiations have demonstrated their value, and they will continue to be needed. Where the barriers to market entry in a particular sector are high and sanctioned by government authorities, we should devote less time to expressing public indignation and concentrate more on quietly but resolutely making Japanese exporters pay a price. One way or another we should seek a greater parity of trade and investment opportunities. If Japan cannot streamline its customs procedures or remove burdensome certification requirements, we should have the wit and the will to subject their exports of key items to the United States to comparable burdens. Reciprocity should be the objective.

Sixth, while it is frequently frustrating to do business in Japan, the belief that our companies can stake out a strong position in Asia without penetrating the Japanese market is a delusion. There has been a discernible tendency of late for U.S. companies to redirect their attention from Japan, with its high costs and burdensome regulations, to more rapidly growing markets elsewhere in Asia. This is matched by a certain "Japan fatigue" among U.S. trade negotiators, who appear eager to devote more of their efforts to the big emerging markets in Korea, China, Indonesia, and India. Some evidence of this shift in priorities is beginning to show up in trade and investment statistics. Direct U.S. investment in Japan remains low. The number of U.S. electronics firms in business in Japan has declined. U.S. business publications in Japan are cutting back. Many financial services firms have moved their regional headquarters to Hong Kong or Singapore. A number of U.S. construction companies have thrown in the towel on the Japanese market. And many U.S. firms have withdrawn from the Tokyo Stock Exchange.

Many of these decisions reflect the fact that Japan is a tough, expensive, and highly regulated market. And Japanese firms, after all, are also relocating many operations overseas. Yet Japan still accounts for nearly two-thirds of the entire East Asian economy, and it is difficult to see how a company can develop an effective regional strategy while ignoring the largest segment of the regional market. Moreover, Japan is the second largest economy in the world and possesses the most efficient manufacturing sector. U.S. companies that wish to achieve world-class status must test themselves against their most difficult competitors on their home turf. If they have no presence in Japan, they will deprive themselves of the ability to tailor products to local tastes, monitor Japanese technological and product developments that they will soon encounter in other markets, and force their rivals to compete in their own market on the basis of price as well as quality.

Nor is pessimism about the USA's ability to compete in Japan warranted. Firms with high-quality products and the perseverance to overcome the costs of market entry in Japan have demonstrated again and again an ability to develop strong profit centers in most segments of that market. In fact, an A. T. Kearney study concluded that U.S. firms have been more profitable in the Japanese market than have Japanese and European companies during the current economic downturn.[6] If our companies succeed in Japan, they can surely compete anywhere; success in Taiwan, or Thailand, or Indonesia, however, offers no comparable guarantee of success in Japan.

Seventh, we must devote particular attention to expanding our foreign direct investment in Japan. Since intrafirm trade now constitutes nearly half of world commerce, the presence of U.S. production operations in Japan will clearly enhance our ability to export to that market. Foreign direct investment in Japan has been growing recently at rates roughly comparable to that in other advanced countries, but because of past restraints, recent growth has been from an extremely modest base.[7] And although formal impediments to foreign direct investment in Japan have been generally dismantled, a host of informal barriers remain. Some of these are now gradually coming down. Land prices have declined significantly. A soft labor market eases the difficulties of recruiting local staff. The prolonged recession has reduced resistance to mergers and acquisitions. And growing concerns about the hollowing-out of Japanese industry should create a more receptive mood toward foreign investments that create local jobs. This is a subject that deserves more attention in both bilateral exchanges between the Treasury and the Ministry of Finance and among APEC members generally. It also requires greater public discussion in the United States. Ross Perot and the labor unions have contributed to a widespread public misimpression that overseas investments invariably encourage the export of jobs. There is little evidence to confirm this. In fact, the 1960s and 1980s, which saw a rapid expansion of U.S. direct investment abroad, were both periods in which employment increased dramatically at home.

Eighth, in the interests of our consumers and our productivity, we should continue to guard against creeping protectionism. Because Detroit faced the full force of Japanese competition in the U.S. market throughout the 1980s, the Big Three are far more competitive today. Those sectors of our economy that have steadily increased their participation in the global system (finance, pharmaceuticals, information technologies, and the like) are acknowledged global leaders. Those that have secured heavy protection from Washington—such as

6. See *Japan Digest* 6, no. 20 (May 29, 1995): 11.
7. For an assessment of recent trends, see Marcus Noland, "Implications of Asian Economic Growth," paper prepared for the Council on Foreign Relations Asia Project, November 1994, p. 19.

textiles and agriculture—have declined in efficiency while absorbing huge governmental subsidies. Protection remains a crutch that breeds dependence and invites inefficiency. Nor can it protect jobs for very long, for Americans generally refuse to pay higher prices for goods and services just because they are produced at home—a healthy instinct from which the Japanese have much to learn.

It will be easier to check protectionist pressure if we retain a sense of proportion about our trade imbalance with Japan. We cannot measure a relationship as diverse and multifarious as ours with Japan merely against monthly bilateral trade statistics, particularly when the familiar methods of compiling such statistics do no justice to our complex trade patterns. For example, they do not adequately account for services trade, yet we are the most competitive supplier of services in the world. Peter Drucker has estimated that our surplus in service exports is about two-thirds the size of our merchandise trade deficit, and that gap is narrowing.[8] Yet prior to early 1994 the Commerce Department did not even hazard an estimate of our service exports in its monthly trade figures.

An increasing percentage of world trade is affected by strategic alliances among U.S. and Japanese companies. Yet many of the transactions embodied in these alliances are likewise missing from the trade statistics. The massive activities of our respective multinationals profoundly influence trade flows through transfers among their divisions. This further skews our bilateral trade statistics with Japan, because U.S. multinationals moved production facilities overseas much earlier than did the Japanese, and ours export a much larger percentage of their products back to the United States. The trade numbers, moreover, do not adequately account for the daily movement of vast sums of capital at a time when the complementarity of trade and investment is greater than ever before. In short, to the extent that we allow trade statistics to color the atmospherics and determine the substantive agenda of the U.S.-Japan relationship, we should at least find a more accurate way of describing the underlying size and scope of our trading patterns.

Finally, it is important to remember that precisely because our economies are interdependent, we retain a crucial stake in Japan's con-

8. See Drucker, "Trade Lessons," pp. 101–2. Drucker attributes our deficit largely to the underestimation of services exports, our profligate use of petroleum, and a decline in both the volume and prices of farm exports.

tinuing growth and prosperity. Some Americans have expressed—and others undoubtedly have felt—a sense a schadenfreude over recent Japanese economic difficulties. This is perhaps understandable but is neither worthy of us nor wise. It neglects our own interests. If Japan's growth rate were higher, our exports would increase faster. And if Japanese profits and wages increased more rapidly and their jobs were more secure, they might more readily open their markets wider to foreign products. Instead of concentrating so single-mindedly on trade disputes, we should therefore offer Japan further encouragement to stimulate consumer spending and business investment. By helping themselves in this way, they would also help us and the rest of the world.

Of course, even if we honor all these guidelines, our trade deficit—with Japan and with the world at large—will not recede overnight. It took a long time to get into our current fix, and it will take considerable effort to get out of it. Yet if we take these various admonitions to heart, we can ease political strains and substantially alleviate our trade imbalance with Japan while positioning our companies to compete more effectively both in Japan and in other markets.

The Future of the U.S.-Japan Alliance

Some Americans question the necessity for an alliance in the post–cold war era. Among Republican leaders, Pat Buchanan is the most outspoken proponent of its termination. Dissolution of the alliance is the logical corollary of the policies promoted by many of the economic nationalists within the Democratic Party as well. To date, however, few within the political mainstream agitate for an end to the Treaty of Mutual Cooperation and Security or the withdrawal of our forward-deployed forces in Japan or Korea. Congress appears content with current cost-sharing arrangements. And the Clinton administration has not only reaffirmed the value it attaches to the alliance but has assured the Japanese that we expect to maintain our current force levels—roughly 100,000—in Asia for the next several decades.

Yet doubts have grown about the necessity for this alliance. Intense trade frictions have raised the levels of mutual distrust, and neither side appears as willing as it was in the past to compartmentalize trade and security issues. Questions have also been raised as to how useful the alliance would prove to be in the face of a full-blown crisis in Korea. As *The Economist* recently put it: "Would it pass the kind of test that NATO failed in Bosnia?"[9] That is, would it be able to function effectively in the face of North Korean provocations?

If this issue has not been on the front burner in Washington and Tokyo, it is in part because the security environment in East Asia is more benign and less threatening than it has been in decades. The balance of forces among the major powers—China, Russia, Japan, and the United States—appears reasonably stable. The prospect of military conflict among them is remote; all are pursuing generally moderate policies in Asia; each is preoccupied with domestic problems; relations among them are more or less amicable; and they have collaborated on occasion to defuse regional conflicts, such as those in Cambodia and Korea.

The U.S.-Japan alliance was forged to prevent the Soviet Union from dominating the Eurasian land mass. Throughout U.S. history, we consistently have acted to prevent powerful and hostile nations from ganging up on us. Today, happily, neither Russia nor any plausible combination of other powers currently threatens to achieve such dominion. And alliances among the other major powers appear currently problematic.

As noted in chapter 7, both a Russo-Japanese and a Sino-Japanese alignment seem extremely unlikely. The reestablishment of a Sino-Russian alliance appears equally implausible. Sino-Russian trade, to be sure, is growing; China can provide Russia with cheap and abundant consumer goods, while Russia can offer China energy resources and needed raw materials. Yet both possess more natural economic associations with others, and a Sino-Russian axis would alienate Russia from the West and China from its neighbors in Asia. Nonetheless, improved ties between Moscow and Beijing have already relieved both of the incentive to deploy large forces along the Sino-Russian border, thereby freeing their hands either to redeploy their ground forces or reduce their size.

To be sure, some legacies of the cold war still fester in Asia. North and South Korea remain antagonistic and heavily armed. Relations between Taiwan and China have improved, but the Taiwan issue

9. "America, Japan and the Unmentionable," *The Economist* 336, no. 7903 (February 25, 1995): 33.

remains unresolved. Territorial disputes abound, and arms purchases are up throughout the region. The cold war security system, centered on the U.S. alliance structure, is fraying around the edges—for example, the Philippines terminated U.S. access to bases at Subic and Clark; the Thai turned down a U.S. proposal to position materiel and equipment offshore; defense relations with New Zealand have been in suspense for a decade; Australia's defense planning now emphasizes greater self-reliance; and key figures in Japan and in Korea question the durability of the United States' commitment to them. Yet no regional security system has emerged to replace it. And in the past, periods during which new military or industrial powers appeared on the scene were marked by intense rivalry and frequent conflicts; today, both China and Japan stand on the threshold of superpower status.

In this more benign yet fluid political setting, the United States has a variety of strategic options. One possibility would be to withdraw our military forces from Asia and confine our security policy largely to the Western Hemisphere. Such a course of action would be historically anachronistic: Asia is the region in which we have our largest and most rapidly growing economic interests, and it is the only area in which a superpower-sized threat to our national security might conceivably emerge in the early twenty-first century. Another option would be to encourage the ASEAN Regional Forum (ARF) in the hope that it might develop into a genuine collective security. But the prerequisites for collective security—a common perception of threats, general agreement about the territorial status quo, and a sense of community underpinned by widely accepted political and philosophical principles—have not yet taken root in Asia. Hence a wider Pacific security community is a goal toward which we should aspire; it is not a reality on which Asian nations are presently prepared to rely. Neither can we.

A third possibility would be to seek to build a NATO-like multilateral alliance in Asia. But this begs the question, against whom would such an alliance be forged? A fourth alternative would be to carve out a role for ourselves as the neutral arbiter of the Asian equilibrium—a role akin to that of England in the European balance of power system. This would amount to a policy Josef Joffe has described as "anti-hege-

10. Josef Joffe, " 'Bismarck' or 'Britain'? Toward an American Grand Strategy After Bipolarity," *International Security* 19, no. 4 (spring 1995): 94–117.

monism without entanglement."[10] It would entail remaining aloof from durable commitments to other major powers, aligning ourselves against the most powerful and aggressive Asian nation only if and when the overall balance of forces appears in jeopardy.

Pursuit of such a strategy of flexible alignment could limit our current defense burdens in Asia while maximizing our diplomatic maneuverability. Our nuclear arsenal would give us the defensive strength to match our power projection capabilities. And we could presumably ignore many local conflicts in Asia on grounds that they would not immediately affect our core national interests.

Chalmers Johnson and E. B. Keehn stated the case for a strategy similar to this in their *Foreign Affairs* article "The Pentagon's Ossified Strategy." They argue that the U.S.-Japan alliance is both outdated and unnecessary; that our strategic guarantee represents a flawed attempt to buy Tokyo's cooperation while preserving the appearance of U.S. strategic hegemony in the Pacific; and that perpetuation of the alliance impedes the development of responsible economic conduct by the Japanese, enables Tokyo to delay further a serious effort to come to terms with its past, and robs us of leverage in bilateral trade negotiations. They are equally critical of the Clinton administration's recent pledge not to alter the size of U.S. forward-deployed forces in the Pacific—a policy which, they argue, gives "Japan and China a few years to consolidate their ascendancy in Asia" at our expense. "Only an end to Japan's protectorate status," they conclude, "will create the necessary domestic political conditions for Japan to assume a balanced security role in regional and global affairs." Instead of preserving the alliance, they urge that the United States play a flexible balancing role among China, Japan, and the ASEAN countries while taking steps to avert what they regard as the real danger, i.e., "armed impotence" and growing dependence on Japanese components for our defense technology.[11]

I agree that the United States should play the role of balancer and broker in the Pacific. But for the foreseeable future I believe we can more effectively acquit those responsibilities with the U.S.-Japan alliance than without it. Flexible access to Japanese bases enables us to project our power efficiently into the western Pacific, and Japan picks up a large share of the cost of our forward presence. Far from compli-

11. See *Foreign Affairs* 74, no. 4 (July/August 1995): 104, 107, 114.

cating our relations with Asian nations, the alliance remains a source of reassurance to virtually all countries in the area. At a time of flux and fluidity in the Asian balance, termination of the U.S.-Japan alliance would generate a host of new uncertainties. Such a drastic step is scarcely warranted in order to encourage the Japanese to come to terms with their past; their desire to play a larger role in Asia is compelling them to do that in any event. Nor is it self-evident that a retreat from defense cooperation with Tokyo would induce more cooperative Japanese policies on trade issues. Unilateral termination of the alliance could just as easily reduce Tokyo's incentives to accommodate our commercial interests, while encouraging it to "tilt" further toward its Asian trading partners.

More broadly, the alliance has provided one of the sources of predictability and stability underlying Asia's phenomenal economic growth. As Joe Nye has put it, political order, to which our alliance with Japan has contributed so much, is like oxygen; we take it for granted unless it is not available.[12] Termination of the alliance could weaken the underpinnings of the region's prosperity and hasten the drift toward renewed Japanese-U.S. strategic rivalry. In that case we would find ourselves for the first time in decades having to organize our Pacific strategy with one eye cocked toward the possibility of future conflict with Japan—a surefire way of generating new defense requirements and new budgetary demands. Could we live without the alliance? We did throughout much of our history, and could again. But Johnson and Keehn exaggerate the benefits of termination and underestimate its risks.

At a minimum, termination of the alliance would raise new questions about Japan's future strategic posture, scarcely an advantage for a status quo power like the United States. At a time when the Sino-Japanese-U.S. triangle is the core of the Asian equilibrium, this could impel Tokyo either toward strategic rivalry with Beijing, or, alternatively, more intimate collaboration with it. Neither would serve our interests in Asia. The former would breed instability and perhaps conflict; the latter could fuel joint efforts to promote more exclusive patterns of pan-Asian regionalism at our expense. And what of the impact on our international credibility—let alone our self-respect—

12. Joseph Nye, "The Case for Deep Engagement," *Foreign Affairs* 74, no. 4 (July/August 1995): 91.

of walking away from security commitments in Northeast Asia at a time when North Korea has not definitively abandoned its nuclear aspirations?

Thus I believe Americans are unlikely to be able to skillfully play the "in-and-out" game the way Castlereagh's England did. We should strive for a different role in promoting a regional equilibrium. We face no imminent need to balance Asian rivals. We do confront the challenge of inducing friends and potential adversaries alike to join in consolidating a generally benign and favorable political and territorial status quo in Asia. As in the past we have a vital interest in preventing potentially hostile powers in that region from ganging up against us. And for that purpose our guideline should be to cultivate better bilateral relations with the key nations of Asia—Japan, China, Russia, Korea, Indonesia, and others—than they enjoy with one another. This requires a policy of active engagement, and in this context our alliance with Japan remains an asset not only with Tokyo but with the other major powers as well. Of course, we also need to provide them all with incentives to continue regarding us as a valued partner and a real or potential ally if trouble should come.

In this connection, our alliance with Japan remains critically important to our position in Asia and our grand strategy in the world. Put most simply, our political, economic, and security interests require a stable balance of power in Asia. No durable equilibrium is likely without our active participation, and our alliance with Japan facilitates our involvement in the Asian balance in an efficient and reassuring way. More specifically, the alliance lends credibility to the United States' commitment to South Korea at a time when developments on the peninsula are in flux. It reduces Tokyo's incentives to cross the nuclear threshold. It provides a potential counterweight to other powers, should they reassert expansionist designs. It facilitates the coordination of parallel diplomatic approaches by Washington and Tokyo to unresolved security problems in Korea and the Taiwan Straits. It enables us cooperatively to protect sea lanes in the Pacific through which much of the world's commerce passes. And it furnishes a possible cornerstone for future regional security arrangements. Needless to add, the Japanese must exhibit sufficient sensitivity to our interests to warrant a security connection. And that means a readiness to extend reciprocal access to their market. Without it, no administration in Washington will be able to sustain political support for the alliance.

Adjustments in the supporting arrangements of the alliance, how-ever, may be required to assure its continuing relevance to the chang-ing security environment in Asia and the demands of politics in Japan and the United States. Two possibilities should be resisted—at least for now: (1) major reductions of U.S. military forces; and (2) an effort to revise the treaty to provide reciprocal defense commitments.

Continuing speculation about U.S. retreat from defense responsi-bilities in the western Pacific fuels uncertainty in the region and induces East Asian nations to prepare to fill a possible power vacuum. Our forces in Asia threaten no one; their presence is widely accepted; and since their financial support is shared by local allies, withdrawing them would generate savings only if they were eliminated from our force structure. Recent Pentagon announcements that the Clinton administration plans no further reductions for an indefinite period may squelch current fears of retrenchment. In that respect it may have some utility. But Asians know that administrations come and go and that such decisions are regularly revisited. In fact, there is nothing magic about the current level of our forces either in Korea or Japan. They were established under quite different circumstances. There is no reason to rule out future adjustments. But it will be important to man-age them in a way that suggests they are prudent responses to chang-ing security conditions in the area rather than merely a by-product of budgetary politics in the United States.

Nor is this a prudent time to encourage Japan to match our com-mitment to come to its defense, if attacked, with a reciprocal commit-ment to the United States' security. Balancing our defense obligations has conceptual appeal, but in practical terms it would require Japan to alter its constitution and substantially expand its military capabilities. Such efforts would alarm Japan's Asian neighbors and unsettle Japan's politics without significantly improving our security. Thus we can safely set this aside.

The most immediate challenges the alliance faces are in the Korean peninsula. At present there are ample reasons for doubting whether current support arrangements would permit effective operational cooperation between the United States and Japan in the event of a conflict. Nor are such contingencies entirely implausible. In 1994 many feared that tough UN sanctions against North Korea might provoke a military response from Pyongyang. Such a reaction would have exposed gaps in the ability of Tokyo and Washington to undertake a coordinated response. For example, Japan's road traffic law forbids the unloading of explosives at night. No Allied Cross-Servicing Agreement exists to facilitate the refueling and resupply of U.S. naval vessels by the Japanese Self-Defense Forces. Arguably, Japanese ships could not even rescue a U.S. vessel damaged by the North Koreans, because that would fall outside their constitutional role of defending Japanese territory. And the lip service the Socialist Party pays to the alliance does not assure their support of operational cooperation between our uniformed services, as indicated by Prime Minister Murayama's reluctance both to deploy Self-Defense Forces and to accept help from U.S. military units at the time of the Kobe earthquake.

The relevance of more detailed contingency planning is thus apparent. So, too, is the need for Japan to review its military roles and missions in the light of post–cold war realities. Obviously, implementation of any new plans or missions presupposes the approval of civilian authorities. But the alliance could not sustain a repetition of the Gulf war experience, particularly if a crisis occurred in Japan's backyard. If Americans are to assume the risks of supporting South Korea in a crisis, they will expect Japan to do far more than merely send checks. Such crises are more likely to be avoided if the alliance is capable expeditiously of forging a coordinated response.

In this connection, developing theater ballistic missile defenses against North Korea is also a possible arena for further collaboration. The U.S.–North Korean nuclear accord promises the dismantling of nuclear facilities some years down the road, but Pyongyang's record of compliance with international obligations is erratic at best. North Korea has pursued the development not only of nuclear weapons but of delivery systems than can reach most parts of Japan. Some elements of the Japanese political and defense establishments have expressed interest in acquiring systems to defend against these North Korean capabilities. Others have demurred.

Should Japan decide that it needed more effective defenses, I believe we should support joint efforts to develop them. We should also expect the Japanese to repay us with reciprocal access to defense-related technology of interest to the Pentagon. But I have long believed that we can safely leave the initiative for cooperation in this field to Tokyo. It is, after all, Japan's security that is potentially at risk. Its initial reaction to U.S. proposals for cooperation in theater ballistic missile defenses revealed a host of political, financial, and diplomatic reservations.

Japanese have lived in the shadow of formidable Chinese and Russian nuclear capabilities for many years without a perceived need for strategic defenses. Their defense budget is currently tight, particularly for procurement. The fluid state of their domestic politics complicates the search for a consensus in support of such capabilities. And our own past debates about strategic defenses suggest that some Asians will regard Japan's acquisition of defensive systems as augmenting its future offensive potential.

There may also be opportunities for further sharing of defense responsibilities in protecting the sea lanes in the western Pacific. But Japan already shares these burdens through its surveillance and patrolling between Tokyo and the Bashi Channel, north of the Philippines. I doubt the advisability of pressing Japan to extend the geographic scope of its involvement in such activities—particularly outside the framework of a multilateral naval task force. For one thing, in the absence of provocation, such a venture is unlikely to get off the ground. If such provocations occur, the ASEAN Regional Forum would provide an appropriate arena in which to discuss ways to augment the role of the Seventh Fleet by contributions from others, including Japan.

Perhaps the most delicate task in managing the alliance relates to China. China's rapid economic growth offers opportunities as well as challenges. It is an engine of growth in East Asia. But its military potential has also captured the attention of its neighbors. And uncertainties as to how it will utilize the power it is accumulating undoubtedly account to some degree for renewed Japanese interest in sustaining the alliance with the United States. Since Russian military power has atrophied in recent years, the Sino-Japanese-U.S. triangle will decisively shape the Asian balance of forces. The nature of our relations with Tokyo and Beijing will have a major bearing on the way they deal with each other. Steady U.S. diplomacy can reduce the likelihood of either Sino-Japanese strategic rivalry or a Sino-Japanese entente in Asia. Without our active involvement in the region, Beijing and Tokyo will be more likely to increase their military spending and pursue national ambitions that could provoke new sources of instability in the neighborhood. Japanese defense capabilities linked to the United States generate fewer apprehensions among the Chinese than do independent Japanese capabilities. And without the alliance, Japan would probably regard its current level of military capabilities as imprudently modest.

The existence of acute tensions in Sino-American relations could tempt Japan to keep the United States at arm's length, if not to capitalize on those differences, at least to avoid having its own relations with Beijing adversely affected by appearing to follow the USA's lead too closely. Intense friction between Washington and Tokyo would further erode Beijing's respect for our judgment and invite it to exploit Japanese-American differences. And while our alliance with Japan may encourage the continued moderation of Beijing's external policy, any U.S. effort to confront China on the Asian continent or in the Taiwan Straits without clear Chinese provocation would jeopardize U.S.-Japan cooperation and alienate other leading Asian nations. Our interests require that we play this triangular game. Playing it effectively will demand more attentiveness and hard-headedness than we have exhibited in the recent past. But the main point is this: we are better positioned to play the game with the alliance than without it.

Reshaping the Political Relationship

Political bonds between Tokyo and Washington are somewhat fragile. The mutual confidence and personal friendship that marked the Ron-Yasu (Reagan-Nakasone), George-Toshiki (Bush-Kaifu), and George-Kiichi (Bush-Miyazawa) relationships are not visible features of the current relationships between our political leaders. (Indeed, senior officials in Washington reportedly sought to condition a 1995 visit to the United States by Prime Minister Murayama on prior assurances of a significant Japanese contribution to the Korean Energy Development Organization.) The extensive turnover in the U.S. Congress and Japanese Diet in recent elections has taken its toll on trans-Pacific ties between legislative leaders. Prolonged guerrilla warfare on trade issues has left a legacy of mistrust between our bureaucracies. Recent incidents related to commemorations of the fiftieth anniversary of V-J Day exposed the sharply diverging perspectives with which our peoples recall that conflict. Within the U.S. government, the locus of much of the policy making with respect to Japan has shifted from agencies interested in collaboration with Tokyo to those (e.g., the U.S. trade representative's office and the National Economic Council) preoccupied with our competitiveness vis-à-vis Japan. And the new generation of bureaucrats coming of age in Japan seems more keenly interested in Asia than in the United States. These problems should not be overstated, for cooperation on many issues remains routine. But the unmistakable erosion of mutual trust between our leaders and the decline in public support for the relationship among our peoples is genuinely troubling.

Perhaps we should also reconcile ourselves to more realistic expectations for the relationship. In some respects, U.S. relations with Japan parallel our links with France. Each country has a proud tradition of self-reliance. Each harbors ambitions for regional leadership, though France is driven by a quest for grandeur while Tokyo principally covets respect and status. Neither Paris nor Tokyo can dispel anxieties about a powerful neighbor with whom it cultivates close ties. Both acknowledge the value of the United States' presence in preserving a regional equilibrium, and both cling to mercantilist trading practices. Of course, there are obvious differences as well— most notably, Japan's reluctance to establish its strategic independence, its preference for low-profile diplomacy, and the ambiguity of many of its public pronouncements.

Washington has long since become accustomed to the independence of French diplomatic efforts. It accommodated, though it did not welcome, France's arm's-length relationship to NATO. Yet our bilateral relationship with Paris has survived and periodically flourished. With Japan, we can no longer anticipate the degree of diplomatic compliance Tokyo exhibited during the cold war. Nor can the Japanese expect Washington to extend an open-ended security guarantee in the absence of a more reciprocal trading relationship. Though we have our share of disagreements with the French, rarely are these cause for widespread speculation about the demise of our entire relationship. With Japan, too, we should strive for agreement where our interests permit, while learning to accept occasional disagreements without assuming they automatically place the relationship as a whole in jeopardy.

Yet we must also strive to improve the political relationship with Tokyo. In that regard a number of suggestions have surfaced. One hardy perennial is the suggestion that we improve our consultative process. Unquestionably, we could develop even more elaborate arrangements for U.S.-Japan consultations. But the problem is not the channels but what is transmitted through them. The difficulties are primarily substantive rather than procedural.

Others suggest greater emphasis on our common agenda. Certainly, it is appropriate to search for major regional and global problems on which our interests converge and to publicize more widely the successes of our collaboration on them. There is already a rich agenda for such cooperation on matters ranging from the environment to joint scientific and technological projects; from supporting AIDS research to financing population control efforts in developing countries; from stamping out narcotics trafficking to putting terrorist groups out of business. These are worthy causes deserving of support. But most such cooperative activities can best be organized on a multilateral basis, and they are consequently unlikely to serve as the focal point for reinvigorating our bilateral relationship.

It is more crucial that we accord priority to the most significant problems. Only parallel efforts by Washington and Tokyo are likely to succeed in dissuading North Korea from its quest for nuclear weapons, to cope with the consequences of Korea's future unification, or to buy the time and preserve the flexibility in Taipei and Beijing necessary for a peaceful resolution of the Taiwan issue. If we pursue divergent courses of action toward Korea, China, or the Taiwan issue, the adverse consequences will be felt throughout our relationship, and our alliance is unlikely to survive.

We might rely more heavily on multilateral fora for policy coordination. As APEC acquires weight in the calculations of key Asia/Pacific powers, we should utilize this forum more in tackling some of the prominent trade issues on our bilateral agenda. Our proposals for economic deregulation will count for more in Tokyo if we weigh in alongside other Japanese trading partners. We have already begun to handle many consultations regarding North Korea on a trilateral basis with Seoul and Tokyo. To the extent possible, Beijing should be drawn into these discussions. Indeed, there is much to be said for regularizing discussions about Northeast Asian problems among the two Koreas, the United States, Japan, China, and Russia, and some steps have already been taken in that direction.

Most important, we should explore a new understanding of the broad trade-offs that underpin our relationship. The basic bargain that underlay the links between Washington and Tokyo for a generation is no longer viable. Japan is too large an economic force in the world to expect our indulgence of the many hidden barriers to its market. And Japan is too proud and too powerful to be expected merely to follow Washington's policy direction. Whether a new understanding can be struck is unclear. President Bush and President Clinton have tried. The results are not yet satisfactory.

From an American standpoint, the general contours of the trade-off are reasonably clear. We need Japan's help in defining and defending reasonable multilateral rules for managing an unruly and dynamic international system. We need a rough equality of opportunity in Japan's markets akin to what we give them in ours. And we need Japan's collaboration in order to forge regional cooperation within a trans-Pacific rather than a Pan-Asian framework. Japan, meanwhile, needs Washington's attentiveness to its interests and views and respect for its independence. It needs our continued cooperation on security matters if central features of its own defense policy (specifically, the three noes—no nuclear weapons, no arms exports, and no major military power projection capabilities) are to survive. And Japan wants acknowledgment of its major power status in the United Nations Security Council. This is a reasonable agenda that offers major benefits to both countries. It remains to be seen whether both governments can muster the political will to assure its realization.

We must devote special efforts to reconciling our respective ambitions in Asia. We have long urged Japan to assume a more ambitious regional and global role. There is no reason to regard a larger and more active Japanese presence in Asia as a threat. But if we are to participate fully in Asia's growing prosperity, we must also look out for our own equities in the region. If we effectively terminate our economic assistance programs in Asia, we cannot expect to compensate by seeking a larger share of supply contracts under Japan's official development assistance program. We cannot badger Asian governments on every political issue that comes along and then complain when public procurement contracts for telecommunications, energy, and transportation infrastructure projects go to Japanese competitors. We cannot expect to keep up with the presence Japan is establishing with its massive foreign direct investment in the Asian market merely by increasing the volume of U.S. portfolio investment in the region. (After the Mexican experience, many developing countries—including some in Asia—are leery of such hot money.) And we cannot hope to shape APEC's institutions in directions congenial to U.S. interests without a steady engagement in the process of building a regional consensus regarding APEC's role and without displaying greater sensitivity to Asian methods of nurturing such a consensus.

Asians are not unhappy to see a healthy measure of competition between the United States and Japan, particularly on economic and commercial issues. It enhances their ability to maneuver between us. Yet on the fundamentals, cooperation between Tokyo and Washington is crucial if regional initiatives are to flourish. In this connection, we should redirect our energies toward determining the common goods needed to build a Pacific Community and working on an equitable arrangement for providing them.

If we fail to overcome the current malaise in our bilateral relationship with Japan, we will find it difficult to muster the cooperation necessary to meet a variety of regional and global challenges. Yet only if we can elevate our concerns beyond current trade disputes will we be able to temper the nationalistic excesses that our economic competition increasingly breeds. It is essential that our political leaders remind themselves and their constituents of the immense benefits U.S.-Japanese cooperation brings to both our peoples. And they must invest the time and effort needed for managing this relationship, which its importance demands. It is high time we cease hurling accusations and recriminations back and forth across the Pacific, roll up our sleeves, and get back to work. That is the best way of assuring that long-standing allies remain firm friends and that commercial competition does not breed geopolitical rivalry.

Index